READING EZRA 9–10 *TU'A*-WISE

RETHINKING BIBLICAL INTERPRETATION IN OCEANIA

Society of Biblical Literature

International Voices in Biblical Studies

General Editors
Monica J. Melanchthon
Louis C. Jonker

Editorial Board
Eric Bortey Anum
Ida Fröhlich
Jione Havea
Hisako Kinukawa
Sam P. Mathew
Néstor Míguez
Nancy Nam Hoon Tan

Number 3
READING EZRA 9–10 *TU'A*-WISE

READING EZRA 9–10 *TU'A*-WISE

RETHINKING BIBLICAL INTERPRETATION IN OCEANIA

Nāsili Vaka'uta

Society of Biblical Literature
Atlanta

Copyright © 2011 by the Society of Biblical Literature

All rights reserved. No part of this work may be reproduced or published in print form except with permission from the publisher. Individuals are free to copy, distribute, and transmit the work in whole or in part by electronic means or by means of any information or retrieval system under the following conditions: (1) they must include with the work notice of ownership of the copyright by the Society of Biblical Literature; (2) they may not use the work for commercial purposes; and (3) they may not alter, transform, or build upon the work. Requests for permission should be addressed in writing to the Rights and Permissions Office, Society of Biblical Literature, 825 Houston Mill Road, Atlanta, GA 30329, USA.

Library of Congress Cataloging-in-Publication Data

Vaka'uta, Nasili.
    Reading Ezra 9/10 tu'a-wise : rethinking biblical interpretation in Oceania / by Nāsili Vaka'uta.
       p. cm. — (Society of Biblical Literature international voices in biblical studies ; v. 3)
    Includes bibliographical references (p.   ).
    ISBN 978-1-58983-620-4 (paper binding : alk. paper) — ISBN 978-1-58983-621-1 (electronic format)
    1. Bible. O.T. Ezra IX-X—Criticism, interpretation, etc. 2. Theology—Tonga. I. Title.
    BS1355.52.V35 2011
    222'.70608999482—dc23
                        2011042795

For

Silia Tupou, Latai, 'Eneasi Jr, Rosrine, George, and Kelesi'ia;

and my loving parents:

'Eneasi and Siokāpesi Vaka'uta

CONTENTS

ACKNOWLEDGMENTS xi
ABBREVIATIONS xiii

INTRODUCING *LAU FAKA-TU'A* 1
   Reading *Tu'a*-wise: An Alter-native 1
   Locating the Boundary 3
   Shifting the Boundary 8
   Defining the Limits 12

PART 1: *TU'UNGA*

CHAPTER 1: DEFINING *LAU FAKA-TU'A* 17
   Tu'unga: Location 18
   Tu'a 19
      Tu'a as a Concept 19
      Tu'a as a Social Class 20
      Tu'a as Colonized Subjects 27
   Lau Faka-tu'a 31
      Faka-tu'a as a Way of Being 31
      Lau Faka-tu'a as a Way of Reading 32

CHAPTER 2: SITUATING *LAU FAKA-TU'A* 35
   The Cultural-Ethnocentric Mode 38
   The Religious-Syncretic Mode 45
   The Experiential-Pragmatic Mode 51
   The Island-Oceanic Mode 58
   Situating *Tu'a*-wise 62

PART 2: *FOUNGA*

CHAPTER 3: THEORISING *LAU FAKA-TU'A* 67

Categories of Analysis 68

- Category 1: *Fonua* 69
- Category 2: *Tākanga* 72
- Category 3: *Tālanga* 74

Key Principles Reconsidered *Tu'a*-wise 76

- Principle 1: Idea of Context 76
- Principle 2: Idea of Text 78
- Principle 3: Idea of Interpretation 80

Theorising *Tu'a*-wise 84

CHAPTER 4: CHARTING *LAU FAKA-TU'A* 85

Methods of Analysis 88

- Method 1: *Lau Fe'unu* 89
- Method 2: *Lau Lea* 91
- Method 3: *Lau Vā* 94
- Method 4: *Lau Tu'unga* 96

Charting *Tu'a*-wise 98

PART 3: *ANGAFAI*

CHAPTER 5: UN-WEAVING EZRA 103

'Ātakai 104

'A-ki-loto 107

'A-ki-tu'a 109

Un-weaving *Tu'a*-wise 116

CHAPTER 6: RELOCATING EZRA 119

Category of Analysis 120

Methods of Analysis 121

Relocating Ezra 9–10 121
   Myth of (Im)purity and the *kakai-e-fonua* 122
   Illusion of Home and the *Kumifonua* 132
Relocating *Tu'a*-wise 141

CHAPTER 7: REVISIONING EZRA 143
   Category of Analysis 145
   Method of Analysis 145
   Revisioning Ezra 9–10 146
      Defining *Fa'ahinga* 146
      Assessing *Vā* 154
      Re-vis[ion]ing *Tākanga* 158
   Revisioning *Tu'a*-wise 160

CHAPTER 8: RE-STOR[Y]ING EZRA 161
   Category of Analysis 161
   Method of Analysis 162
   Re-stor[y]ing Ezra 9–10 162
      Analysing Tufunga lea 162
      Analysing Tō'onga lea 168
   Re-stor[y]ing *Tu'a*-wise 176

CONCLUSION 179
BIBLIOGRAPHY 183
GLOSSARY OF TONGAN TERMS 205

ACKNOWLEDGMENTS

I want to express my heartfelt gratitude to those who have enabled me to bring this book into publishable form. None of them is responsible for any shortcoming herein.

To my former doctoral advisors at the University of Auckland, Prof Elaine M. Wainwright and Dr Tim Bulkeley, for their guidance, and for allowing this work to be different.

To Jione Havea (United Theological College, Sydney) for reading the manuscript, and his on-going support and encouragement.

To the editors of the Society of Biblical Literature's IVBS series, especially Dr Monica Melanchthon, for accepting the manuscript. I am also indebted to Leigh Andersen, Managing Editor of SBL, for making the final form of this work less problematic.

To those who shaped my life *tu'a*-wise: my wife and best friend, Silia Tupou—for her unfailing love, understanding and support—and my children, Latai, 'Eneasi, Rosrine, George, and Nāsili Jr.—for being my rock and source of joy. *Mālō 'aupito* for all that you have brought into my life, and for making me a better person.

To my late father, 'Eneasi—for his wisdom and vision—and my mother and best teacher, Siokapesi, for who I am.

To those who have supported me but are not mentioned by name, you are greatly appreciated. *Tauange ke langilangi'ia 'a e 'Otua pea ke 'aonga foki 'a e ngāue faka-tu'a kuo fai ni.*

Mālō mo e tu'a'ofa!

ABBREVIATIONS

AAAG	*Annals of the Association of American Geographers*
AAR	American Academy of Religion
AIQ	*American Indian Quarterly*
APJA	*The Asia Pacific Journal of Anthropology*
BCP	Blackwell Companion to Philosophy
BibInt	*Biblical Interpretation*
BSac	*Bibliotheca Sacra*
CFTL	Clark's Foreign Theological Library
CoPac	*The Contemporary Pacific*
CS	*Cultural Studies*
CSPHS	Contemporary Studies in Philosophy and the Human Sciences
CTHP	Cambridge Texts in the History of Philosophy
DunRev	*Dunwoodie Review*
EB	The Expositor's Bible
EcuRev	*Ecumenical Review*
Edge	*The Edge: The E–Journal of Cultural Relations*
Exc	*Exchange*
GBS	Guides to Biblical Scholarship
GPBS	Global Perspectives on Biblical Scholarship
ICC	The International Critical Commentary
Int	Interpretation: A Bible Commentary for Teaching and Preaching
JAMs	*Journal of Asian Missions*
JBL	*Journal of Biblical Literature*
JEMs	*Journal of Ethnic and Migration Studies*
JIS	*Journal of Intercultural Studies*
JPH	*The Journal of Pacific History*
JPS	Jewish Publication Society
JPS	*The Journal of the Polynesian Society*
JSJ	*Journal for the Study of Judaism*
JSOT	*Journal for the Study of the Old Testament*

JSOTSup	JSOT Supplement Series
JTSA	*Journal of Theology for Southern Africa*
KJV	King James Version
KSS	Key Sociologist Series
LHB/OTS	Library of Hebrew Bible/Old Testament studies
LTQ	*Lexington Theological Quarterly*
MT	Masoretic Text
NAC	New American Commentary
NCBC	New Century Bible Commentary
NIBC	New International Bible Commentary
NICOT	New International Commentary on the Old Testament
NIV	New International Version
NKJV	New King James Version
NRSV	New Revised Standard Version
OBT	Overtures to Biblical Theology
OTL	Old Testament Library
OTM	Old Testament Message
OTS	Old Testament Series
PJT	*Pacific Journal of Theology*
PTMS	Pittsburgh Theological Monograph Series
RBL	*Review of Biblical Literature*
RCT	Routledge Critical Thinkers
RPG	Routledge Philosophy Guidebooks
SAQ	*The South Atlantic Quarterly*
SBibLit	Studies in Biblical Literature
SBL	Society of Biblical Literature
SBLDS	SBL Dissertation Series
SBLMS	SBL Monograph Series
SemeiaSt	Semeia Studies
SHS	The Scripture and Hermeneutics Series
SPEP	Studies in Phenomenology and Existential Philosophy
STS	Second Temple Studies
SWC	*Studies in World Christianity*
TBC	Torch Bible Commentaries

TBP	The Bible and Postcolonialism
TBTC	The Bible in the Twenty–First Century
TOTC	The Tyndale Old Testament Commentaries
TUMSR	Trinity University Monograph Series in Religion
VT	*Vetus Testamentum*
WBC	Word Biblical Commentary
WPCC	*Westminster Papers in Communication and Culture*

INTRODUCING *LAU FAKA-TU'A*

No reading is neutral or innocent, and by the same token every text and every reader is to some extent the product of a theoretical standpoint, however implicit or unconscious such a standpoint may be.

Edward Said[1]

The pact of interpretation is never simply an act of communication between the I and the You . . . The production of meaning requires that these two places be mobilized in the passage through a Third Space.

Homi Bhabha[2]

READING *TU'A*-WISE: AN ALTER-NATIVE

Reading *tu'a*-wise (Tongan: *lau faka-tu'a*) is an attempt to interpret the Bible through the "eye-/I-s"[3] of *a* Tongan commoner (*tu'a*).[4] The

---

[1] Edward Said, *The World, The Text and The Critic* (London: Vintage, 1983), 241.
[2] Homi K. Bhabha, *The Location of Culture* (London/New York: Routledge, 1994), 53.
[3] This play on words implies that to read through one's *eyes* is at the same time a reading from one's "I"—one's reading carries along one's subjectivity and idiosyncrasies. My *eyes* are conditioned by my "I"; the way "I" read texts is shaped by the things that define my "self" as a person. That is why I use the singular "commoner"; though I read as a *tu'a*, I cannot claim that I read for all Tongan commoners, nor am I prescribing in this work a way of reading for them. However, my "eye-/I-s" is not a solitary subject, but a collective one. As soon as "I" read, "I" am always connected to a community that "I" am a part of. The "I" in that sense is also a "we." I read as an individual *tu'a*, yet my *tu'a*-ness can only be defined by being in a *tu'a* community. Without that community, I cannot read *tu'a*-wise.
[4] Chapter 1 will deal in detail with the concept of *tu'a* and its significance to the whole work. The intention is not to trace correspondences between biblical texts and my context (that is application). Nor am I seeking to employ existing approaches to biblical interpretation in my context (that is adaptation). I seek rather to develop a new approach to reading the Bible; to interpret biblical texts in a different way.

primary concern of this book is to develop, on the one hand, an "alter-native"[5] approach to biblical interpretation from a Tongan standpoint and to depart, on the other hand, from theories and methods that dominate biblical scholarship. *Lau faka-tu'a* puts more emphasis on contextualizing the "pact" of biblical interpretation rather than the Bible *per se*.

Contextualizing interpretation and contextualizing the Bible are two separate tasks. The former is about employing contextual or, more specifically, indigenous categories of analysis for interpretation, whereas the latter is about applying the insights from one's reading to one's situation or tracing correspondence between a text and one's context. One is about methodology; the other is application. *Lau faka-tu'a* seeks to offer "an–other" way of reading. The work as a whole is woven and organized with three interrelated objectives.

The first objective is to develop a theoretical framework or a *way of reading*[6] that is informed by Tongan cultural perspectives and knowledge in general, and the experiences of Tongan *tu'a* in particular. Tongan *ways of being* (i.e. the ways they act, relate, and behave) and *ways of knowing* (i.e. the way they think, understand, and construct knowledge) will provide the ontological and epistemological foundations of this Tongan *way of reading*. They offer the directions for interpretation and provide the insights for the formulation of methods.

The second objective is to chart a methodology for the analysis of biblical texts based on the proposed theoretical framework. This involves developing new methods and tools of analysis, rather than borrowing and employing existing methods of biblical interpretation. The main reason for such an undertaking is the fact that existing methods were neither developed within a vacuum nor should be regarded as universally applicable. Instead, a reading perspective of some sort that reflects a particular social and cultural location shaped each method.

The third, and final, objective is to put the theory and methodology to the test by reading Ezra 9–10[7] from multiple dimensions.

---

[5]The term "alter-native" indicates that the approach I will develop in this work is not just another approach, but it seeks to alter existing approaches using native insights, and, if necessary, it will also alter what is native.

[6]The phrase "way of reading" is preferable because it does not presuppose a systematic and organized approach, but an open-ended one. Openness and fluidity are characteristically Tongan and Oceanic.

[7]A text that reflects not only the mechanisms that drive the politics behind the reconstruction programme of the returnees in the postexilic Yehud community, but also the risks involved. This provides a glimpse into the psychological orientation that drives a large portion of biblical postexilic literature. In a sense, Ezra 9–10 is postexilic imagination in microcosm. It reflects in many ways the issues that the *tu'a* reader

Each reading will adopt a particular perspective and employ a certain method of analysis. These readings will allow readers to assess whether or not this Tongan reading of biblical texts makes any difference and if it offers alternative insights and/or voices.

These objectives do not proceed from abstract to concrete, nor do they shift from theory to practice. The theoretical framework to be developed and methods charted are not based upon abstract ideas, but on actual practices. They constitute a *practice-based* approach to biblical interpretation. Most importantly, the three objectives seek to affirm one key question: *Can a Tongan reading of biblical texts make a difference in biblical scholarship?* The whole work is structured in a way to demonstrate that such a move is a tenable alternative.

LOCATING THE BOUNDARY

The kind of reading that this work proposes falls within the emerging area of contextual biblical interpretation (CBI),[8] which is an umbrella name for various approaches to biblical interpretation that seek "[t]o foster justice, transformation, and liberation through the process of

---

experiences within the class-based Tongan society, and the postcolonial context of Oceania. Chapter 5 will set the limit of the text.

[8]This hermeneutical mode is also known by various names: Justin Ukpong prefers the name "inculturation hermeneutics" in Justin Ukpong, "Inculturation Hermeneutics: An African Approach to Biblical Interpretation," in *The Bible in a World Context* (ed. Walter Dietrich and Ulrich Luz; Grand Rapids: Eerdmans, 2002), 17–32. R. S. Sugirtharajah speaks of "vernacular hermeneutics" in R. S. Sugirtharajah, "Vernacular Resurrections: An Introduction," in *Vernacular Hermeneutics* (ed. R. S. Sugirtharajah; Sheffield: Sheffield Academic Press, 1999), 11–17. Larry W. Caldwell comes up with the term, "ethnohermeneutics," in Larry W. Caldwell, "Towards the New Discipline of Ethnohermeneutics: Questioning the Relevancy of Western Hermeneutical Methods in the Asian Context," *Journal of Asian Missions* 1, no. 1 (1999): 23–43.

I prefer the term "contextual" since it clearly locates the task in its proper setting, on the one hand, and avoids the misconception that comes with the various nuances of the terms "inculturation," "vernacular," and "ethnohermeneutics." As Josef Estermann acknowledged, "inculturation" presupposes some kind of dualistic philosophical world–view, which is problematic when considering the subject and object of the process: who is inculturating what? Consult Josef Estermann, "Like a Rainbow or a Bunch of Flowers: Contextual Theologies in a Globalized World," *Pacific Journal of Theology* II, no. 30 (2003): 8–9. Likewise, what is considered the "vernacular" alters and shifts from one place to another. The term "ethnohermeneutics," albeit acknowledging the fact that no hermeneutics is presuppositionless, leans toward ethnocentric orientation. Whatever name one uses, they all point to the rootedness of the interpretive task in culture. This rootedness does not endorse ethnocentrism; it favours an ethnocritical stance, where one has the liberty to engage one's culture critically. After all, there is no pure culture.

interpretation,"[9] and take the *social location* of the real readers (as opposed to the so-called *original* and *implied* readers) as their point of departure. CBI is marked by at least the following characteristics.

First, it is *context-based*. It is rooted in the situation of the real reader and takes into account the issues that threaten the lives of those within that context. CBI deals with realities such as social discrimination and violence, among numerous others. Politically, it is sensitive to instability, and also seeks to expose exploitation and corruption. It resists any forms of political domination. Economically, it is concerned with the challenge of globalisation, economic exclusion, and extreme poverty. The point being made is: *the context of the reader draws the agenda* and *provides the conceptual frame of reference*[10] for the hermeneutical task.

Second, it is *culture-sensitive*. It demonstrates a particular interest in resurrecting local cultures; those once suppressed and ignored by the dominant culture of the oppressors/colonizers. It draws on particular language traditions or cultural insights, and employs them as lenses for reading the Bible. Meanings of biblical texts are viewed through the eyes of the reader's culture. CBI also suspects cultural oppression in both context and text, and thus seeks to retrieve positive aspects of local cultures. This makes CBI, as Sugirtharajah points out, postmodern in its eagerness to celebrate the local and postcolonial and in its capacity to upset and displace the reigning imported theories.[11]

Third, CBI is *people-centred*, especially those who are poor and marginalized. Those who read contextually are not isolated subjects, but members of a community of people with whom they share experiences. They do not distance themselves from that community, but they immerse themselves in their daily lives and share their sufferings and their struggles.[12] Through the task of interpretation, contextual readers read the bible from where their people are, allowing them the opportunities to voice out their understanding of the biblical text. Simply put, the people are taken as active subjects of interpretation, not just mere audience.[13]

---

[9]David Rhoads, "Introduction," in *From Every People and Nation: The Book of Revelation in Intercultural Perspective* (ed. David Rhoads; Minneapolis: Fortress, 2005), 4.

[10]As promoted in Ukpong, "Inculturation Hermeneutics: An African Approach to Biblical Interpretation," 23.

[11]Sugirtharajah, "Vernacular Resurrections: An Introduction," 12.

[12]See Musimbi Kanyoro, "Reading the Bible from an African Perspective," *Ecumenical Review* 51, no. 1 (1999): 19.

[13]See Gerald O. West, "Local is Lekker, but Ubuntu is Best: Indigenous Reading Resources from a South African Perspective," in *Vernacular Hermeneutics* (ed. R. S. Sugirtharajah; Sheffield: Sheffield Academic Press, 1999), 37.

Fourth, CBI is *liberation-focused*. CBI is satisfied with neither mere reading of the text nor retrieval of information. It seeks through the reading task to bring about change. It aims to transform and to make a difference. In the words of Sandra M. Schneiders, "the comprehensive object of biblical interpretation is not merely information but transformation."[14]

Fifth, and finally, CBI is *faith-driven*. The majority of contextual readers are involved in the task of interpretation to make sense of their faith, and bring it closer to where they are. Each reader approaches the Bible with predetermined ideas about the Bible. In many cases, contextual readers struggle to reconcile the truth-claims of the Bible with the realities of their daily lives.[15]

All these aspects point to the situatedness of interpretation. That is, hermeneutics, of any type or form, is always situated within a particular historical and social milieu, and therefore conditioned by the worldviews, values, cultures and ideologies of that setting. As such, none is neutrally positioned or universally binding. Each approach to biblical interpretation (scientifically designed or not) is socioculturally dyed.[16] The approach developed herein—*lau fakatu'a* (*tu'a* reading or reading *tu'a*-wise)—shares the above characteristics and limitations of CBI.

Raising awareness in biblical scholarship to the situatedness of interpretation came via some significant developments in both the humanities and social sciences. Pushing forward this development were ordinary peoples in different contexts, who struggled to free themselves from the various oppressive regimes they encountered in real life. At the forefront of such struggles were the feminist and black liberation movements of the 1960s. Different forms of CBI seek to participate in

---

[14]Sandra M. Schneiders, *The Revelatory Text: Interpreting the New Testament as Sacred Scripture* (Collegeville: Liturgical, 1999), xvii.

[15]See David Tuesday Adamo, "African Cultural Hermeneutics," in *Vernacular Hermeneutics* (ed. R. S. Sugirtharajah; Sheffield: Sheffield Academic Press, 1999), 69.

[16]Mary C. Callaway acknowledges this by saying, "A review of critical work over a period of years shows how emphases change because the exegetes' own historical contexts inevitably colour their work. It is easy from a distance to see the effect of Darwin's theory on Wellhausen's reconstruction of Israel's religion"; see Mary C. Callaway, "Canonical Criticism," in *To Each Its Own Meaning: An Introduction to Biblical Criticism and Their Applications* (ed. Steven L. McKenzie and Stephen R. Haynes; Louisville: Westminster John Knox, 1993), 123. I, as a Tongan reader who hails from a particular social location, do not intend to follow the theoretical and methodological maps charted by other contextual readers. I attempt to redirect the course of contextual hermeneutics towards Oceania. Meaning-making is only possible due to sociocultural conventions that enable understanding and communication. Without such conventions, interpretation would be an impossible task.

these movements for liberation through the process of interpretation. But as with every movement, there are always issues involved; CBI has its own share, and some are as follows.

The first is what I call *naïve contextualism*. This contextual tendency celebrates local cultures as valid sites for interpretation, and rightly calls for a departure from Eurocentric/colonial readings of the Bible. The problem however is that those who utter this call have failed in many instances to acknowledge and condemn the "sins" of their own culture. David Adamo, for example, calls for an African cultural hermeneutics that "immerses" the interpreter in African culture, to become an insider.[17] He ignores, however, the reality that African cultures also contribute to the African situation of conflict and poverty. While there is a need to appreciate the value of local cultural resources, one must acknowledge that no culture is innocent. Every culture, native or foreign, has its own dark side. Each culture therefore must undergo critical scrutiny to expose oppressive forces that for the most part affect the well-being of people within that culture, and the way they read the Bible. Failure to critically engage with one's own culture would be problematic for interpretation.

The second is *reversed contextualism*.[18] This refers to the use of contextual linguistic "guises" for non-contextual concepts. Instead of employing local concepts for reading, reverse contextualism simply translates foreign concepts into the vernacular. Such practice may be linguistically valid, but it is not hermeneutically. Each context has its own cultural heritage. That heritage needs to be the basis for developing approaches, rather than using foreign ideas dressed up in local linguistic outfits.

The third issue is *purist contextualism*. This refers to a tendency to assume contextual/cultural homogeneity, which thus ignores the reality that every culture is a hybrid, and always multifaceted. Some African approaches[19] strangely refer to African culture in the singular sense, ignoring this diversity. Contextual readers need to acknowledge the multifarious and heterogeneous character of cultures.

---

[17]Adamo, "African Cultural Hermeneutics," 66–90.

[18]I coined the term "reversed contextualism" to indicate the idea that "contextualization" is a process that needs to begin from one's own context and culture (from inside), rather than dictated by issues and ideas that are borrowed from other cultures (from outside).

[19]For examples, Musa W. Dube, "Readings of *Semoya*: Batswana Women's Interpretation of Matthew 15:21–28," *Semeia* 78 (1996): 111–129, Ukpong, "Inculturation Hermeneutics: An African Approach to Biblical Interpretation," 17–32.

The fourth issue is *ethnocentric contextualism*. This involves the temptation to put too much hope in indigenous epistemologies and insights. I do not question the fact that indigenous epistemologies have some valuable contributions. That is one of the major drivers behind this work. However, one needs to be aware that every construction of knowledge has some ideological tendency.[20] In my case, I am required to do some critical self-analysis in order to understand my prejudices, biases, and limitations.

The fifth, and final, issue is *hegemonic contextualism*. While contextual approaches attempt to "dehegemonize"[21] the colonial (or "Euro-stream") reading of texts, on the one hand, it is important not to create new hermeneutical hegemonies, on the other hand. Contextual interpretation needs to be theorised considerably, making sure that it does not unleash any oppressive force in its pursuit of liberation and justice.

These issues, and the characteristics discussed above, provide guidelines and cautions for the approach that Chapters 3 and 4 outline respectively. The issues also mark two important points. First, CBI, like all approaches, has pitfalls. Second, CBI needs constant change and

---

[20] Knowledge in Tonga, prior to arrival of Europeans (beachcombers, traders, missionaries, colonizers, etc.), was a property of chiefs (*hou'eiki*). As the only subjects with souls, they were also the ones with minds. In contrast, the *tu'a* (including my ancestors) was viewed as soulless and ignorant, lacking the ability to think and create knowledge. The chiefs, as a way of strengthening their grip on power and legitimizing their rule, moulded and shared only knowledge that was necessary for people to have. Views of the world and society were very much determined and dictated from the top. The majority of the people were indoctrinated with the illusion that it was their destiny to serve. Such propaganda was conveyed in the form of myths (cf. 'I. Futa Helu, *Critical Essays: Cultural Perspectives from the South Seas* (Canberra: Journal of Pacific History, 1999), 73.) and genealogies, among others. Myths were ideologically shaped to serve the interests of the elite class. Genealogies were also constructed for the same reason. See Phyllis Herda, "Genealogy in the Tongan construction of the past," in *Tongan culture and History* (ed. Phyllis Herda, et al.; Canberra: Department of Pacific and Southeast Asian History, Research School of Pacific Studies, ANU, 1990), 21. To do justice to history was the effect of this programme of indoctrination that proved to be the most severe, psychologically and socio-politically. Psychologically, the inferiority mentality never ended. It prevailed in the mind of the *tu'a/me'avale* (commoners/ignorant ones) across centuries and millennia. The lack of critical thinking that often characterizes learning among Tongans (as in other Oceanic islands) is one of the many prolonged effects.

[21] A term coined by David W. Gegeo and Karen Ann-Watson Gegeo to describe the need for Pacific Island scholars to find their "own research and epistemic frameworks rather than continue to rely exclusively on those of the colonizer." See David W. Gegeo and Karen Ann-Watson Gegeo, "How We Know: Kwara'ae Rural Villagers Doing Indigenous Epistemology," *The Contemporary Pacific* 13, no. 1 (2001): 55, 57.

improvement. The approach theorized and charted in the forthcoming chapters will seek not only to avoid the pitfalls, but also to offer some options for improvement.

SHIFTING THE BOUNDARY

This work is prompted by various rationales; each has its own significance. It is prompted, first of all, by a need to develop an approach to biblical interpretation that is non-elitist and culturally relevant. Biblical interpretation has long been "a cult of professional expertise"[22] that caters only for the interests of scholars in the field, but with lack of consideration for non-expert readers like Tongan commoners (*tu'a*). This need came to my attention some years ago when I taught a course on biblical hermeneutics and exegesis to a group of Tongan students who enrolled in the Tongan programmes of study at the Sia'atoutai Theological College (STC)[23] in Tonga. As required by the curriculum, the various theories and methods of biblical interpretation were to be taught in the Tongan language, despite the fact that there was lack of resources and tools in Tongan, and only a few of those students could read English textbooks. At the end of their programme of study, the students still found it hard to apply what they had learned in class to their readings of the Bible. Most continued to be dependent on lecture notes and interpretations of several texts that I shared with them. It was not until I met one of our Tongan Methodist lay ministers (*Setuata Faka-Konifelenisi*)[24] that the idea of contextual interpretation struck me. STC hosted a programme for its ex-students every Wednesday in 1992 to 1993, where biblical studies faculty updated them on matters related to biblical interpretation. After a session on how to interpret lectionary readings for Good Friday and Easter Sunday, this Methodist lay minister approached me and asked if he could share with me his own reading of the Easter narrative. He started by talking about the seating of the

---

[22] Said, *The World, The Text and The Critic*, 2.

[23] Sia'atoutai Theological College is run by the Free Wesleyan Church (Methodist Church) of Tonga and it offers degree programmes both in English and Tongan. STC offers these programmes to cater for the needs of those who are interested in theological education but find it hard to speak, read and write in English. It is one, if not the, oldest theological institutions in the region as it was first established in 1841 in Neiafu, Vava'u (a group of islands to the north of Tonga's main island, Tongatapu).

[24] The name of this particular person is Tupou Malolo of Fahefa, Tongatapu, who passed away shortly after our conversation. His knowledge of Tongan culture and dedication to the preaching of the Scripture made him one of the best Tongan preachers I had ever met, despite having a limited theological training.

matāpule (chiefs' attendants or spokespersons) in formal Tongan occasions. If it was a funeral, the *matāpule* would be seated to the left side of the presiding chief; in case of celebration, the *matāpule* would be seated to the right. He then referred back to the resurrection text and pointed out that at the tomb, the angels who announced the resurrection were seated to the right side of the place where Jesus was laid to rest, thus indicated something to celebrate. The seating of *matāpule* served as his reading lens. My interest in contextual interpretation began from that conversation; from the same occasion, this project was conceived.

The second rationale is a need to *re[th]ink* (rethink and rewrite) biblical interpretation from an Oceanic, particularly Tongan, standpoint. This is motivated by the opportunity allowed by the contextual turn in biblical studies, on the one hand, and the uncharted space, as well as critical tendencies, exposed by the contextual biblical literature[25] on the other hand. Contextual hermeneutics opens up the opportunity to claim a space in biblical scholarship for Tongan perspectives; it allows my approach to be different, rather than being homogenized into a particular academic disciplinary norm. This is to be established upon the fact that:

> (i) Oceania is contextually different and culturally diverse. I am not claiming Oceanic or Tongan "exceptionalism."[26] I simply hope that this work would contribute, in its own uniqueness, to the great cause others have remarkably advanced from their respective contexts.[27]

---

[25] I am referring here to works in biblical studies that are upfront about how the readers' contexts shape the way they read the Bible.

[26] I use the term in the same sense as in James Clifford, "Indigenous Articulations," *The Contemporary Pacific* 13, no. 2 (2001): 473.

[27] See Jione Havea, "The Future Stands Between Here and There: Towards an Island(ic) Hermeneutics," *Pacific Journal of Theology* II, no. 13 (1995): 61–68. Fernando F. Segovia and Mary Ann Tolbert, eds. *Reading from this Place: Social Location and Biblical Interpretation in the United States* (Vol. 1. Minneapolis: Fortress, 1995). Choi Hee An and Katheryn Pfisterer Darr, eds. *Engaging the Bible: Critical Readings from Contemporary Women* (Minneapolis: Fortress, 2006), Randall C. Bailey, ed. *Yet With A Steady Beat: Contemporary U. S. Afrocentric Biblical Interpretation* (Atlanta: SBL, 2003), Charles H. Cosgrove et al., *Cross-Cultural Paul: Journeys to Others, Journeys to Ourselves* (Grand Rapids: Eerdmans, 2005). Walter Dietrich and Ulrich Luz, eds. *The Bible in a World Context: An Experiment in Contextual Hermeneutics* (Grand Rapids: Eerdmans, 2002), Bob Ekblad, *Reading the Bible with the Damned* (Louisville: Westminster John Knox, 2005), Graeme Goldsworthy, *Gospel–Centered Hermeneutics: Foundations And Principles Of Evangelical Biblical Interpretation* (Downers Grove: InterVarsity, 2006). Gary A. Phillips and Nicole Wilkinson Duran, *Reading Communities, Reading Scripture* (Harrisburg: Trinity, 2002), David Rhoads, ed. *From*

(ii) Tongan culture, like that of any other country, has its own ways, perspectives, and values. Continental and discipline–based hermeneutics and methodologies, which arise from different circumstances, are insufficient for understanding our "connected life worlds"[28] and for serving the interests of Oceanic/Tongan readers of the Bible.

The third rationale is the need to demystify the dominant fundamentalist view of the Bible amongst Tongans. Tongans (especially those in the "Methodist household")[29] view the Bible as *"folofola"* (a Tongan term reserved only for words of a paramount chief or a king) and is therefore *tapu* (sacred).[30] Because of its sacredness, it demands nothing less than reverence and obedience. Whatever it says is seen largely as an expression of the *finangalo 'o e 'Otua* (will of God). In that sense, the Bible is *the* book.

In most Tongan families, especially Protestants, the Bible is the only book in their possession, and the only book some people have ever

---

Every People and Nation: The Book of Revelation in Intercultural Perspective (Minneapolis: Fortress, 2005), Fernando F. Segovia, *Decolonizing Biblical Studies: A View from the Margins* (New York: Maryknoll, 2000). . *Interpreting Beyond Borders* (Sheffield: Sheffield Academic Press, 2000), George M. Soares-Prabhu, *The Dharma of Jesus* (Maryknoll: Orbis, 2003). R. S. Sugirtharajah, *Asian Biblical Hermeneutics and Postcolonialism: Contesting the Interpretations* (Sheffield: Sheffield Academic Press, 1999), *The Bible and the Third World: Precolonial, Colonial and Postcolonial Encounters* (Cambridge: Cambridge University Press, 2001), *The Postcolonial Bible* (Sheffield: Sheffield Academic Press, 1998), *Postcolonial Criticism and Biblical Interpretation* (Oxford: Oxford University Press, 2002), *Postcolonial Reconfigurations: An Alternative Way of Reading the Bible and Doing Theology* (London: SCM, 2003), *Voices from the Margin: Interpreting the Bible from the Third World* (London: SPCK, 1991). Miguel A. De La Torre, *Reading the Bible from the Margins* (Maryknoll: Orbis, 2002), Justin S. Ukpong et al., *Reading the Bible in the Global Village: Cape Town* (Atlanta: SBL, 2002), Gerald O. West, ed. *Reading the Bible Other-wise: Socially Engaged Biblical Scholars Reading with Their Local Communities* (Atlanta: SBL, 2007), Gerald O. West and Musa W. Dube, *The Bible in Africa: transactions, trajectories, and trends* (Leiden: Brill, 2000).

[28]Houston Wood offers this timely observation: "Disciplines that separate the spiritual from the political, literature from history, or economics from psychology, for example, misconstrue how most people in Oceania live. . . Disciplines are part of the homogenization of the world." See Houston Wood, "Cultural Studies for Oceania," *The Contemporary Pacific* 15, no. 2 (2003): 340.

[29]Methodism in Tonga is more than just one denomination; it includes the Free Wesleyan Church of Tonga, Church of Tonga, Free Church of Tonga, Free Constitutional Church of Tonga, and the Tokaikolo Church. The phrase "Methodist household" refers to these churches.

[30]Another sense of *tapu* is to place a prohibition upon something; that is, the Bible is strictly prohibited to be treated with disrespect.

read. It is considered embarrassing not to have a Bible, whether or not one reads it. Regarded by the people as endowed with divine *mana* (life-sustaining power), the Bible is kept with utmost respect and care. No one is allowed to eat in front of it or to abuse it in any manner or form. Such an act would, according to most, bring a curse upon oneself or one's family. This attitude goes to the extent that people do not welcome a new translation of the Bible that uses vocabularies that are meaningful to the present generation of Tongans.[31] The general attitude to the Bible hinders every move to re-educate people about the Bible and its interpretation.[32]

The Bible in Tonga is also seen as a container of answers to all problems. All issues, political or otherwise, are mostly judged based on biblical insights; or at least on someone's reading of biblical texts. That happened because of the prevalence of Protestant views of the Bible, especially the reformist doctrine of *sola scriptura*, which gives the Bible the sole authority for life and faith. The Bible offers the first and final word; there is no space for *an–other* word.

In many Tongan churches, both in Tonga and abroad, are groups who meet regularly to read and interpret biblical texts, especially the readings from the common lectionary. These groups are known by one of these labels: *"kalasi malanga" (preachers' class), "kulupu talanga" (discussion group)* or *"pakipaki folofola" (breaking scriptures)*. The name *"kalasi malanga"* is used for groups which consist mostly of Methodist lay preachers who seek to improve their interpretation of the Bible and their preaching. *"Kulupu tālanga"* means "group discussion"; that is, those groups meet simply to discuss biblical texts in light of everyday issues. The term *"pakipaki folofola,"* as Jione Havea has indicated,[33] literally means "breaking scriptures," and it indicates how members of these groups share their insights on biblical passages in the same manner as in the *breaking of bread* in the Christian sacrament of the Last Supper. Most of the groups are largely formed by *tu'a* people that have no formal training in biblical interpretation. What a biblical text "says" to each participant is the only thing that matters. Through *sharing*,

---

[31]As the "Word of God," no one is good enough to re-translate it. The irony is that missionaries translated the two Tongan versions of the Bible, and both are more than a century old. They both used difficult Tongan vocabularies that belong to a bygone era.

[32]It has gained an *'eiki* status that demands respect from readers and requires a literal reading, the kind of reading that does not take into account how one's reading might affect the well-being of the community. For some ideas on the fundamentalist position on the Bible, see George M. Marsden, *Understanding Fundamentalism and Evangelicalism* (Grand Rapids: Eerdmans, 1991), J. I. Packer, *"Fundamentalism" and the Word of God* (Grand Rapids: Eerdmans, 1958).

[33]See Jione Havea, "Numbers," in *Global Bible Commentary* (ed. Daniel Patte; Nashville: Abingdon, 2004), 43.

the participants are enlightened. Reflection and sharing thus serve as the dominant modes of meaning making.

It is ironic that Tongan commoners would read and value the Bible; a text so influential in the construction of their identity; a text that legitimized colonial practices and perceptions, on the one hand, and validated the suppression of Tongan cultures, on the other. How can such a text be sacred? The Bible, like any other text, is not guiltless. And neither are its readers. It is also ironic that a *tu'a* would employ aspects of Tongan culture for reading the Bible. Tongan culture has in a sense disowned the *tu'a*. Tongan culture, like any other, is neither pure nor innocent!

Despite all this, those within the *tu'a* class cannot live without the Bible or the culture (Tongan) that gives meaning to their lives. The Bible is so embedded in Tongan culture, which thus makes it difficult to take one without the other. One shapes the other, and vice versa. What is required, at least, is to adopt an approach to the Bible that could expose the dehumanizing elements that are engraved in its texts in order to bring out their transformative *mana*. Such an approach should neither be an attempt to offer expert advice nor to re-place the mode of reading most *tu'a* are practicing. Rather, it is an attempt to create more reading options for the *tu'a* community to be able to free themselves from the restrictions imposed on them by academic readings of the Bible, and to rise above what Tongan culture allotted to them.

DEFINING THE LIMITS

This book is divided into three main parts. Each part is guided by a key Tongan concept; when combined they reflect not only the objectives outlined above, but also the three main components of the reading that I develop.

Part 1 is guided by the Tongan concept of *tu'unga* (variant: *tu'u'anga*), which generally means "location, status or position." *Tu'unga* indicates, on the one hand, my social location, status and position as a *tu'a* reader; it provides, on the other hand, the location of *tu'a* reading as an alter-native approach to biblical interpretation. Defining the *tu'unga* of the reader is significant in the sense that no reader participates in the act of reading in a vacuum. Every reader reads from a particular location or setting, and s/he does so as a person who is socially located and positioned in relation to power and resources. Similarly, identifying the *tu'unga* of a particular reading, such as the one proposed in this work, is crucial because no reading is created *ex nihilo*.

Every reading, like readers, is situated in a particular location, on the one hand, and is built upon existing scholarship, on the other hand. These insights determine the concerns of the two chapters in Part 1. Chapter 1 defines my *tu'unga* as a *tu'a* reader, whereas Chapter 2 provides the *tu'unga* for my proposed reading in the theoretical and methodological landscapes of CBI. The two chapters set the stage for the development of *lau faka-tu'a* proper in the second part.

Part 2 focuses on developing *lau faka-tu'a* proper by outlining its key elements. Like Part 1, it is informed by another Tongan concept, *founga* (variant: *fou'anga*). The term designates "points of entry" or "transitory spaces." With regard to biblical interpretation, *founga* encompasses both the theoretical and methodological dimensions of a particular reading or approach. The *founga* offers several *points* where a reader can *enter* a text in the event of reading; it also provides the necessary methods and tools for the analysis of texts. The concept of *founga* underlies the concerns of the two chapters in this second part. Chapter 3 discusses the theoretical underpinning of *tu'a* reading; it outlines its key *points of entry* or what is referred to in the discussion as *categories of analysis*. These points or categories draw the agenda for *tu'a* reading. Chapter 4 deals with the methodological dimensions of *tu'a* reading by charting several methods of analysis. Both chapters will indicate that *tu'a* reading is not only a *practice-based cross-cultural* approach, but is also *multidimensional*.

Part 3 offers a *tu'a* reading of Ezra 9–10, displaying the categories and methods of *lau faka-tu'a*. As with the first two parts, this final part dwells on the Tongan concept of *angafai* (*anga* way; *fai* doing = way of doing or practice). *Angafai* shows how to go about doing a particular task; in this case, *angafai* demonstrates the way to go about reading biblical texts *tu'a*-wise. Most importantly, *angafai* indicates that *tu'a* reading is more than just a theory or method; it is actually a practical alter-native for biblical interpretation. The four chapters that constitute this part will manifest this alter-native. Chapter 5 un-weaves the *fe'unu* (strands) of Ezra 9–10 and its *'ātakai* (contexts) by employing the *lau fe'unu*[34] method of analysis. Chapter 6 offers a *fonua* reading of the text based on the *lau tu'unga*[35] and *lau lea*[36] methods. Chapter 7 gives Ezra

---

[34] The word *fe'unu* refers to materials made from the pandanus leaves for mat weaving. In Chapter 4, texts are visualized as mats and the acts of writing as weaving. To read texts is therefore an act of un-weaving.

[35] I defined *tu'unga* above as location, status, or position. In Chapter 4, it has another meaning; referring to the foundation, basis, or charter that validates claims made in biblical texts. To read *tu'unga* is to look for elements within the text that justify certain claims to power and domination.

9–10 a *tākanga* reading, and uses the *lau vā*[37] method. The last treatment of Ezra 9–10 in Chapter 8 provides a *tālanga* reading which is facilitated by some aspects of the *lau lea* method.[38]

The Conclusion will then bring the three parts together, and highlights the significant aspects of the work. Herewith I will evaluate the implications this work has for biblical interpretation, and provide some insights for further development of contextual hermeneutics in Oceania.

---

[36]The word *lea* is Tongan for "words, language, speech or the act of speaking." To read *lea* (*lau lea*), as will be discussed in Chapter 4, is to pay attention to the rhetoric of the text, the employment of language, and different ways of speaking.

[37]This method provides a social dimension for *tu'a* reading, yet it is more than just a social reading. The term *vā* indicates both horizontal and vertical relations. In that sense, the *lau vā* method does not merely preoccupy itself with examining the social aspects of texts, but also the sacred. That shows the fact that in Tonga, and most parts of Oceania, there is no dichotomy between the sacred and the secular.

[38]None of these categories and methods have been utilised in biblical interpretation before. They are used herein to demonstrate what Tongan hermeneutics can contribute to biblical scholarship.

PART 1: *TU'UNGA*

CHAPTER 1
DEFINING *LAU FAKA-TU'A*

> The *'eiki/tu'a* relationship applied throughout society to relations that have been contrasted hitherto in the literature as either political or consanguineal . . . All relations in Tongan society were inherently political since they involved relations between statuses that were regarded as superior and inferior in a particular context.
>
> Kerry E. James[39]
>
> The role of culture in keeping imperialism intact cannot be overestimated, because it is through culture that the assumption of the 'divine right' of imperial powers to rule is vigorously and authoritatively supported.
>
> B. Ashcroft and P. Ahluwalia[40]

Biblical interpretation has always been, and still is, a situated task. Every interpreter reads from a specific location in time and space, belongs to a certain community, and thus reads the Bible with eyes that are conditioned by his or her own experiences, preconceptions, values, beliefs, and interests. No interpreter is socially virginal; each is located, conditioned and engaged. This chapter seeks to define my *tu'unga* (location) as a *tu'a* reader and its significance to the work as a whole. The discussion below is thus divided into three sections. The first section focuses on defining my social location. The second section clarifies my location by defining *tu'a*, and the third section discusses *lau faka-tu'a*. All sections provide the basis for the approach this work will outline in Chapters 3 and 4.

---

[39] K. E. James, "The Female Presence in Heavenly Places: Myth and Sovereignty in Tonga," *Oceania* 61, no. 4 (1991): 296.

[40] B. Ashcroft and P. Ahluwalia, *Edward Said* (London: Routledge, 2001), 4.

TU'UNGA: LOCATION

Social location, as defined by David Rhoads, refers to

> [t]he way people experienced privilege and power and the way people are exploited, marginalized, or oppressed. Social locations include *race and ethnicity, gender, age, economic level, religious community, political stance, social class, occupation, education* (formal and informal), *sexual orientation, health, disabilities, legal status*, among other things.[41]

Based on that definition, I will now provide a brief synopsis of my social location as Tongan *tu'a* reader of the Bible. First, I am an ordained minister of the Free Wesleyan Church of Tonga (FWCT), and have considered myself a Christian (though some perceived me otherwise). I grew up in a morally conservative family that treated the Bible with utmost respect and reverence. Second, my education journey began at a kindergarten in 'Eua Island (east of Tongatapu, the main island of Tonga), which was operated by the wife of an Australian expatriate who worked in a FWCT agricultural college. I had my primary school education at the Government Primary School at my hometown, and former capitol of Tonga, Mu'a. From there, I passed the entry examination into the only English–speaking secondary school in Tonga at the time, Tonga High School, where I was on punishment duty (PD) several times for speaking in Tongan. After passing both the New Zealand School Certificate (NZSC) and the New Zealand University Entrance examinations (NZUE), I entered the FWCT's Sia'atoutai Theological College in 1988 to do undergraduate studies. Since then, I have been involved with theological education through teaching and postgraduate studies. Third, I lean politically towards a more democratic Tonga, despite having many reservations about the way movements for democracy have being conducted in recent years. Socially, I would like to see some transitions in the Tongan society towards genuine freedom and justice as the majority of the population are struggling to survive on a daily basis. Fourth, I am a son who loves his parents very much, a husband to a loving wife, and a father of five wonderful children. Fifth, I grew up in a family who (like most Tongan families) struggled

---

[41] Rhoads, "Introduction," 15.

financially (despite having both parents working). Sixth, I am a displaced Tongan. I no longer live in Tonga, and have yet to settle in Aotearoa New Zealand, despite being a permanent resident. I am constantly drifting between my memories and imaginations; between what I have left behind and what is yet to come. Finally, I am a heterosexual male who is culturally positioned as a commoner, a *tu'a*.[42] The concept of *tu'a* is the most influential in defining one's identity and place in Tongan society; hence, it deserves a closer analysis.

TU'A

TU'A AS A CONCEPT

The term *tu'a* carries spatial, temporal, physical, psychological, and cultural meanings. Spatially it indicates the *exterior* as opposed to interior; the *periphery* as opposed to the centre. In this sense, *tu'a* entails the fringes, the margins, the edges, the boundaries,[43] and subjects who are positioned, or have found themselves, in/on such a space. Temporally, *tu'a* designates that which is beyond time (Tongan: *tu'a taimi*) or that time that is yet to come. In this sense, *tu'a* carries an eschatological/apocalyptic overtone. The implication of this temporal sense is that another world is not only possible but is surely coming. Physically, it refers to the *rear* side, especially of the human body; that is, the back, the behind, or that which is *out of sight* as opposed to that which is *in sight*. *Tu'a*, in this sense, points to the *"unseen"* subjects as opposed to the *"seen."* In its psychological sense, *tu'a* signifies a state of mind or an attitude (for examples, *tu'a-melie* hope, *tu'a-naki* confidence, *tu'a-tamaki* despair). Culturally, *tu'a* marks a particular social class, and ways of life associated with it. This is the so-called *commoner* class in the Tongan socio-religious hierarchy (see Figure 1).[44]

---

[42]The whole book is organized around this particular position.

[43]Hence, we speak of *tu'a fale* (outside the house), *tu'a kolo* (outside the village), and so on.

[44]See Adrienne L. Kaeppler, "Rank in Tonga," *Ethnology: An International Journal of Cultural and Social Anthropology* 10, no. 2 (1971): 174–193. Also K. E. James, "Is There a Tongan Middle Class? Hierarchy and Protest in Contemporary Tonga," *The Contemporary Pacific* 15, no. 2 (2003): 309–336.

TU'A AS A SOCIAL CLASS

This identification—*tu'a* as commoners—was authored by non-Tongan writers to depict the group of people at the underside of the Tongan society. The term "commoner" however is a misnomer, since the meanings *tu'a* encompasses categorised those who are in that class together with slaves and animals,[45] and that is far more dehumanising than being an ordinary person.[46] Being a *tu'a* is worse than being a commoner. To some chiefs, if not all, *tu'a* are like dogs.[47] They may be imprisoned in the great stone burial vault of deceased chiefs to die.[48] They were in fact regarded by chiefs "as mere chattels to be used exclusively for their own benefit."[49] This was the situation into which Christianity arrived, and it continues onto the present.

The *tu'a* class as a social construction, however, is driven to an extent by the collusion of various mechanisms, both internal and external. Internally, the Tongan worldview, shaped largely by its belief system and values, is the strongest architect of Tonga's class-based society. The *tu'a* identity is defined in relation to the class at the helm of the Tongan society, the *'eiki* (insider/chief). Those in the *'eiki* class, on the one hand, are of divine origin, for they are descendants of the gods; hence they, according to Tongan culture, deserve the privilege they have. Those in the *tu'a* class, on the other hand, are descendants of maggots; it is their deserved duty to serve.[50] The *'eiki* have souls, and are destined to continue their existence in the after-life; the *tu'a* are (like non-human creatures) soulless, and therefore have no place in life or death.[51] Culturally speaking, members of the *tu'a* class do not belong in the

---

[45]They are addressed at most times with terminologies reserved only for animals. For instance, the children of the *tu'a* are often referred to as *'uhiki*, a term used especially for animals and their offspring. Ironically, and unfortunately, such stereotypes have found their way into the psyche of the *tu'a* and, instead of resisting such designations, they regard them as an expression of humility.

[46]A person born of *tu'a* parents is sometimes referred to as *tu'a posiposī* (literally, "farting commoner").

[47]Edward Winslow Gifford, *Tongan Society* (Honolulu: Bernice P. Bishop Museum, 1921), 286.

[48]Ibid, 321.

[49]S. Latukefu, *Church and State in Tonga, 1822–1875* (Canberra: ANU Press, 1974), 22. See also Elizabeth Wood–Ellem, *Queen Salote of Tonga: The Story of an Era 1900–1965* (Auckland: Auckland University Press, 1999), 66.

[50]I am invoking here one Tongan myth of origin, which talks about how one of the sky gods in the form of a bird tossed a worm into three pieces and eventually turned them into three human beings—*Ko Hai, Ko Au,* and *Momo*. Such a myth is both demoralizing and humiliating for the *tu'a*.

[51]Gifford, *Tongan Society*, 328.

society in which they were born and bred; they are a displaced class. This *'eiki-tu'a* dynamics dictates every relation in the Tongan society, at all level (macro and micro).[52]

It is sufficient at this point to say that this is a cultural form of control and domination, manufactured to preserve the *status quo* and maintain the privilege of power in the hands of an elite minority, the *'eiki* (chiefly) class. This dynamic manifests itself in many forms. Politically, the *tu'a* class continues to struggle for a more democratic representation in the decision making process. Economically, the *'eiki* class owned most of the resources, and that includes high tech resources like orbital allotment in space, and internet domain names. In the realm of religion, the *'eiki* class are also given high status, and they collude with religious administration at most times to the detriment of the people, the *tu'a*.

This underprivileged location underpins this whole work, and shapes its limitations. As an individual male *tu'a* reader, I do not speak for all the *tu'a*, though I belong to that class. I do not speak for all Tongans, though I am Tongan. I am an ordained church minister, but I do not share the current views of the Free Wesleyan Church of Tonga particularly with regard to its stance on the Bible and its interpretation. Likewise, this work can never represent the diversity of Oceanic perspectives, though Tonga is in that region. Nonetheless, this work, and the view presented herein, is one small step on the rugged pathway to transformation.

Being a *tu'a*, nevertheless, is not a given of existence; it is a *construction* of Tongan culture. This construction has been maintained throughout the centuries by both cultural and colonial mechanisms, which are *ipso facto* means of domination. Tongan culture is maintained by a strict cultural code called *tapu* (root of *taboo*). The term serves as a spatio-temporal marker that draws the distinction between the *'eiki* and the *tu'a*, between what is sacred and what is not, between permission and prohibition.[53] *Tapu* is a strict cultural boundary that tolerates neither intrusion nor transgression. To cross the boundary is a cultural "sin." *Tapu* functions also as a socio-political means of defining and claiming space. It demands certain obligations, and thus becomes the basic governing factor for all social relationships in Tongan society.

In the religious realm, certain practices were, and still are *tapu* at sanctuaries and designated places; adherents of the gods were given

---

[52]See James, "The Female Presence in Heavenly Places: Myth and Sovereignty in Tonga," 287–308.

[53]See J. Martin, *Tonga Islands: William Mariner's Account* (2 vols.; vol. 1; Edinburgh: Constable and Co. & Hurst, Chance and Co., 1827), lxxxv.

proper directions for worshipping. In the social sphere, the *tapu* system is evident in family relationships. Children are not allowed to cross into their father's designated space in the house, or to eat what is left of their father's meal, among other things. Brothers are also forbidden from staying with their sisters under the same roof, and from entering any of their sisters' designated domains.

Edward W. Gifford distinguished two kinds of *tapu*: inherent and temporary. Sanctuaries and the persons of chiefs, for example, were inherently *tapu*; other things such as food products reserved for feasts were temporarily *tapu*. He explained further:

> Temporary tapus [sic] may be placed by a chief, by a priest, or by a modern practitioner skilled in curing as well as "causing" ailments. Tapus [sic] placed by chiefs seem to have been backed by no supernatural sanction. Tapus [sic] placed by a priest called for the vengeance of a god upon the tapu breaker.[54]

The notion of *tapu* also had an impact on knowledge and understanding. Certain types of knowledge were considered *tapu*.[55] Words and ideas of chiefs (*'eiki*) were *tapu*. Commoners (*tu'a*) were expected to accept them with reverence and obedience. To criticize is to violate the *tapu*, and it therefore jeopardizes the norm of *tauhi vā* (keeping social relation or respecting space).

Knowing how to keep one's *vā* (space, relation) is vital. The *tu'a* simply cannot transgress the *'eiki* space; to do so is to violate the sacredness of that space. If a *tu'a* needed to enter that space, special permission and protocol would be sought and observed. Similarly, intermarriage between *'eiki* and *tu'a* was, and still is, *tapu*. Any cross-marriage would, according to tradition, contaminate the purity of the *'eiki* bloodline, and if it did happen, it often resulted in the dissolution of the marriage and/or the disowning of the *'eiki* person involved. The *'eiki* class prefers to marry their own cousins (to the extent of incest) for the sake of maintaining their constructed *myth of purity*.

The second cultural mechanism is *lea* (language). Tongan language is three-tiered: one for the highest *'eiki*, the second for those with *'eiki* ties, and the third for the *tu'a*, *pōpula* (slaves) and *monumanu*

---

[54] Gifford, *Tongan Society*, 342.
[55] The best example is the knowledge of sex and sexuality. Sex issues had, and continue to have, no place in public and family discourses. The chance of sex education getting into the curriculum of schools in Tonga is unlikely, at least for now.

(animals). For example, *hā'ele* is the word used to describe the mobility of the highest ranking *'eiki* person (or *tu'i*); *me'a* is for other *'eiki* members, and *'alu* or *lele* for the *tu'a*, slaves and animals. The same applies to the act of eating: it is *fafa'o* (to stuff one's mouth) or *kai* for the *tu'a*, *'ilo* for the *'eiki* in general, and *taumafa* for the *tu'i* (highest chief). With reference to the act of speaking, it is *lea* (to speak) or *fakahoha'a* (to disturb or interrupt) for the *tu'a*, *me'a* for the *'eiki* class, and *folofola* for the *tu'i*. *Folofola* is the word employed by Bible translators to describe the Bible as God's word.

These levels of the Tongan language also applied in the religious arena. The gods were addressed or spoken of using words reserved only for the highest chief.[56] Words employed for the members of the *'eiki* class were used for priests, whereas words for the *tu'a* were used for those below the religious structure, who are again *tu'a*. In that sense, a *tu'a* is an outsider in all areas of Tongan society. This linguistic mechanism further upheld the myth that the *'eiki* class had some divine connections, and the *tu'a* class was there to serve. Politics of language reinforced the domination of the *'eiki*, on the one hand, and contributed to the persistent subjugation of the *tu'a*, on the other hand.

The third cultural mechanism is pre-Christian Tongan *values*. Some of the fundamental ones are *faka'apa'apa*, *tauhi vā*, *mamahi'i me'a*, and *loto tō*.[57] *Faka'apa'apa* is the most important of all Tongan values. It demands "unconditional respect" and has its origin in the Tongan traditional *kava* ceremony. In this ceremony, there is *no place* for the *tu'a*. Participants are only the highest ranking chief (*tu'i*), other chiefs (*'eiki*) and their spokespersons (*matāpule*). Chiefs are seated in an oval-shape called *'alofi*, with their spokespersons positioned between them. The role of each *matāpule* is to speak on behalf of his chief, and to taste the *kava* beforehand to make sure that it is not poisoned. Seated at the top (*olovaha*) of the *'alofi* is the *tu'i* with two *matāpule* on each side. These two have higher status than the rest, and are called the *'apa'apa*. They perform the same role as the other *matāpule*, but ultimately they are there to provide security and guard the *tu'i* with their lives. In that sense, the term *faka'apa'apa* means "to act like the *'apa'apa*"; every Tongan,

---

[56]Take for example the words for the English "children": *'alo* for children of *tu'i* and *hou'eiki*, but *'uhiki* or *fanganga*, and sometimes *fanau*, for the children of *tu'a* and animals.

[57]These four are listed in Masiu Moala, *'Efinanga: Ko e Ngaahi Tala mo e Anga Fakafonua 'o Tonga* (Nuku'alofa: Lali Publications, 1994), 23. See also a discussion of Tongan values in Finau 'O. Kolo, "Historiography: The Myth of Indigenous Authenticity," in *Tongan Culture and History* (ed. Phyllis Herda, et al.; Canberra: Australian National University, 1990), 2–4.

especially the *tu'a*, is expected to serve, respect and protect the *tu'i* and those in the *'eiki* class unconditionally and wholeheartedly. The cognate term *'apasia* ("awe" or "reverence") has the same origin as *faka'apa'apa* and it signifies mostly one's proper attitude to the highest chief or the divine. The *faka'apa'apa* value however has gone beyond the confinement of the *kava* ceremony to become the most fundamental basis for all social relations; if reciprocally performed, it is Tongan ethics at its core. Without this value, the structure and order of Tongan society will collapse.

The second pre-Christian value is *tauhi vā*.[58] As briefly mentioned, *tauhi vā* literally means "to keep (*tauhi*) or respect one's relation or space (*vā*)." This is a socio-spatial mechanism that requires every Tongan to maintain right relationships with, and respect for the spaces of, others. As a value constructed by the *'eiki* class, it serves as a reminder to the *tu'a* class of their *fatongia* (duties): to serve the *'eiki* in order to maintain right relationship with them. Otherwise, the *tu'a* would jeopardize their own well-being. *Faka'apa'apa* safeguards *tauhi vā*.

The third value is *mamahi'i me'a* or *mateaki*, which basically means "totally devoted to performing one's duty." Like the foregoing values, this one demands unreserved dedication and zeal. To serve the *'eiki* class, the *tu'a* is expected to do so, even at the cost of their own lives. That is what *mateaki* is really about: to die for something or someone. History reveals that many *tu'a* did carry their service to that extent; all for the sake of the *'eiki*.[59]

The fourth value is *loto tō*, which can be translated as "loyalty" and/or "humility." Tongan culture values loyal, yet modest, people. The *'eiki* class expects not only loyalty from the *tu'a*, but also humility in the way they carry out their duties, and when they present themselves in public. The importance of this value does not abolish the politics that drove it initially. It helps to maintain peaceful co-existence, on the one hand, but it serves as a means of controlling the *tu'a* from any attempt to rise above their culturally constructed position.

All these cultural values are social ideals to be practiced as *fatongia* (duties, obligations, responsibilities). An ideal Tongan would be a person who is characterised with *faka'apa'apa, tauhi vā, mateaki*, and *loto tō*. Ironically, no matter how much a *tu'a* performed his or her duty, she or he continued to be a *tu'a*. His *tu'a*-ness is the basis upon which

---

[58] See an articulation of the concept in Tevita 'O. Ka'ili, "*Tauhi vā*: Nurturing Tongan Sociospatial Ties in Maui and Beyond," *The Contemporary Pacific* 17, no. 1 (2005): 83–114.

[59] Gifford, *Tongan Society*, 108–131, 327–329.

these values are expected to be practiced. Being a *tu'a* is necessary for maintaining these values. Without the *tu'a*, the *fatongia* expected from them would cease to be.

The fourth mechanism for validating the social position of those in the *tu'a* class was the Tongan *meta-story*; that is, those in the *'eiki* class are destined to rule; the *tu'a* are to serve. This meta-story is expressed in myths, legends, folktales, folk music, and genealogies.[60] One Tongan origin myth portrays the origin of *tu'a* as a maggot.[61] That stands in contrast to the origin of the *'eiki*, who are descendants of an earthly mother, Va'epopua, and the sky god, Tangaloa.[62] That gives the *'eiki* a demi-god status.

Another story is about a female *tu'a*, by the name of Kava'onau, who was sacrificed by her *tu'a* parents when a high ranking chief unexpectedly paid a visit to their island, 'Eueiki.[63] Having nothing else to prepare for the chief, the parents killed their only daughter and cooked her in an *'umu* (an underground oven). However, before the *'umu* was ready, the chief discovered the incident, and ordered the *'umu* not to be opened. The *'umu* became a grave, upon which two plants grew: one was intoxicating (*kava*), the other sweet (*tō*, sugarcane). This story praises the sacrifice of the life of an innocent and leprous female *tu'a* for the sake of a male *'eiki*. It has found a place at the heart of Tongan culture as a model *par excellence* of how the *tu'a* should serve the *'eiki*. On the flipside, the story implies that to be a *tu'a* and a female could make

---

[60]These stories are recorded in publications such as the following: *Tongan Myths and Tales* (Honolulu: Bishop Museum, 1924). E. E. Collocott, "Tongan Myths and Legends, III," *Folklore* 35, no. 3 (1924): 275–283. Elizabeth Bott, *Tongan Society at the Time of Captain Cook's Visits: Discussions with Her Majesty Queen Salote Tupou* (Wellington: The Polynesian Society, 1982).

[61]*Tongan Society at the Time of Captain Cook's Visits: Discussions with Her Majesty Queen Salote Tupou*, 89.

[62]Collocott, "Tongan Myths and Legends, III," 279.

[63]Here is one version of the myth: "There was a man and his wife, named Fevanga and Fefafa, who had a daughter named Kava'onau. They lived at Faimata in Eueiki. The Tui Tonga named Loau went travelling and reached Eueiki after dark. He went around and looked about the country, but found nobody except the couple and their child. A solitary *kape* plant (*Arum costatum*) grew near their house, and Loau placed his mat over it for shelter. The couple set about getting food for his reception. As they had nothing they killed their child, who was a leper, and roasted her. When the food was cooked, it was taken and presented to Loau. Loau knew it was their child who was cooked and he ordered them to take her again and bury her properly. Loau said that a plant would grow from the grave and that they must tend it. When the plant was large enough they dug it up and sailed with it to Haamea (in Tongatabu)." Another version identifies the two plants as kava and sugarcane. See Gifford, *Tongan Myths and Tales*, 71–75.

oneself a mere object of sacrifice upon the altar of chiefly service.[64] Kava'onau, from a *tu'a* perspective, indicates the uncertain condition to which Tongan female *tu'a* are exposed.[65]

The fifth, and final, cultural mechanism that shapes the construction of the *tu'a* is the ancient Tongan *belief system*. As there was no clear distinction in Tonga between the sacred and secular, one's status in the society reflected one's stand in the religious realm and vice versa. Chiefs ranked high in both religion and politics. "Every chiefly person possessed some degree of *mana* or supernatural power."[66] This ancient belief had its origin and legitimacy in the myth about the semi-divine origin of 'Aho'eitu, the first Tu'i Tonga,[67] from whom his successors derived their spiritual authority. That gave him "supreme sanctity,"[68] dynastic pre-eminence, and a theocratic status. Temporal and spiritual powers, therefore, were combined in the person of the Tu'i Tonga.

Priests (*kau taula*) were second only to the principal chiefs in matters of both religion and politics. Their roles and status corresponded largely to the gods they were serving, but were accountable to the needs and instructions of their respective chiefs. Priests played a mediating role between the gods and the families. Some stayed in sanctuaries; others did not. They performed sacrifices and determined the quantity and quality of the offerings. In cases concerning illness of chiefs, the offerings went as far as body parts, such as cutting the finger joints (*kau'inima*) or killing a person.[69] The *tu'a* people were the ones who often suffered when sacrificial demands were higher than what they had to offer.

The authority of the *'eiki* class towered above the whole society. The gods and priests were, in a way, at the service of the chiefs. One group served or used the other to uphold its own interests. However, religious figures were in no way equal in rank and authority to chiefs. The priesthood, in a way, was serving two masters: gods and chiefs. Chiefs worshipped the gods as much as they liked themselves to be worshipped. Contrariwise, the *tu'a* remained as they were as "the lowest order of all, or the bulk of the people."[70] In some cases, the *kau popula*

---

[64]Such a sacrifice however aligned well with the agenda of the Christian missionaries as they gave the myth some legitimacy by reading it alongside the narratives of the passion of Christ.

[65]This finds a parallel in modern Tonga as the *'eiki* class continue to use *tu'a* females as sexual objects, who eventually become mothers of illegitimate sons and daughters who have *'eiki* ties yet with no *'eiki* privilege.

[66]Latukefu, *Church and State in Tonga, 1822–1875*, 4.

[67]Ibid, 1.

[68]Ibid, 2.

[69]Gifford, *Tongan Society*, 321.

[70]Martin, *Tonga Islands: William Mariner's Account*, 91.

(slaves)—usually prisoners of war—enjoyed privileges that the *tu'a* never had.[71]

TU'A AS COLONIZED SUBJECTS

Tonga was never formally colonized; yet the rushing tides of colonialism affected Tonga considerably. This impact however did not transform the Tongan society in a manner that was accommodating for the *tu'a*. What it did at best was colonial *translation* and *cloning* at all levels of the Tongan society. Robert C. Young offers some insights on this translation process:

> A colony begins as a translation, a copy of the original located elsewhere on the map . . . No act of translation takes place in an entirely neutral space of absolute equality. Someone is translating something or someone. Someone or something is being translated, transformed from a subject to an object.[72]

Politically, the colonial authorities schemed with the most prominent figures in the *'eiki* class in order to establish a foothold in the decision making process. New political flavours were introduced and these functioned not to transform but to strengthen the traditional political setup. The best example is the translation of the Tongan traditional hierarchy into a colonial version of the British monarchy and hierarchy. This political influence brought a concept alien to Tongan culture, a text in the form of a constitution, which proclaimed, on paper, the emancipation of "commoners" (the colonial translation of *tu'a*), on the one hand, but gave more power to chiefs/nobles (*'eiki*), on the other hand.

Running alongside this political influence was the introduction of a new belief system in the form of Christianity that brought with it its own worldview and social values, based largely on another "text," the Bible. This strange "text" functioned as the foundational guide for religion and society as the constitution was for politics. Together they took over the place, and assumed the authority of the traditional Tongan

---

[71]This was due mainly to the slaves being treated as members of their captors' household, and these captors were mostly chiefs. See Latukefu, *Church and State in Tonga, 1822–1875*, 6.

[72]Robert C. Young, *Postcolonialism: A Very Short Introduction* (Oxford: Oxford University Press, 2003), 139, 140.

cultural "texts" that had shaped the lives of Tongans for millennia. This involved the suppression of many Tongan cultural practices (dances and rituals, for examples), and did very little to transform the situation of the *tu'a*.

As the colonial officials did in the political arena, so too in the area of religion, the Christian missionaries sided mostly with high-ranking chiefs in order to successfully establish their mission in Tonga. These chiefs in turn used the missionaries for their own political agenda. As a result, the Christian mission became a new embodiment of the old Tongan religion, where the *'eiki* continued to enjoy a privileged status at the cost of the Tongan *tu'a*. Religious affiliation of the *tu'a* was determined by that of their respective chiefs or the most powerful *'eiki*. The church of the chief was expected also to be the church of his subjects. To affiliate otherwise was considered a mark of contempt and disloyalty.

In the society, missionaries formed a new class equivalent in status to the ancient Tongan priests. As in other areas, the old must give way for the new. Tongan priests were relegated to a lower position and eventually vanished together with their religion. The missionaries became more powerful and were seen by Tongans as a new *'eiki* class, and therefore the *tu'a* served them in a chiefly manner. That at times created tensions between them and the traditional *'eiki* class, which subsequently resulted in political turmoil and church secessions.[73] Christianity introduced the western system of education, which trained the people for the first time to read and write. That created a literary subculture that was considered superior over Tongan oral traditions and indigenous modes of learning. The consequences of those events were heavy on the *tu'a* class as they continued to be outsiders in both the religious and political circles.

The impact of colonialism went beyond religion and politics to the psyche of the people. It caused the development of two significant notions: "the native (mind)" and the "colonial mind." Stewart Firth, an Australian historian and expert on Pacific history, recounts the colonial attitude to the natives:

> The colonizers' most significant ideological achievement was the invention of the Native, a category embracing all non-Europeans. The Native—singular and masculine—

---

[73] Secessions marked the development of Methodism in Tonga since 1885. See Nāsili Vaka'uta, "Religion and Politics: Issues Surrounding Ecclesiastical Politics and Political Development in Tonga" (MA Thesis, University of the South Pacific, 2000).

lacked European virtues such as application and foresight. His mind—the Native Mind—worked in mysterious ways.

> [t]he natives have no expressions for ideas quite unknown to them, such as gratitude, chastity, modesty, humility . . . [74]

Similarly, an Australian woman asked Hortense Powdermaker (an American anthropologist), in New Zealand at a dinner party: "Don't you think that the natives [Maori] are just like human beings?"[75] Thirdly, a Governor of New Guinea in 1919 held this view of the native in defence of corporal punishment:

> The Native is a primitive being, with no well developed sense of duty or responsibility. A full belly and comfortable bed are his two chief desiderata.
>
> The native frequently mistakes kindness for weakness
>
> With a native as with an animal—correction must be of deterrent nature.[76]

The portrayal of the natives did not only come from Europeans.[77] Other imperial powers also played a role. Japanese regarded the Micronesians as a third-class people (under Koreans and Okinawans):

> Micronesians . . . had no 'concept of progress' and 'no sense of industry or diligence. Theirs is a life of dissipation: eating, dancing, and carnal pleasure absorb their waking hours. For these reasons they have not

---

[74] Stewart Firth, "Colonial Administration and the Invention of the Native," in *The Cambridge History of the Pacific Islanders* (ed. Donald Denoon, et al.; Cambridge: Cambridge University Press, 1997), 262.

[75] Ibid.

[76] Ibid, 263.

[77] The native became a homogenized category for all non-Europeans. Indonesian natives were once described as "insensitive to ethics: he represents not only the absence of values but also the negation of values. He is, let us dare to admit, the enemy of values, and in this sense he is the absolute evil." See Christopher R. Duncan, "Savage Imagery: (Mis)representations of the Forest Tobelo of Indonesia," *The Asia Pacific Journal of Anthropology* 2, no. 1 (2001): 45.

> escaped the common traits of tropic peoples: lewd customs, barbarity, laziness and debauchery."[78]

These depictions of the natives were not mere colonial discourses. On many occasions, the natives became *victims of the words* when these were enacted. In *Colonization and Christianity*, colonial brutal acts against the natives are documented:

> In these colonies, no idea of any right of the natives to the soil, or any consideration of their claims, comforts, or improvements, seem to have been entertained. Colonies were settled, and lands appropriated, just as they were needed; and if the natives did not like it, they were shot at.[79]

A bishop in Sydney speaks of the colonial impact on the natives in these words:

> They are [the natives] in a state which I consider one of extreme degradation and ignorance; they are, in fact, in a situation much inferior to what I suppose them to have been before they had any communication with Europe.[80]

The construction of the native and the end results of that process put the natives at risk. *Tu'a*, as natives, also faced the same predicaments. In addition to this was the creation of the *"colonial mind,"* which left a psychological mark on the mind of the so-called "natives," and thus gave them a mindset that was self-contradictory and self-annihilating. This entailed preference for western lifestyles over traditional ones, western cultures over the local, western religion over Tongan religion, western values over Tongan values. The prevalence of such mentality in the Tongan society upheld the legitimacy of the *status quo*, and validated the traditional relationship between the *'eiki* class and the *tu'a*, rather than creating a more liberating alternative.

The colonial mentality also gave the "natives" a new notion of place that divided countries and peoples into "empire" and "colonies," as well as "centres" and "margins." This sense of place was defined by

---

[78]Firth, "Colonial Administration and the Invention of the Native," 263.

[79]William Howitt, *Colonization and Christianity: A Popular History of the Treatment of the Natives by the Europeans in all their Colonies* (London: Longman, Orme, Brown, Green, & Longmans, 1838), 471.

[80]Cited in ibid, 476.

power and was limited to land space, ignoring the vast ocean space in which Tonga is a part. Emerging from this perception was the name "Pacific" which connoted inferiority, smallness and peripherality.[81] With that mentality, local places were marked as centres (*kolo*), in which the *'eiki* class should be; other places were peripheral, such as *motu* (islands) and *'uta* (bush), and were considered the proper place for the *tu'a*. This geographical manifestation of the colonial mind pushed the *tu'a*, geographically and emotionally, *out of place*.

LAU FAKA-TU'A

FAKA-TU'A AS A WAY OF BEING

The term *faka-tu'a* indicates *a way of being*; it refers to the "ways of the *tu'a*" (how they live, relate, speak, think, behave, create knowledge and make meanings). A *tu'a* participates in events of interpretation in accordance with the ways of the *tu'a*. The term however has various nuances. When uttered by a member of the *'eiki* class, it serves as a *derogatory* remark on ideas, practices, and presentations that deviate from the norm and expectations of the *'eiki* class.[82] When used by a *tu'a* it has two possible functions: first is to express a sense of *humility* (especially in the presence of others, and those of higher social status), and second is to mark *resistance* (particularly when someone refuses to be dictated by the status quo). In the presence of others, a *tu'a* would proudly present oneself *tu'a*-wise as a genuine acknowledgment of one's limitations, and sincere respect for others. If a *tu'a* invited a guest, one would hear the expression, *"Ko e fakaafe faka-tu'a pē"* ("It is only a *humble* invitation"). When speaking in public, a *tu'a* would utter: *"Ko e fakahoha'a tu'a pē"* (I speak as a *tu'a*—meaning, I speak with a *humble and respectful* heart). In this sense, *faka-tu'a* conveys two important points: (i) a *tu'a* is neither insensitive to ethic nor an enemy of values; s/he is ethically sensitive and morally *response-able*; (ii) a *tu'a*, like any other, has worth and values, and thus deserves respect.

---

[81] The name "Pacific" describes the region as scattered islands in a vast ocean; such a perception limits the definition of the region to land-space, and thus disregards its greatest asset: the ocean-space. Hau'ofa proposes an enlarged vision in the notion of Oceania: a sea of islands. See 'Epeli Hau'ofa et al., eds. *A New Oceania: Rediscovering Our Sea of Islands* (Suva: Institute of Pacific Studies, USP, 1993), 6.

[82] In such situations, one would hear: *"Me'a faka-tu'a mo'oni ko ho'o lea"* (I cannot believe you have spoken in a *tu'a* manner or as a *tu'a*); *"tuku e sio faka-tu'a ko ia"* (get rid of that *tu'a* perspective).

A *tu'a* cannot be forced to act otherwise. Even if a *tu'a* succumbs to acting, s/he will always be a *tu'a*, and *faka-tu'a* will always be the way to be. *Faka-tu'a* allows the *tu'a* to *re-story/re-tell* and *re-stores* their identity and ways! *Faka-tu'a* is the *tu'a* rising from the underside of society to confront agents of domination. It is also the *tu'a* resisting being treated as objects, for they are active subjects in their own rights.

From the perspective of *'eiki*, however, the "ways of the *tu'a*" (*faka-tu'a*), like *tu'a* themselves, are inferior to the "ways of the *'eiki*" (*faka-'ei'eiki*). When the term *faka-tu'a* is attached to an action, idea, word, or behaviour, it serves as a degrading tag. *Anga faka-tu'a* (behaving *tu'a*-wise) depicts certain behaviour as informal and socially unacceptable. *Lea faka-tu'a* (speaking *tu'a*-wise) is used mostly for a person who is speaking in plain language or in an informal and unorganized manner. *Fakakaukau faka-tu'a* (thinking *tu'a*-wise) portrays one's thoughts as inferior and nonsensical. *Teunga faka-tu'a* (dressing *tu'a*-wise) refers to a code of dressing that is considered casual, or a person who does not present herself or himself properly in public or in chiefly occasions. Finally, *mo'ui faka-tu'a* (living *tu'a*-wise) is the word for a person who does not know his/her proper responsibility or has not taken his/her *tu'a* duty seriously. This is why the *tu'a* is linked with two stereotypes: *me'avale* and *kainanga-e-fonua*. The term *me'avale* portrays the *tu'a* as "ignorant or foolish ones," whereas *kainanga-e-fonua* depicts them as "waste of the land" or "eaters of the soil" (like earthworms). In that sense, an ordinary Tongan (myself, for example) is (from the point of view of culture) a worthless and ignorant outsider.

LAU FAKA-TU'A AS A WAY OF READING

The term *lau faka-tu'a* designates a *way of reading*. The word *lau* means to "read, count, or talk." When combined with *faka-tu'a* it refers to reading, counting or talking *tu'a-wise* (in the way of the *tu'a*). The idea of *faka-tu'a* in this work has a dual function: *it describes the orientation of the approach I am developing* (*tu'a* reading), and *offers an ethical basis for the practice of that approach*. Hermeneutically speaking, *faka-tu'a* functions as an ethic of interpretation.

As a *tu'a*, I participate in the act of reading with respect and humility, and am not ashamed to admit the limits of my reading. *Faka-tu'a* carries the *subjectivity* of the *tu'a*, which includes their experiences, aspirations, beliefs, values, concerns, and imaginations. *Faka-tu'a* offers displaced subjects in biblical texts the opportunity of speaking, rather than being spoken to/for; of seeing, rather than being gazed at/upon. *Faka-tu'a* is taking seriously the identity and desire of *tu'a* subjects in the event of reading.

Lau faka-tu'a will bring into the reading task the experiences of and issues surrounding the *tu'a* class, and engage in the reading task with attention to the well-being and aspirations of their fellow *tu'a*. A *tu'a* reader cannot be obsessed with his/her own well-being, because s/he is not a *subject-in-isolation* but a *subject-in-community*. One's reading is shaped by, and should therefore give account to, the community.

Lau faka-tu'a also seeks to prevent any dehumanizing tendency by unveiling forces of domination such as constructions of identity, discourse, meta-stories, value-systems, and belief-systems. In the process of reading, a *tu'a* reader has to identify both the *'eiki* and *tu'a* subjects in and around biblical texts. By *'eiki* subjects, I am referring to characters, motifs, and aspects elevated by both texts and readers to a dominant status. By *tu'a* subjects, I am referring to characters, motifs and aspects of texts that are unread and displaced by texts and readers alike; aspects that texts and readers tend to put at the *rear*, the *behind*, and *out of sight*. The *'eiki* subjects are those privileged by the flow of texts; *tu'a* subjects are the underprivileged. It is the task of a *tu'a* reader therefore to give the underprivileged subjects of texts a reading.

CHAPTER 2
SITUATING *LAU FAKA-TU'A*

> No one reads the Bible in a vacuum. Each of us reads the Bible within some venue, within a setting, within some place of contextualization—wherever it may be—and knowing one's place is key to biblical interpretation.
>
> Michael Hull[83]

> If social location shapes reading, then it is important to be honest and self-conscious about one's social location in approaching any act of interpretation ... It is appropriate to read from a particular 'place' and with particular interests. Not only do interpreters necessarily bring a preunderstanding to the text that enables them to understand at all, they also bring commitments, a stake in the outcome of interpretation, *a will to interpret in a certain direction.*
>
> Charles H. Cosgrove[84]

This chapter maps the terrain of contextual biblical interpretation, and aims to open a gap for Oceanic reading of the Bible. Contextual biblical interpretation owes its place in biblical scholarship largely to the influence of postcolonialism. This intellectual phenomenon, as William Kelly describes, can be thought of in the following senses: (i) an attempt to deconstruct Western thought within various academic disciplines, (ii) an investigation of the realm of the colonial and its aftermath, and (iii) a theory with two archives:

> One is the writing of people whose subjectivities have experienced the influence of colonization; and the other

---

[83]Michael Hull, "Knowing One's Place: On Venues in Biblical Interpretation," *Dunwoodie Review* 26 (2003): 83.

[84]Charles H. Cosgrove, "Introduction," in *The Meanings We Choose: Hermeneutical Ethics, Indeterminacy and the Conflict of Interpretations* (ed. Charles H. Cosgrove; London: T&T Clark, 2004), 3.

is the writing of those involved in resistance to colonialism, its ideologies, and their present forms.[85]

Postcolonialism came out of the context of Commonwealth or Third World Literature studies, which were literary productions during and after colonialism in colonies in Asia and Africa.[86] R. S. Sugirtharajah views postcolonialism as "a way of engaging with the textual, historical, and cultural articulations of societies disturbed and transformed by the historical reality of colonial experience."[87] In a similar vein, Robert J. C. Young offers this definition,

> [P]ostcolonialism seeks to intervene, to force its alternative knowledges . . . It seeks to change the way people think, the way they behave, to produce a more just and equitable relation between the different peoples of the world.[88]

Fernando Segovia locates the emergence of postcolonialism in biblical studies in the 1980s, due to growing frustration with existing paradigms of interpretation as well as major transformations across the disciplines of the human and social sciences.[89] Postcolonialism owes its theorization and practice to three influential scholars: Edward Said (influenced by Michel Foucault's notion of discourse),[90] Gayatri Spivak (influenced by Jacques Derrida's notion of deconstruction),[91] and Homi Bhabha (utilizing some important psychoanalytical concepts, especially the poststructural version of Jacques Lacan).[92] They gave postcolonial

---

[85]William Kelly, "Postcolonial Perspective on Intercultural Relations: A Japan-U.S. Example," *The Edge: The E–Journal of Cultural Relations* 2, no. 1 (2001): 1.

[86]R. S. Sugirtharajah, "A Postcolonial Exploration of Collusion and Construction in Biblical Interpretation," in *The Postcolonial Bible* (ed. R. S. Sugirtharajah; Sheffield: Sheffield Academic Press, 1998), 91.

[87]Sugirtharajah, *Postcolonial Criticism and Biblical Interpretation*, 11.

[88]Young, *Postcolonialism: A Very Short Introduction*, 7.

[89]Fernando F. Segovia, "Postcolonial and Diasporic Criticism in Biblical Studies: Focus, Parameters, and Relevance," *Studies in World Christianity* 5, no. 2 (1999): 178.

[90]Edward Said, *Orientalism* (London: Penguin, 1978). "Opponents, Audiences, Constituencies, and Community," in *The Politics of Interpretation* (ed. W. J. T. Mitchell; Chicago: University of Chicago Press, 1982/1983), 7–32. *The World, The Text and The Critic.*

[91]See Gayatri C. Spivak, *Death of a Discipline* (New York: Columbia University Press, 2003).

[92]Kelly, "Postcolonial Perspective on Intercultural Relations: A Japan-U.S. Example," 1.

studies its dual functions as a *reading strategy* (based on the insights of Said and Spivak), and as *a state or condition* (based on Bhabha's work).[93]

The postcolonial turn presupposes a real flesh and blood reader[94] who lives amongst a people situated in a particular sociocultural location in time and space. From such a location, the reader approaches the Bible with the goal of exposing oppressive mechanisms encoded in the text, and those that impede emancipation in the reading community. Here the reader is no longer trapped in history or in texts, but is located in different real–life settings. Such a turn inspired the publication of various articles and volumes,[95] allowing real readers from wherever they are to read the Bible in the light of their own situations and experiences.

Contextual biblical interpretation is about real readers. Broadly speaking, the current approaches in this emerging area of biblical scholarship can be categorized into four modes namely, *cultural-ethnocentric*, *religious-syncretic*, *experiential-pragmatic*, and *island-oceanic*.[96]

---

[93] Sugirtharajah, "A Postcolonial Exploration of Collusion and Construction in Biblical Interpretation," 93.

[94] Fernando Segovia has used the phrase "real flesh and blood readers" repeatedly in his works to mark the difference between the subject of cultural reading and the implied readers or subjects in philosophical hermeneutics. See Fernando F. Segovia, "Cultural Studies and Contemporary Biblical Criticism: Ideological Criticism as Mode of Discourse," in *Reading from this Place: Social Location and Biblical Interpretation in Global Perspective* (ed. Fernando F. Segovia and Mary Ann Tolbert; Minneapolis: Fortress, 1995), 7.

[95] Scholars who have in different ways utilized the insights from this discipline include Cosgrove et al., *Cross-Cultural Paul: Journeys to Others, Journeys to Ourselves*, Daniel Patte, "Introduction," in *Global Bible Commentary* (ed. Daniel Patte; Nashville: Abingdon, 2004), David Rhoads, ed. *From Every People and Nation: The Book of Revelation in Intercultural Perspective* (Minneapolis: Fortress, 2005), Segovia, *Decolonizing Biblical Studies: A View from the Margins*, Fernando F. Segovia and Mary Ann Tolbert, eds. *Reading from this Place: Social Location and Biblical Interpretation in Global Perspective* (Vol. 2. Minneapolis: Fortress, 1995), *Reading from this Place: Social Location and Biblical Interpretation in the United States*, Sugirtharajah, *Asian Biblical Hermeneutics and Postcolonialism: Contesting the Interpretations, The Bible and the Third World: Precolonial, Colonial and Postcolonial Encounters, The Postcolonial Bible, Postcolonial Criticism and Biblical Interpretation, Postcolonial Reconfigurations: An Alternative Way of Reading the Bible and Doing Theology, Vernacular Hermeneutics* (Sheffield: Sheffield Academic Press, 1999), *Voices from the Margin: Interpreting the Bible from the Third World*, Gerald O. West, *The Academy of the Poor: Towards a Dialogical Reading of the Bible* (Sheffield: Sheffield Academic Press, 1999), *Reading the Bible Other-wise: Socially Engaged Biblical Scholars Reading with Their Local Communities*.

[96] I have coined the above names to represent at least the diversity of readings in each mode, and in the area of contextual biblical interpretation in general.

The cultural-ethnocentric mode seeks either to revive aspects of cultures previously suppressed by colonialism, read the Bible as a product of culture, or to simply juxtapose the cultures and worldviews that shaped the Bible with the readers' own. Since it is a popular mode amongst African scholars, I will discuss two works on African hermeneutics as illustrations.

The religious-syncretic mode focuses particularly on the faith traditions and belief systems encoded in the Bible, on the one hand, and the resurrection of native belief systems and religious texts, on the other hand. This mode will be illustrated from works of Asian biblical scholars.

The experiential-pragmatic mode comprises readings from contexts of social, economic, and political oppressions. It also pays close attention to questions of race, class, gender, and ethnicity. This mode is well demonstrated in works of Latin American biblical scholars.

The final mode, island-oceanic, is still an emerging approach that seeks to read the Bible with island and/or oceanic imagination. Whereas the other modes are situated in continental contexts, the island-oceanic mode emerges from the non-continental context of Oceania. This mode will be illustrated from the works of Jione Havea. I will conclude the discussion of each mode by outlining not only its significant contributions, but also the gaps that invite alternatives.

THE CULTURAL-ETHNOCENTRIC MODE

> The biblical story is an unfinished story; it invites its own continuation in history; it resists the covers of the Bibles and writes itself on the pages of the earth... My experience has taught me that a written book does not only belong to its authors – it also belongs to its readers and users.[97]

This mode encompasses, and presupposes, readings that view the Bible as a product of culture,[98] and therefore employs aspects of readers'

---

[97]Musa W. Dube, "Towards a Postcolonial Feminist Interpretation of the Bible," *Semeia*, no. 78 (1997): 12, 14.

[98]Examples of such works include Wim Beuken and Seán Freyne, eds. *The Bible as Cultural Heritage* (London: SCM, 1995), Mark G. Brett, *Ethnicity and the Bible* (Leiden: Brill, 1996), Jacob A. Loewen, *The Bible in Cross-Cultural Perspective* (Pasadena: William Carey Library, 2000), Rhoads, ed. *From Every People and Nation: The Book of Revelation in Intercultural Perspective*, Gerd Theissen, *The Bible and Contemporary Culture* (Minneapolis: Fortress, 2007), Elaine Mary Wainwright and Philip Leroy Culbertson, eds. *The Bible in/and Popular Culture: A Creative Encounter* (Atlanta: SBL, 2010).

cultures as categories of analysis. I coin the term "cultural-ethnocentric" to highlight the point that any cultural reading of the Bible always carries an ethnocentric tendency. The term "ethnocentric" does not merely mean elevating one's own culture above all others, but it also serves as a reminder that to be culturally situated is itself ethnocentric since it involves the retrieval and celebration of one's culture amongst others. The call by L. W. Caldwell for an *ethnohermeneutics* is akin to this position.[99] He underlines the fact that hermeneutics is not presuppositionless. It always has some ethnocentric aspects, whether we like it or not. Whatever name one is using, they all point to the rootedness of the interpretive task in culture.[100]

---

[99] See Caldwell, "Towards the New Discipline of Ethnohermeneutics: Questioning the Relevancy of Western Hermeneutical Methods in the Asian Context," 23–43.

[100] S. Wesley Ariarajah offers an alternative in what he called *intercultural hermeneutics*. It is a hermeneutic that arises "out of experience, out of the need to make sense of an inter-religious reality, and out of the struggle to find meaning in the midst of and with the help of religious-cultural realities in which one finds oneself" – Wesley Ariarajah, "Intercultural Hermeneutics–A Promise for the Future?," *Exchange* 34, no. 2 (2005): 191. The importance of this intercultural hermeneutics, according to Ariarajah, "has to do with the need for an intercultural theology and missiology in a religiously plural world" (191). In his article "Thinking about Vernacular Hermeneutics in a Metropolitan Study," R. S. Sugirtharajah identifies three key aspects of cultures that are utilized by readers. The first aspect is the *ideational*, which includes worldviews, values and rules. The second is the *performative* aspect that encompasses rituals and roles. The third is the *material* aspect which comprises elements such as language, symbols, food, clothing and so on. Sugirtharajah draws a correspondence between these aspects of cultures with three modes of "vernacular" readings, which he referred to as *conceptual correspondences*, *narrative enrichments*, and *performantial parallels*. The conceptual mode "seeks textual and conceptual parallels between biblical texts and the textual or conceptual traditions of one's own culture" (98). The narrative mode reemploys "some of the popular folktales, legends, riddles, [and] plays . . . that are part of the common heritage of the people, and place[s] them alongside biblical materials in order to draw out their hermeneutical implications" (100). The performantial mode "utilizes ritual and behavioural practices which are commonly available in a culture" (102). While these categories do shed light on the cultural appropriation of the Bible, they do not acknowledge that contextual hermeneutics is more than cultural. It involves social, economic, ecological and political issues as well. See R. S. Sugirtharajah, "Thinking about Vernacular Hermeneutics Sitting in a Metropolitan Study," in *Vernacular Hermeneutics* (ed. R. S. Sugirtharajah; Sheffield: Sheffield Academic Press, 1999), 98. The use of the term "vernacular" however is misleading on two accounts. First, the literature on contextual hermeneutics is mostly, if not all, in English. Second, methodologies and research values for doing contextual hermeneutics are, from a *tu'a* and Oceanic perspective, still very much Eurocentric and continentally-biased. I use the term *continentally-biased* to mark the clear preference in biblical studies for projects from continental scholars (for examples, Asian and Asian-American, African and Afro–American, Latin American, and so on), rather than those from non-continental contexts, like Oceania. In that sense, *tu'a* reading is not just another contextual project; it seeks to

The orientation of the cultural-ethnocentric mode is perceptible in numerous published works, but I will limit the discussion to works of two African biblical scholars: Justin Ukpong and Musa Dube. Justin Ukpong proposes *inculturation hermeneutics*. He defines it as "a contextual hermeneutic methodology that seeks to make any community of ordinary people and their sociocultural context the subject of interpretation of the Bible."[101] As such, it articulates and emphasizes the use of the conceptual frame of reference of the people doing the reading in the interpretation process. Its goal is "sociocultural transformation focusing on a variety of situations and issues."[102] Its ethos is cultural diversity and identity in reading practices. Inculturation also has a twofold task. The first is to appraise the cultural-human dimension of the Bible in respect of its attitude to, and evaluation of, "other" peoples and cultures; it views the Bible (culturally and ideologically) not as an innocent text, but God's word in human language, implying human culture with its ideology, worldview, orientation, perspective, values, and disvalues. It also raises the need for a critical ethical reading in terms of its stance toward other peoples and cultures in the light of basic human and biblical values of love and respect for others, justice, and peace. The second task is reading the Bible to appropriate its message for a contemporary context; this involves engaging a biblical text in dialogue with a contemporary contextual experience to appropriate its message in today's context.

Ukpong's approach is clearly shown in his earlier article on the Parable of the Shrewd Manager in Luke 16:1–13.[103] He reads the parable from the context of the exploited peasant farmers of West Africa and the international debt burden of the Two-Thirds World. He then situates the parable within the theological framework of Luke's critique of the rich/riches and within the socio-historical context of the parable. While Ukpong advocates a multicultural approach to interpreting the Bible, which I think is an inevitable move, he still regards the biblical canon as the boundary for meaning making and suggests that contemporary readers should not read meanings into the text. To Ukpong, contemporary *cultures can inform the readers but should not transform the texts*. Here lies my problem with inculturation, which confirms what

---

de-continentalize and *de-hegemonize* biblical scholarship, on the one hand, and *re-contextualize* contextual hermeneutics itself, on the other.

[101] Ukpong, "Inculturation Hermeneutics: An African Approach to Biblical Interpretation," 18.

[102] Ibid.

[103] "The Parable of the Shrewd Manager (Luke 16:1–13): An Essay in Inculturation Biblical Hermeneutic," *Semeia* 73 (1996): 189–210.

Joseph Estermann finds, namely, that the term presupposes "some kind of dualistic philosophical world-view, which is problematic when considering the subject and object of the process: who is inculturating what?"[104] As long as the Bible maintains its essentialist status, the cultures of readers will continue to be missiological objects, vulnerable to suppression.

Another important contribution to cultural reading of the Bible comes from the works of the Motswana feminist scholar, Musa Dube. In most of her works, Dube calls for a postcolonial feminist interpretation of the Bible,[105] which takes into account not only colonialism and its impact on African cultures, but also the experiences of African women as opposed to those of males generally and white women. To Dube, the problem with biblical interpretation lies not only in the fact that it is predominantly Eurocentric and androcentric, but that white female interpreters fail to condemn such orientation, and thereby subscribe to it. This continues to maintain the superiority not only of European and male perspectives, but also of white females over their coloured counterparts. Dube argues,

> The failure of Western feminists to recognize and to subvert imperialist cultural strategies of subjugation means that their advocacy for women's liberation has firmly retained the right of the West to dominate and exploit non-Western nations. . . This position has complicated the relationship of international women's movements, hindering the formation of strategic coalitions that go beyond narrow identity politics.[106]

With regard to the Bible, Dube writes,

> For me to read the Bible as an African woman and from my experience, therefore, is to be inevitably involved with the historical events of imperialism. Indeed, to read the Bible as an African is to take a perilous journey, a sinister journey, that spins one back to connect with dangerous memories of slavery, colonialism, apartheid, and neo–colonialism. To read the Bible as an African is

---

[104]Estermann, "Like a Rainbow or a Bunch of Flowers: Contextual Theologies in a Globalized World," 8–9.

[105]See Musa W. Dube, *Postcolonial Feminist Interpretation of the Bible* (St. Louis: Chalice, 2000), "Towards a Postcolonial Feminist Interpretation of the Bible," 11–26.

[106]*Postcolonial Feminist Interpretation of the Bible*, 24.

to relive the painful equation of Christianity with civilization, paganism with savagery.[107]

Dube prescribes four elements of postcolonial feminist interpretations. First, one must recognize that patriarchal oppression overlaps with, but is not identical to, imperialism. Second, one must recognize the methods and strategies of subjugation in cultural texts and reality. Third, one needs to identify the patterns of resistance it evokes from the subjugated. Fourth, there is also a need to recognize the use of the female gender in colonial discourse as well as explicate how post-colonialism exposes some women to double or triple oppression.[108] With these insights, Dube offers a reading of Matt 15:21–28.[109] This reading incorporates perspectives of Batswana women on the text, obtained by using questionnaire and taping sermons. She also employs the concept of *semoya*, which in Setswana means "of the spirit."[110] *Moya* or spirit in Botswana culture symbolizes the continuing presence of God among the believers. One manifestation of the spirit is healing. *Moya* in that sense is an agent of restoration. Dube's aim is to "take seriously the subjectivity and agency of the women's own interpretation" and to draw from them useful models of reading,[111] *semoya* reading. This reading is founded upon the experiences of women in the African Independent Churches (AICs), and it comprises these four aspects. First, *semoya* as a mode of reading "resists discrimination and articulates a reading of healing: healing of race and gender relations; of individuals, classes, and nations."[112] This aspect of *semoya* presupposes that there is something good for all people within the gospel. Second, *semoya* reading also exhibits wisdom, courage, the creativity which integrates different religious faith in the service of life, and difference. It rejects the imposition of Christianity as the only valid religion. It promotes "a mode of reading that allows one to encounter and to acknowledge the strengths and weaknesses of our different cultures, and to respectfully learn cross-culturally."[113] Third, *semoya* offers an alternative feminist model of liberation that breaks free from the patriarchal constraints. Fourth, it

---

[107] "Towards a Postcolonial Feminist Interpretation of the Bible," 13.

[108] *Postcolonial Feminist Interpretation of the Bible*, 43.

[109] "Readings of *Semoya*: Batswana Women's Interpretation of Matthew 15:21–28," 111–129. See also *Postcolonial Feminist Interpretation of the Bible*, 184–195.

[110] *Postcolonial Feminist Interpretation of the Bible*, 187.

[111] "Readings of *Semoya*: Batswana Women's Interpretation of Matthew 15:21–28," 111.

[112] Ibid, 124.

[113] Ibid, 125.

articulates political resistance and survival against structural forces behind poverty, unemployment and so on.

Dube's approach brings to the fore two important points. First, there is no readymade strategy for cultural reading of the Bible; each culture creates the agenda. Second, it highlights what Dube and Gerald West allude to elsewhere as "reading with."[114] This mode, according to Fernando Segovia, has both socio-religious and socio-political aspects. Socio-religiously, the Bible is considered a significant text in the lives of African people symbolising the presence of God. This, however, is very ambiguous since it has been used for oppressive purposes. Socio-politically, "reading with" is concerned with prolonged political crisis and particularly the suffering of the poor and needy.[115] In the process of interpretation, *reading with* encompasses various features: attitude of the poor and marginalized to the Bible, relationship between popular reading and critical reading, and *speaking–with* rather than "listening to" or "speaking for."[116] The point of departure for *reading with* is "community consciousness."[117]

Positive though it sounds, other aspects of such a reading call for serious consideration. While "reading with" advocates the importance of perspectives other than those in academia, on the one hand, it poses, on the other, the risk of turning those *whom we read with* into "hermeneutical resources," which thus continues to exalt the "cult of professionalism" (Said)[118] and Eurocentric tendencies that contextual and postcolonial critics are trying to resist. From a *tu'a* perspective, popular readers of the Bible are not "resources" but dialogue partners, and they are definitely not "ordinary readers" (West) in the strict sense of the word. The term "ordinary readers" gives the false impression that professional and expert perspectives are in some sense "extra-ordinary" and superior. The acknowledgement of other perspectives should go hand in hand with appreciating the fact that "others" may have knowledge that trained readers do not have as well as insights that cannot be found in books and in lecture rooms. *Reading with* should go beyond

---

[114]See Gerald O. West and Musa W. Dube, "An Introduction: How Have We Come to 'Read With,'" *Semeia* 73 (1996): 7–17. See also West, *The Academy of the Poor: Towards a Dialogical Reading of the Bible*. "Local is Lekker, but Ubuntu is Best: Indigenous Reading Resources from a South African Perspective," 37–51.

[115]Fernando F. Segovia, "Reading-Across: Intercultural Criticism and Textual Posture," in *Interpreting Beyond Borders* (ed. Fernando F. Segovia; Sheffield: Academic Press, 2000), 67.

[116]Ibid, 69.

[117]Ibid.

[118]Said, *The World, The Text and The Critic*, 2.

"resourcing" others to "being taught and informed by others" as human beings who are capable of expressing their perspectives in their own words, and in their own language. This criticism may sound unfair, but the fact that Dube herself asks the questions and analyses the results from the women she "reads with" draws the limits to her postcolonial feminist agenda. At the end of the day, the reading belongs to Dube, and not the women of AICs.

The insights from both Ukpong and Dube do not exhaust the perspectives of other readers who employ their cultures in the process of interpretation. Laura Donaldson, a Native American scholar, rereads the story of Ruth through the eyes of a native American woman, shifting the focus to Orpah as a paradigmatic native who values her own culture and tradition rather than being assimilated into a foreign one like Ruth.[119] George Mulrain, from the Caribbean, encourages the use of mythologies and imagination in the interpretive task.[120] An important article by Randall C. Bailey, an African American, warns against ignoring one's own cultural bias in interpretation.[121] Bailey shares this concern with an African feminist reader, Musimbi Kanyoro. Kanyoro acknowledges, on the one hand, that the "culture in which a text is created or read plays a very important role in its hermeneutics."[122] On the other hand, she calls for a critique of cultures as a means of "seeking justice and liberation for women in Africa."[123]

The turn to indigenous and native cultures is prompted by several reasons. First, there is an increasing awareness amongst non-European readers that every reading is cultural, and meanings can only be cashed in the currency of one's own linguistic world and culture. Second, there is also an interest in retrieving native cultural resources and traditions, particularly those suppressed by colonialism and Christianity. Third, there is the need amongst those who are displaced to reclaim and reconstruct their identity by reemploying aspects of their cultures. These tendencies, Sugirtharajah observes, enable indigenous cultures to survive, thus reversing the missionary condemnation of

---

[119]Laura Donaldson, "The Sign of Orpah: Reading Ruth Through Native Eyes," in *Vernacular Hermeneutics* (ed. R. S. Sugirtharajah; Sheffield: Sheffield Academic Press, 1999), 20–36.

[120]George Mulrain, "Hermeneutics within a Caribbean Context," in *Vernacular Hermeneutics* (ed. R. S. Sugirtharajah; Sheffield: Sheffield Academic Press, 1999), 116–132.

[121]Randall C. Bailey, "The Danger of Ignoring One's Own Cultural Bias in Interpreting the Text," in *The Postcolonial Bible* (ed. R. S. Sugirtharajah; Sheffield: Sheffield Academic Press, 1998), 66–90.

[122]Kanyoro, "Reading the Bible from an African Perspective," 18.

[123]Ibid, 19.

indigenous cultures.[124] Speaking as a *tu'a*, the cultural-ethnocentric mode and its celebration of cultural diversity is a way forward in the practice of biblical interpretation. It means that Oceanic cultures, especially Tongan, have their own values and can serve as valid sites for interpretation. Celebrating the value of one's culture however is one thing; being displaced by one's culture is another. To ensure that cultures make a positive contribution to hermeneutics and promote transformation in society, they have to be critically scrutinised to avoid reviving their dehumanising and oppressive aspects.

THE RELIGIOUS-SYNCRETIC MODE

[O]nce we liberate ourselves from viewing the biblical text as sacred, we can feel free to test and reappropriate it in other cultures.

Kwok Pui Lan[125]

The religious-syncretic mode comprises readings of the Bible that juxtapose the religious traditions of readers with those featured in biblical texts. Since most traditional belief systems and religious texts were suppressed by colonialism, readers in this mode have an interest in resurrecting native religious texts, belief systems and traditions. I have chosen the works of R. S. Sugirtharajah,[126] Kwok Pui Lan,[127] and George M. Soares-Prabhu[128] to illustrate this mode.

---

[124]Sugirtharajah, "Thinking about Vernacular Hermeneutics Sitting in a Metropolitan Study," 92–115.

[125]Kwok Pui Lan, "Discovering the Bible in the Non-Biblical World," in *Voices from the Margin: Interpreting the Bible from the Third World* (ed. R. S. Sugirtharajah; London: SPCK, 1991), 310.

[126]See also Sugirtharajah, *Asian Biblical Hermeneutics and Postcolonialism: Contesting the Interpretations*, *The Bible and the Third World: Precolonial, Colonial and Postcolonial Encounters*, *The Postcolonial Bible*, *Postcolonial Criticism and Biblical Interpretation*, *Postcolonial Reconfigurations: An Alternative Way of Reading the Bible and Doing Theology*, *Vernacular Hermeneutics*, *Voices from the Margin: Interpreting the Bible from the Third World*.

[127]Some of her works include *Discovering the Bible in the Non-Biblical World* (New York: Orbis, 1995), "Overlapping Communities and Multicultural Hermeneutics," in *A Feminine Companion to Reading the Bible* (ed. Athalya Brenner and Carole Fontaine; Sheffield: Academic, 1997), "Sexual Morality and National Politics," in *Engaging the Bible* (ed. Choi Hee An and Katheryn Pfisterer Darr; Minneapolis: Fortress, 2006).

[128]See George M. Soares-Prabhu, "Laughing at Idols: The Dark Side of Biblical Monotheism," in *Reading from this Place: Social Location and Biblical Interpretation in Global Perspective* (ed. Fernando F Segovia and Mary Ann Tolbert; Minneapolis:

Sugirtharajah, situating himself within the religiously pluralistic context of Sri Lanka and India, proposes an *inter-faith hermeneutics* that "addresses the question of using the Christian Scripture in a multifaith context, and the need for biblical scholars to be sensitive to the people of other faiths in their interpretative task."[129] One key issue that he identifies as crucial in a pluralistic context is *conversion*, since it endorses cultural dislocation and resocialisation. To Sugirtharajah, religious conversion means not only a shift from one religion to another,

> but also more importantly from one community to another. Therefore conversion to Christianity means not only experiencing, relating to and realizing the ultimate reality in a totally different way, but also stepping into an utterly strange social and religious milieu. It is a change of outlook and an orienting of one's life to a different focal point, but it also means leaving one's own cultural heritage and joining a Christian community whose style of worship and church structure follow Western cultural patterns.[130]

Conversion in that sense, to Sugirtharajah, raises a lot of questions: Is one religion superior to the other? Is there an aspect in a convert's culture that should be preserved? How can one's tradition be utilized to interpret the new faith? Should one leave one's own cultural social tradition entirely in accepting another faith? To answer these questions, Sugirtharajah directs his attention to narratives that talk about Paul's conversion, where he finds two approaches: *conquest approach* and

---

Fortress, 1995), 109–131. Other scholars with a similar approach include M. Thomas Thangaraj and Temba L. J. Mafico. The former, from a Tamil Christian perspective, seeks to Cross-read biblical texts with Vedic texts; see M. Thomas Thangaraj, "The Bible as Veda: Biblical Hermeneutics in Tamil Christianity," in *Vernacular Hermeneutics* (ed. R. S. Sugirtharajah; Sheffield: Sheffield Academic Press, 1999), 133–143. The latter, Mafico, rereads the divine Yahweh 'Elohim from an African standpoint. Refer to Temba L. J. Mafico, "The Divine Yahweh 'Elohim from an African Perspective," in *Reading from this Place: Social Location and Biblical Interpretation in Global Perspective* (ed. Fernando F. Segovia and Mary Ann Tolbert; Minneapolis: Fortress, 1995), 21–32. A recent article also leans towards the same mode; see Barend F. Drewes, "Reading the Bible in Context: An Indonesian and a Mexican Commentary on Ecclesiastes: Contextual Interpretations," *Exchange* 34, no. 2 (2005): 120–133.

[129] R. S. Sugirtharajah, "Inter-faith Hermeneutics: An Example and Some Implications," in *Voices from the Margin: Interpreting the Bible from the Third World* (ed. R. S. Sugirtharajah; London: SPCK, 1991), 352.

[130] Ibid, 353.

reorientation approach. The former defines Paul's conversion as being conquered by Christ; his mission therefore is to conquer others for Christ. This approach functions at two levels. Theologically, "it projects a Paul who is deeply dissatisfied with the arid spirituality of his own faith"; missiologically, "it sees Paul's conversion as a warrant to take the Christian message to all parts of the world."[131] The latter approach, reorientation, describes Paul's conversion as a rehabilitation within Judaism, from one sect to another, rather than a transition from one religion to another. His life is not seen as being without faith but with a new understanding of his task. From a multifaith perspective, Sugirtharajah concludes that both approaches are insensitive to people of other faiths. He therefore proposes an alternative which he calls a *dialogical approach.* This approach "acknowledges the validity of the varied and diverse religious experiences of all people and rules out any exclusive claim to the truth by one religious tradition."[132] The implication for the hermeneutical task is to enlist the liberation aspect of each religion to bring harmony and social change to all people.

Sugirtharajah's concern is taken up by Kwok Pui Lan, but from the standpoint of a Chinese woman.[133] The driving force behind Kwok's work is the fact that for

> [m]any centuries the Christian Scriptures had been taken as the norm to judge other, non-biblical cultures. Seldom do biblical scholars and others feel the need to rediscover the Bible through the issues raised by people whose lives are not shaped by the biblical vision.[134]

The problem for Kwok is twofold: first, the rigidity of the biblical canon and its universal truth-claims; second, how the less than one percent Christians in China interpret the Bible to a majority of non-Christian Chinese. The agenda for biblical interpreters therefore is to reconsider the validity of the Christian claims, and to be aware of the politics of truth and interpretation. Kwok points out that interpretation is not just a religious matter, but a political one as well. It can be used either as instrument of domination or liberation. She then poses three vital

---

[131] Ibid, 355.
[132] Ibid, 356.
[133] I will focus only on the version of her work that appears in the *Voices from the Margin*; see Kwok, "Discovering the Bible in the Non-Biblical World," 299–315.
[134] Ibid, 299.

questions: Who owns the truth? Who interprets the truth? What constitutes truth?[135]

Truth, from a Chinese standpoint, is not a Christian or Western monopoly, but can be found in other cultures and religions as well. Similarly, the interpretation of truth is not the sole task of Christians and the West. Western readings of the Gospel, Kwok argues, tend to alienate those in the Third World from the struggle against material poverty and other oppressions in society. She speaks of Western reading as a "thin-sliced" and "pre-packaged" understanding that was shipped all over the world. As such, Christianity serves as the "running dog of imperialism."[136] Each culture and religion, to Kwok, has the right to redefine truth for itself. In response to the last question (What constitutes truth?), Kwok points to the difference between Chinese and Western understanding. Unlike the Western interest in the metaphysical and epistemological aspects of truth, the Chinese focus more on the moral and ethical visions of a good society; they emphasise the relation between knowing and doing. Truth, from a Chinese viewpoint, is "not merely something to be grasped cognitively, but to be practiced and acted out in the self-cultivation of moral beings."[137] She explains further that

> [t]he politics of truth is not fought on the epistemological level. People in the Third World are not interested in whether or not the Bible contains some metaphysical or revelational truth. The poor, women, and other marginalized people are asking whether the Bible can be of help in the global struggle for liberation.[138]

Like Sugirtharajah, Kwok sees interpretation as *dialogical imagination*. The Chinese understanding of dialogue is talking to each other, and it implies mutuality, active listening, and openness to what the other has to say, rather than a "dialogue of the deaf" (Dube).[139] This involves conversation between biblical stories and Asian stories; between Christian and non-Christian religions. It is also an attempt, in Kwok's words, "to bridge the gap of time and space, to create new horizons, and to connect the disparate elements of our lives in a meaningful whole."[140]

---

[135]Ibid, 301, 302, 303.
[136]Ibid, 303.
[137]Ibid.
[138]Ibid, 304.
[139]Dube, *Postcolonial Feminist Interpretation of the Bible*, 39.
[140]Kwok, "Discovering the Bible in the Non-Biblical World," 305.

Soares-Prabhu's works consolidate the message Sugirtharajah and Kwok have promoted. In his article "Laughing at Idols," Soares-Prabhu offers an Indian reading of Isa 44:9–20 where he exposes the dark side of biblical monotheism, on the one hand, and the misrepresentation of idol worship, on the other.[141] Soares-Prabhu situates himself in the complexity of the Indian world, which to him is defined by the three dialectically interrelated factors of poverty, religiosity, and caste. His key reading category is what he called the "Indian Mind," a mode of thinking that is context-sensitive rather than context-free; it prefers the concrete (such as persons and events) as opposed to the abstract; it is inclusive not exclusive; it experiences all reality as an interconnected and interdependent whole, which is therefore cosmocentric as opposed to Western anthropocentricism.[142] Indian thinking is also tolerant of ambiguity; it interests itself more in "seeing the divine image" than in hearing the divine word; it prefers polytheism over the monotheistic tendency of the Bible and the West. In sum, the Indian Mind is "intensely visual, pluriform, inclusive, cosmocentric."[143] This Indian mode of thinking provides the foundation for Soares-Prabhu's Indian reading of Isa 44:9–20.

He traces back the monotheistic and anti-idol orientation of Isa 44:9–20 to the Babylonian exile, which to him was an attempt of the so-called "Yahweh alone movement" to assert the exclusive worship of Yahweh, and portray Yahweh as the sole saviour of Israel, thus encouraging and supporting a shift from Israel's polytheistic past. He also despises the satirical nature of the text, arguing that such a tendency is unimaginable in such a religious text from an Indian perspective. The most problematic feature of the text for Soares-Prabhu is its misunderstanding of idolatry and its anti-gentile bias. Isaiah 44:18–20 portrays idol worshippers as those who practice "left-over religion"; they bow to idols made from blocks of wood left from those that they used to cook their food. Speaking from a religiously pluralistic and idol worshipping context, he rejects this portrayal of idolatry as a misrepresentation. Idolatry, argues Soares-Prabhu, is not worshipping a mere block of wood, but is something that mediates the "real presence" of the divine, similar in some ways to the mediation of the "real presence" of Jesus in the "consecrated" bread and wine of the Christian Eucharist. To bow down to an idol is not to submit to a block of wood,

---

[141] Soares-Prabhu, "Laughing at Idols: The Dark Side of Biblical Monotheism," 109–131.
[142] Ibid, 112.
[143] Ibid, 116.

but to a god made present in the idol. "The sin of idolatry . . . lies wholly in the eye of the beholder."[144]

Soares-Prabhu traces in Isaiah's anti-idol polemic text an ironic element. That is, the very reason that motivates Isaiah's condemnation of idolatry in others is the element of idolatry in Israel's own religion. "We see ourselves . . . in the mirror of our own destructive criticisms," remarks Soares-Prabhu.[145] Idols or images, to him, do not have to be material. Mental images of the divine are as idolatrous as the material ones. So, the claim that Yahweh cannot be represented by a material image is superseded by mental images that portray Yahweh in anthropomorphic terms; a God who speaks, punishes, pardons, is jealous, ordains laws, commands, promises, and who leads people in war, destroys their enemies, and demands strict "ethnic cleansing" to guard against apostasy. Such a portrayal, argues Soares-Prabhu, belongs to Panikkar's euphemism for idolatry, that is, *iconolatry*. Isaiah's monotheistic and anti-idol tendency is therefore an inadequate understanding of God. "If Yahweh is truly God . . . then he [sic] must be the God not just of Israel but of all other peoples (of all idol worshipers!) as well."[146] He further elaborates:

> God's concern cannot be monopolized by a single people but must reach out to all. God's all–pervasive presence cannot be restricted to any one temple or to any one "holy" land but must encompass the world. The gods that people worship cannot, then, be false gods or no gods. They may be (as Hinduism would say) inadequate representations of God. But they cannot be "nothing." Every attempt to reach God must relate in some way to the only God that is.[147]

The anti-idol attitude of Isaiah also gives rise to his anti-gentile bias, which exposes the dark side of biblical monotheism. Such an exclusivist position breeds intolerance and hatred, which thus hinders any movement towards liberation and transformation. Soares-Prabhu's reading provides two important implications. First, interpreters should acknowledge religious plurality and difference in the process of interpretation. Second, the religious and cultural orientation of the Bible is not always

---

[144] Ibid, 124.
[145] Ibid, 125.
[146] Ibid, 126.
[147] Ibid.

applicable, and it is certainly not the only claim there is. The Bible should be critically read for the sake of transformation.

The three works discussed provide clear insights into the mode of reading that I have called "religious-syncretic." This mode urges the practice of biblical interpretation to go beyond the doorsteps of academia and the confinement of traditional Western hermeneutics, to acknowledge that there is more to sacred texts and religion than the Bible and Christianity. It raises the readers' consciousness in regard to the following: First, it acknowledges the fact Christianity is not the only faith there is, and the Christian Scripture is not only one amongst many sacred texts, but it is also an alien document within many cultures that endorse a strange worldview and belief system. Second, Christianity, as an agent of Western civilization and imperialism, does not hold the sole key to salvation and truth. Third, the survival of Christianity and the Bible in such a pluralistic context depends largely on how much Christians appreciate the existence of other faiths and other sacred texts. Fourth, Christianity and its Scriptures only occupy a very limited space in the world's religious geography. Its truth claims need to be measured alongside others.

The multifaith and dialogical tendencies of the religious-syncretic mode open up possibilities for the interpretive tasks, and direct attention to the significance of all belief systems and religious traditions, including ancient Tongan religion. Nevertheless, religion of any kind, like culture itself, does not come naked or virginal; it is always ideologically "dressed" and, to a certain degree, "prostituted." As I have discussed in Chapter 1, there is nothing in Tongan religion for the *tu'a*. The *tu'a* therefore cannot put any hope in a religion that predetermines his/her status and destiny. For that reason, *tu'a* reading does not belong in this religious-syncretic mode.

THE EXPERIENTIAL-PRAGMATIC MODE

> The abject . . . is racially excluded and draws me toward the place where meaning collapses . . . from its place of banishment, the abject does not cease challenging its master. . . The abject is perverse because it neither gives up nor assumes a prohibition, a rule or a law; but turns them aside, misleads, corrupts; uses them, takes advantage

of them, the better to deny them. It kills in the name of life . . . it lives at the behest of death.[148]

This mode is experience–based and orients towards praxis. It encompasses different forms of oppression—personal, national, regional, and global—that people experience in their daily lives, from socio-political issues,[149] economic exclusion,[150] ecological degradation,[151] material poverty,[152] as well as discriminations in terms of sexual orientation,[153] race,[154] gender,[155] class,[156] ethnicity,[157] and residential

---

[148] Julia Kristeva, *Powers of Horror: An Essay on Abjection* (trans. Leon S. Roudiez; New York: Columbia University Press, 1982), 15.

[149] Norman K. Gottwald and Richard A. Horsley, eds. *The Bible and Liberation: Political and Social Hermeneutics* (Rev. ed.; Maryknoll: Orbis, 1993). See Naim Ateek, "Pentecost and Intifada," in *Reading from this Place: Social Location and Biblical Interpretation in Global Perspective* (ed. Fernando F. Segovia and Mary Ann Tolbert; Minneapolis: Fortress, 1995), 69–81. Also Monica J. Melanchthon, *Dalits, Bible, and Method* (2005 [cited November 2005]); available from http://www.sbl-site.org/Article.aspx?ArticleId=459.

[150] Nestor Miguez, "Apocalyptic and the Economy: A Reading of Revelation 18 from the Experience of Economic Exclusion," in *Reading from this Place: Social Location and Biblical Interpretation in Global Perspective* (ed. Fernando F. Segovia and Mary Ann Tolbert; Minneapolis: Fortress, 1995), 250–262.

[151] Norman C. Habel, ed. *Readings from the Perspective of Earth* (Sheffield: Sheffield Academic Press, 2000).

[152] Gustavo Gutierrez, "Song and Deliverance," in *Voices from the Margin* (ed. R. S. Sugirtharajah; London: SPCK, 1991), 129–146. See also Elsa Tamez, "Reading the Bible Under a Sky Without Stars," in *The Bible in a World Context* (ed. Walter Dietrich and Ulrich Luz; Grand Rapids: Eerdmans, 2002), 3–15.

[153] Robert E. Goss and Mona West, eds. *Take Back The Word: A Queer Reading of the Bible* (Cleveland: Pilgrim, 2000).

[154] West, "Local is Lekker, but Ubuntu is Best: Indigenous Reading Resources from a South African Perspective," 37–51. See Cain Hope Felder, "Racial Motifs in the Biblical Narratives," in *Voices from the Margin* (ed. R. S. Sugirtharajah; London: SPCK, 1991), 172–188. Also Makhosazana Keith Nzimande, "Postcolonial Biblical Interpretation in Post-Apartheid South Africa: The *gvirah* in the Hebrew Bible in the light of Queen Jezebel and the Queen Mother of Lemuel" (Ph.D., Texas Christian University, 2005).

[155] Elaine M. Wainwright, "A Voice from the Margin: Reading Matthew 15:21–28 in an Australian Feminist Key," in *Reading from This Place: Social Location and Biblical Interpretation in Global Perspective* (ed. Fernando F. Segovia and Mary Ann Tolbert; Minneapolis: Fortress, 1995), 132–153. See Yani Yoo, *"Han*–Laden Women: Korean 'Comfort Women' and Women in Judges 19–21," *Semeia* 78 (1997): 37–46. Also Dalila Nayap–Pot, "Life in the Midst of Death: Naomi, Ruth and the Plight of Indigenous Women," in *Vernacular Hermeneutics* (ed. R. S. Sugirtharajah; Sheffield: Sheffield Academic Press, 1999), 52–65. Tina Pippin, "The Heroine and the Whore: The *Apocalypse of John* in Feminist Perspective," in *From Every People and Nation: The Book of Revelation in Intercultural Perspective* (ed. David Rhoads; Minneapolis: Fortress, 2005), 127–145. Joseph Pushpa, "Trailblazers: Elizabeth Schüssler Fiorenza and

status.[158] Examples of this mode can be found in many published volumes that feature readings from diverse contexts and experiences.[159] I will focus my attention on insights from works of two Latin American biblical scholars, Elsa Tamez and Pablo Richard, plus one queer critic, Mona West.

Elsa Tamez, in a reading of 1 Timothy, situates herself in the southern *barrios* (neighbourhood) of San Jose, Costa Rica.[160] She describes the context as overpopulated, unhealthy and poor, where many women have become involuntary heads of households because their husbands have either abandoned them for another woman, migrated to the United States or have been unable to support their families due to alcohol abuse. The best they can do is to survive one day at a time.

George M. Soares Prabhu," in *On the Cutting Edge: The Study of Women in Biblical Worlds* (ed. Jane Schaberg, et al.; New York: Continuum, 2004), 53–68.

[156]See Itumeleng J. Mosala, "Race, Class, and Gender as Hermeneutical Factors in the African Independent Churches' Appropriation of the Bible," *Semeia* 73 (1996): 43–57. Also George M. Soares-Prabhu, "Class in the Bible: The Biblical Poor a Social Class?," in *Voices from the Margin* (ed. R. S. Sugirtharajah; London: SPCK, 1991), 147–171.

[157]Brad Ronnell Braxton, "The Role of Ethnicity in the Social Location of 1 Corinthians 7:17–24," in *Yet With A Steady Beat: Contemporary U. S. Afrocentric Biblical Interpretation* (ed. Randall C. Bailey; Atlanta: SBL, 2003), 19–32. See also Justo L. González, "*Revelation*: Clarity and Ambivalence: A Hispanic/Cuban American Perspective," in *From Every People and Nation: The Book of Revelation in Intercultural Perspective* (ed. David Rhoads; Minneapolis: Fortress, 2005), 47–61.

[158]Harry O. Maier, "A First-World Reading of *Revelation* among Immigrants," in *From Every People and Nation: The Book of Revelation in Intercultural Perspective* (ed. David Rhoads; Minneapolis: Fortress, 2005), 62–81.

[159]For examples, An and Darr, eds. *Engaging the Bible: Critical Readings from Contemporary Women*, Bailey, ed. *Yet With A Steady Beat: Contemporary U. S. Afrocentric Biblical Interpretation*, Athalya Brenner and Carole Fontaine, eds. *A Feminist Companion to Reading the Bible: Approaches, Methods, and Strategies* (Sheffield: Academic, 1997), Cosgrove et al., *Cross-Cultural Paul: Journeys to Others, Journeys to Ourselves*, Dietrich and Luz, eds. *The Bible in a World Context: An Experiment in Contextual Hermeneutics*, Ekblad, *Reading the Bible with the Damned*, Goss and West, eds. *Take Back The Word: A Queer Reading of the Bible*, Daniel Patte, ed. *Global Bible Commentary* (Nashville: Abingdon, 2004), Rhoads, ed. *From Every People and Nation: The Book of Revelation in Intercultural Perspective*, Jane Schaberg et al., eds. *On the Cutting Edge: The Study of Women in Biblical Worlds. Essays in Honor Elisabeth Schussler Fiorenza.* (New York: Continuum, 2004), Segovia, ed. *Interpreting Beyond Borders*, Segovia and Tolbert, eds. *Reading from this Place: Social Location and Biblical Interpretation in Global Perspective, Reading from this Place: Social Location and Biblical Interpretation in the United States*, Sugirtharajah, ed. *The Postcolonial Bible, Vernacular Hermeneutics, Voices from the Margin: Interpreting the Bible from the Third World*, Ukpong et al., *Reading the Bible in the Global Village: Cape Town*.

[160]Elsa Tamez, "1 Timothy," in *Global Bible Commentary* (ed. Daniel Patte; Nashville: Abingdon, 2004), 508–515.

Tamez also acknowledges that the *barrios* are also the home of highly religious women who have emerged as leaders of the community. Engaging 1 Timothy from such a context, to Tamez, is a challenging task for the following reasons. First, it is hard to find an image of God as a liberator who hears the cry of the poor. Second, it prohibits women teaching and endorses silence (1 Tim 2:12). Third, it legitimizes the submission of slaves to their masters (6:12).[161] What people want in that situation is a God who sides with them when society is against them. To reread 1 Timothy requires envisioning a process of reconstruction and being ready to reject some of its teachings. She argues that 1 Timothy should be understood as a text that arose in response to a well-known problem: "the authority of rich people who believe that their power and wealth gives them the right to rule over the community and its leaders."[162] She therefore provides two reading insights. First, it is important "to discern the face of the poor, including gender, race and class. Second, there is a need "to rewrite the letter for our own time."[163]

Tamez's reading carries the following implications. First, biblical interpretation is more than just a search for meanings. It requires a careful look at how meanings of texts might affect those in the context of reading, in the community. Second, reading from the situation of women, the poor and the oppressed poses difficult questions that expose the hurtful side of biblical texts. Third, if freedom and well-being are to be realized through the process of interpretation, readers should first have the liberty to reject the negative aspects of texts.

The next illustration of the experiential-pragmatic mode comes from Pablo Richard, a Chilean biblical scholar. In his article, "Reading the Apocalypse," Richard acknowledges his routed background: born in Chile, ordained as a Roman Catholic priest in Santiago, trained in biblical studies in Rome and Jerusalem, studied sociology in Paris, and has been working in Central America.[164] Like Tamez, he locates himself in the context of Costa Rica, but his concern is with the regional and global political and economic problems that have affected the lives of the people. In his words,

> The conditions of exclusion and extreme poverty in Latin America led me to a new and liberating reading of

---

[161] Ibid, 509.
[162] Ibid, 514.
[163] Ibid, 515.
[164] Pablo Richard, "Reading the *Apocalypse*: Resistance, Hope, and Liberation in Central America," in *From Every People and Nation* (ed. David Rhoads; Minneapolis: Fortress, 2005), 146–164.

the whole Bible . . . The *Book of Apocalypse* teaches us today to search for the spiritual and ethical power capable of destroying the Imperial Beast and to build our hope for the possibility of "another world."[165]

Richard approaches Rev 13 from the perspectives of grassroot movements and Christian communities. He sees his main objective as being of service to God's people; his inspiration comes from liberation theology. The interpreter's role, to him, should begin in one's own communities, cultures, and grassroots social movements. He speaks of his own context as "arduous and dangerous" due to "oppression and exclusion by an economic, cultural, and military system of globalization led by the United States government, operating as an imperial, arrogant, and cruel power." It also generates "greater poverty, misery, exclusion, and ecological devastation." One of the key factors is globalization, which is experienced negatively "as a force that excludes the masses and destroys nature."[166]

Reading the Bible, the Apocalypse in this case, from that context, it is seen as God's word, which serves as a source for hope and life, survival and resistance. It also offers an inspiration for alternatives and utopias. It gives the poor the idea that a different world is possible. Such a notion displays hope, and is particularly important for a context of chaos and exclusion. With that understanding, Richard formulates ten keys for reading the *Apocalypse*, and they constitute a method that he defines as "historical and spiritual exegesis."[167] Four of those keys are as follows. First is the *alternative world*. The Apocalypse, according to Richard, points to an historical and political utopia. Second, the Apocalypse is also seen as *resistance*, which thus calls for a radical transformation of the church and a new expression of Christian witness in the world. The third key is *present eschatology*; it views the death and resurrection of Jesus as the central element of historical transformation; "if Christ has risen, then the time of the resurrection and of God's reign has begun."[168] The fourth key is what he calls *one history*. The Apocalypse, Richard observes, is about history; and history in the Apocalypse has two dimensions: empirical and visible ("earth"); deeper and transcendent ("heaven"). "The *Apocalypse* does not offer *another*

---

[165]Ibid, 146.
[166]Ibid, 147.
[167]Ibid.
[168]Ibid, 148.

world, alienated and divorced from our history. Rather, it offers an *alternative* world here and now."[169]

Applying these reading keys to Rev 13, Richard argues that it is "a critical analysis—a fundamentally theological analysis—of the Roman Empire's structure of oppression."[170] It expresses the Christian community's life and conscience in the context of being oppressed by the Empire. He explains further:

> They lived within the Empire, but they were excluded from its life; they lived as people under a death sentence, because they did not worship the idolized Empire. The Christian community represents resistance against the Empire. They were a community of faith that discovered Satan's presence in the Empire.[171]

Reflecting on his own context, Richard takes the *Apocalypse* as providing the paradigm for reading the Bible and interpreting his situation. He concludes:

> Our empire [that is, the United States] is more dangerous than the Roman Empire of old, because for the first time in the history of mankind there is an empire capable of killing most of humanity and forever destroying our planet earth . . . The world looks in terror as this empire transforms itself into a Beast.[172]

To envision and foster transformation and liberation requires resisting and defeating "the Beast." Only in so doing do we have hope of a possible new world, "a society in which everyone has a place in harmony with each other and nature." That is only possible however "when citizens of the empire reject the mark of the Beast and exclude themselves from the market, in solidarity with the wretched of the earth."[173]

Richard's reading has the following implications. First, the Bible has positive elements that can inspire resistance and liberation. Second, the experiences of those in the Bible correspond in some ways to the present situations; their response to oppression can offer insights to those

---

[169]Ibid.
[170]Ibid, 158.
[171]Ibid.
[172]Ibid, 164.
[173]Ibid.

in the present. Third, local problems people experience have global causes; and global solutions have to be sought locally. There are however aspects of Richard's reading that need critical evaluation. First, he fails to acknowledge that there are local contributions to their contextual distress and suffering, not just external and imperial ones. Second, because of that lack of acknowledgement, he also fails to critique the corruptions that marred both churches and governments. Speaking *tu'a*-wise, I would have begun from local problems and solutions before leaping into external ones. Third, limiting the focus to the biblical canon is itself excluding, given the fact that religion in Latin America is more than Christianity or Roman Catholicism.

The final illustration is from a queer reading of the Hebrew Exodus by Mona West.[174] Queer reading encompasses two kinds of readers: (i) gay and lesbian readers who seek to read the Bible based on their sexual orientation and experience; (ii) readers who are not gay or lesbian but adopt the perspective as a valid alternative to biblical interpretation. In her article, "Outsiders, Aliens, and Boundary Crossers," West offers a very significant and transformative reading of the Exodus tradition, as a response to the intolerance of society towards queers. To her, "coming out," or admitting one's sexual orientation, remains a significant event for many queers. Many queers, anticipating the social consequences, prefer to remain hidden and silent. But to West, the Hebrew Exodus—as a story of coming out, exile, and transformation—provides inspiration for queers to "come out" of the "closet of death" and enjoy the journey towards life: "silence equals death,"[175] that is, silence is the stuff of the dead, not of the living. She remarks:

> Queers are aliens and outsiders in a hostile environment. Because of their sexual orientation, queers are excluded from the rites and sacraments of the church . . . Coming out of the closet is a powerful, liberative act for queers. It is life giving. It is risky. It is the ultimate act of boundary crossing. Queers have refused to be silent. Like the Hebrews, queers cry out against the dominant culture, refusing to accept outsider status. In the act of

---

[174]Mona West, "Outsiders, Aliens, and Boundary Crossers: A Queer Reading of the Hebrew Exodus," in *Take Back The Word: A Queer Reading of the Bible* (ed. Robert E. Goss and Mona West; Cleveland: Pilgrim, 2000), 71–81.

[175]Ibid, 74.

coming out, queers cross over and discover a new identity and a new name for God.[176]

Like the fleeing Hebrews, West observes, many queers have faced the challenge of journeying into wilderness, accepting exile from their religious enslavement and oppression. As such, the wilderness becomes a "revelatory location of spiritual renewal and transformation."[177] It is the retelling of the stories of their own "coming out and wilderness transformations that ignites subversive memories of movement of queer lives from enslavement to freedom, from death to life."[178]

This queer reading of the Hebrew Exodus by West offers some significant insights. First, contextual reading needs to go beyond cultural and religious confinements and consider specific issues such as the experience of queers. Second, a queer reading of the Bible does not necessarily call for a rejection of the Bible, but its rereading and re-appropriation. Third, the methods of reading and perspectives of readers determine meanings of texts.

There are significant insights that this mode offers. First, experience of every sort shapes one's reading of texts. In that sense, the experiences of *tu'a* readers provide a basis for *tu'a* reading. Second, readings in this mode, and from diverse experiences of oppressions, are not just mere attempts at establishing alternative hermeneutical perspectives; nor are they seeking to offer expert contributions to academic professions. They are in fact pleas written with tears, begging for immediate actions that could possibly transform stressful situations. Third, experience differs from one situation to another. Even those who dwell in the same situation and share similar challenges emerge from that situation with different experiences. Latin American readers may have shared similar situations of oppression, corruption and poverty, but the impact of such a situation is experienced differently.

THE ISLAND-OCEANIC MODE

> I read as an islander for whom land- and text-space are crucial and placement signifies survival . . . I read from the place where the ocean meets (is)land, where surf and turf come face to face, from/at the beach, where waves shape and reshape, place and displace, both

---

[176]Ibid, 74–75.
[177]Ibid, 71.
[178]Ibid.

island-space and selfhood. I read from/at the place of arrival [a]nd departure.[179]

The island-oceanic mode of reading utilizes features of island life (where there is more sea-space than land-space), and experiences of peoples who live in such a context. This mode emerges from the context of Oceania and is best illustrated from the works of Jione Havea, a Tongan biblical scholar who is, arguably, the first to adopt and promote such a stance. Havea develops what he calls "island(ic) hermeneutics"[180] (Tongan: *lau faka-motu*). The term *lau* means "to read, interpret, recite, or count"; *faka-motu* indicates the "ways of the *motu*/island." Havea also takes into account other meanings of *motu*: "gaps, breaks, fractures." While *lau faka-motu* is shaped by island life and experiences, its focus is on recovering gaps, breaks and fractures in biblical texts and in readings of texts. This interest in *motu*, to Havea, is not something alien to island life, but it reflects the reality of life in the island:

> Because land-space is limited, South Pacific islanders are oriented toward the ocean, our island boundary, albeit a fluid boundary, and an extension of our land. Into the ocean we search for food, under and above the surfs, from one island to the next. We are oceanic and transoceanic.[181]

From this notion, Havea draws two related moods for the approach he calls *transtextuality*. It is oriented toward the boundary (ocean, margin, limit), on the one hand, and has the tendency to celebrate, on the other, because "celebration and merriment are parts of our lives."[182] The emphasis falls on the "boundary (ocean) that links texts (islands), the fluid expanse in between texts, in/through which readers are encouraged to cross playfully but calmly."[183] To Havea, there is a difference between islandic and continental notions of boundaries. He explains,

---

[179]Jione Havea, "A resting king David: 2 Samuel 7 and [dis]placements" (paper presented at the AAR/SBL (Post-Structuralist Research on the Hebrew Bible section), San Francisco, November 22–24 1997).

[180]"The Future Stands Between Here and There: Towards an Island(ic) Hermeneutics," 61–68.

[181]*Elusions of Control: Biblical Laws on the Words of Women* (Atlanta: SBL, 2003), 4.

[182]Ibid.

[183]Ibid.

> The understanding of a boundary as something that *decisively* limits, as a *solid* barrier that categorically prevents crossing . . . is a continental notion that is inapt for the islandic experience.[184]

Islandic boundaries are not

> [e]rected on land to separate one territory from another . . . [i]t is the ocean which separates and defines what is-land from what is-not-land . . . [it] is fluid (it moves). . . . The islandic understanding of boundary then is not only something that limits and separates, but also something that provides and links.[185]

The islandic experience of dipping into that fluid boundary offers Havea the categories of analysis for *lau faka-motu* (island hermeneutics; transtextuality):

> When an islander dips into the ocean, away from the shores of certainty, she rides up the wake (Tongan: *ma'ahi*) and down the gap (Tongan: *matua*), while looking out for breaking waves, to face the wake behind the gap. She cannot jump from one *ma'ahi* to the next without descending the *matua*, and she cannot stay on a *ma'ahi* without being pushed backward.[186]

He also adds:

> When regular waves break unexpectedly (*ngalu fakaofo*) the islander realizes that changes have taken place somewhere. The disturbances she faces on the surf were triggered at the underside of (that is, beneath and beyond) the waves. She cannot determine what caused *ngalu fakaofo* but she can feel them in the *ma'ahi* (wake) and *matua* (gap). The forces at the underside are real, but they resist representation; they cannot be captured, but they touch and disturb the islander. From this view I

---

[184]"The Future Stands Between Here and There: Towards an Island(ic) Hermeneutics," 63.
[185]Ibid, 64.
[186]*Elusions of Control: Biblical Laws on the Words of Women*, 6.

draw two undercurrents of transtextuality: the affects (agency) and elusiveness of the Other.[187]

These island experiences and oceanic imagination suggest the categories of analysis for *lau faka-motu*. First, as islanders ride up the *ma'ahi*, *lau faka-motu* looks for main points and dominant subjects in and of texts. Second, as islanders surf down the *matua*, *lau faka-motu* is also concerned with recovering the ignored and repressed subjects in and of texts. Third, as islanders face the unpredictable disturbances of the *ngalu fakaofo*, *lau faka-motu* attends the agency and elusiveness of subjects at the underside of texts. Havea's reading of Num 30 is shaped by these categories.[188] In Part I of *Elusions of Control*, he offers three different readings of Num 30, which focus on the idea of vow in the Hebrew Bible. The first is an analysis of the dominant subjects ("subjects of the law") in and of Num 30, the second attends to the ignored subjects ("subjects of the text") in and of Num 30, and the third focuses on the repressed subjects ("subjects of the unconscious") in and of Num 30. Each reading exposes what Havea calls the "illusion of control." In Part II of the same work, Havea circumreads the vow of Num 30 with other texts, where he seeks to reveal the "elusion of control." Here he focuses on three biblical female characters. The first is Jephthah's daughter, who is "a daughter that no man knew."[189] The second is Hannah, Samuel's mother, whom Havea identifies as "a wife no man controlled."[190] The last is Tamar who is "a woman no man unveiled."[191]

Havea's *lau faka-motu* is significant for the following reasons. First, it brings into biblical scholarship (and contextual biblical interpretation in particular) an alternative reading perspective that exposes the illusion of the dominant modes of reading, and eludes the control of continental approaches as well. At last, voices from the islands are not imagined but heard. Second, the way Havea theorizes the island/oceanic experiences and imaginations reflect our *lōlenga faka-motu* (island ways of life), thus establishing the island ways of being as a valid site for biblical interpretation. Third, Havea's work recovers a gap in biblical scholarship where other perspectives from Oceania could emerge.

---

[187]Ibid, 7–8.

[188]Another work that features some of his categories is "Shifting the Boundaries: house of God and politics of reading," *Pacific Journal of Theology* II, no. 16 (1996): 55–71.

[189]*Elusions of Control: Biblical Laws on the Words of Women*, 99–127.
[190]Ibid, 129–156.
[191]Ibid, 157–180.

I, as a *tu'a* reader, welcome the gap, and accept the challenge Havea foregrounds. I want, however, to point out the limits of Havea's work from my standpoint. First, whereas Havea uses the oceanic boundary and its features as his point of departure, I opt to begin in-land, from the experiences and imaginations of real people in the community, the Tongan *tu'a*/commoners. Second, whereas Havea derives the concern of *lau faka-motu* from the relationship between "wakes," "gaps," and "undercurrents," I derive mine from the actual relationships between *'eiki* and *tu'a* in Tongan society. Third, it is important to note that the "wakes" do become "gaps" and vice versa. By implication, the ignored and repressed in Havea's work will eventually become dominant subjects; the dominant can be ignored and repressed. This insight gives the *tu'a* a false impression that s/he could eventually become a *'eiki*. The *tu'a* is capable of resistance, but that will not change who s/he is, from the point of view of Tongan culture. Fourth, and finally, my approach attempts to be more specific than Havea's. I will not talk about island experiences and islanders in general; *there is more in the islands than being an islander; "islanders" are not a homogeneous group*. Some islanders are more privileged than others. Privilege to most *tu'a* is just a figment of their imagination; it is the stuff of dreams. Dreams however provide the basis for *tu'a* reading, which will be the concern of the next two chapters.

SITUATING *TU'A*-WISE

My main concern thus far is to situate *tu'a* reading within the terrain of contextual hermeneutics. For that purpose, I have discussed four broad modes of contextual hermeneutics, each providing distinctive approaches to the Bible. I have also illustrated each mode with readings from various contexts (namely, Africa, Asia, Latin America, and Oceania), and have dialogued with each of them and queried their implications for a reader like myself who not only resides in a non-continental context, like Oceania, and who also originates from a country that is small in terms of land space, yet so exclusivist in its attitude to the majority of its occupants, the *tu'a*. The challenge of such a context is not to reclaim one's culture, as endorsed by the cultural-ethnocentric mode. To do so is to reimpose upon the *tu'a* the very force that has continually hindered their liberation for years. The *religious-syncretic* mode offers no hope as well. To resurrect the Tongan belief system is to wake up the "devil" that had haunted *tu'a* throughout their lives. *Tu'a* reading however is, in some sense, at home with the experiential-pragmatic mode. First, it allows the *tu'a* an opportunity to bring their experience into conversation with readers who struggle with exclusion in the society, such as queers, and those on the margin of the Bible, like the aliens. Second, it allows *tu'a* readers to read the Bible for themselves from their own situations, and acknowledges the fact that such a reading will always be different, particular, and unique. The last mode, island-oceanic, opens the gap through which the *tu'a* reader emerges. The next chapter will explore in greater depth *tu'a* reading and its hermeneutic orientations.

PART 2: *FOUNGA*

CHAPTER 3
THEORISING *LAU FAKA-TU'A*

> The challenge for all of us . . . is not whether incorporating indigenous perspectives and wisdom in higher education is right or wrong, but whether we are ready to give other ways and other voices a chance.
>
> Konai Helu-Thaman[192]

> It is ironical from the viewpoint of our epistemological quest that a region [i.e. Oceania] with one of the largest number of the world's languages should continue to conduct its research and scholarship in a language that created and sustained the colonial process.
>
> Subramani[193]

This work thus far has provided the definitions of terms that are central to the whole project, namely, *tu'a*, *faka-tu'a* and *lau faka-tu'a* (Chapter 1), and a brief survey of the various modes and issues that characterize contextual (indigenous or vernacular) approaches to the Bible (Chapter 2). This chapter and the next will focus on *lau faka-tu'a* (*tu'a* reading) proper by outlining its theoretical and methodological components respectively.

The forthcoming discussion is divided into two sections. The first section deals with three categories of analysis that will guide the reading process. These categories are all Tongan concepts (*fonua*, *tākanga*, and *tālanga*) that reflect the aspirations of Tongan commoners,

---

[192]Konai Helu–Thaman, "Decolonizing Pacific Studies: Indigenous Perspectives, Knowledge, and Wisdom in Higher Education," *The Contemporary Pacific* 15, no. 1 (2003): 15.

[193]Subramani, "Emerging Epistemologies" (paper presented at the Conference on South Pacific Literatures, Emerging Literatures, Local Interest and Global Significance, Theory Politics, Society, Noumea, New Caledonia, 20–24 October 2003).

on the one hand, and provide alter-native interpretive perspectives, on the other hand. The second section reconsiders some of the key hermeneutical questions from a Tongan standpoint; questions such as *context, text,* and *interpretation*. Answers to these questions will serve as guiding principles for *lau faka-tu'a*, and will inform the methodology that will be charted in Chapter 4.

CATEGORIES OF ANALYSIS

Tu'a reading approaches the Bible with three categories of analysis: *fonua, tākanga, and tālanga*. The use of Tongan concepts is not merely a response to challenges that come with context-based interpretations of the Bible; it is also a reaction to the challenge made by both Konai Helu-Thaman (a Tongan academic and poet) and Subramani (an Indo-Fijian literary critic) above (in reference to Pacific Studies). While Helu-Thaman is urging the academy to give "other ways and other voices a chance," Subramani stresses the irony of not doing so. *Lau faka-tu'a* is one of those "other ways," and I am neither pleading for recognition nor claiming exceptionalism. I am simply saying that "this is one way of doing it," that is, to read *tu'a-wise*.

The need for this alternative reading is based on the following reasons. First is to enable a reading of the Bible through lenses other than those already utilised in existing approaches to biblical interpretation. Second is to equip the reader with insights for readings that are culturally unique and contextually specific to the context of reading. Third is to take into account seriously the experiences and perceptions of those whom I intend to read the Bible with: Tongan *tu'a*. The intention is certainly not consumer satisfaction; it is about offering an alternative *way of reading*.

The need for an alternative approach to biblical interpretation is motivated by, at least, three reasons. First, perspectives from Oceania are virtually unheard of in biblical scholarship, which is due in part to the lack of consideration in the field for insights from *non-continental* contexts like ours; it is also partly due to the lack of contribution to the field from scholars in the region. Both factors have created a gap in biblical scholarship that is yet to be bridged. The challenge for Oceanic biblical scholars, I believe, is to bridge that gap by taking the initial move; hence, this work. Second, the Bible, as a foreign text, needs to be read anew through Oceanic cultural lenses and in the light of our diverse contexts. The reason for this is we can only "cash" the value/meaning of foreign texts in the "currency" of our own cultural heritage. Third, and finally, each way of reading reflects certain ways of being[194] and ways of knowing. No reading is created *ex nihilo*.[195]

CATEGORY 1: *FONUA*

A *tu'a*, being culturally displaced, yearns for a sense of place. Place is vital to the survival of the *tu'a*. To claim a place, *tu'a* reading is conceived from the Tongan concept of *fonua*.[196] The word *fonua* is often translated as "land," but *fonua* is more than the solid ground we call earth. It epitomises the following.

First, it symbolizes the *manava* (womb). As a woman's *manava* is a home to a fetus, so is the *fonua* to its inhabitants. It is *a place of origin*; a place where life is conceived, sustained, and nurtured.[197] Likewise, as a *manava* shapes the identity of a new born, so the *fonua* defines a people's sense of belonging.[198] To be at home in the *fonua* implies *rootedness* (attachment, connectedness)[199]; on the contrary, to be

---

[194] As indicated in the work by Mary F. Foskett and Jeffrey Kah-Jin Kuan, eds. *Ways of Being, Ways of Reading: Asian American Biblical Interpretation* (St. Louis: Chalice, 2006).

[195] One may not agree with the direction adopted here, especially from a work of this kind that is expected to adhere to certain norms of research (largely dictated by Western standards). But the need for such a move is to provide some alternative perspectives for biblical interpretation.

[196] See a note on *fonua* in Bott, *Tongan Society at the Time of Captain Cook's Visits: Discussions with Her Majesty Queen Salote Tupou*, 69. Also 'Okusitino Māhina, "The Poetics of Tongan Traditional History, *Tala-e-fonua*: An Ecology-Centred Concept of Culture and History," *The Journal of Pacific History* 28, no. 1 (1993): 112.

[197] To abuse the *fonua* is like abusing one's mother. Similarly, to abuse women is not only to dishonour their value and dignity but also the life-giving *mana* (power) they have.

[198] Wherever a Tongan is, *fonua* is always home as long as one keeps a connection with the land and the people in any way or form. Tongans may migrate overseas, but Tonga will always be their *fonua*, their home. To keep a sense of home, Tongans resort to building Tongan diasporic communities, particularly in the form of churches. There they re-imagine and recreate the ways and practices of the *fonua*. In diaspora, people negotiate amongst them a sense of place, a "home." To lose one's connection with the *fonua* (land and people) is to become *homeless*! This notion of home is also the basis for referring to people's graves as *fonua*; hence the term *fonua-loto* (land–within). A grave, as *fonua*, offers not only a home for the dead, but also an opportunity for returning home, to the *manava* (womb) and to one's ancestors. In this sense, *fonua* symbolizes the Tongan life cycle!

[199] This echoes D. L. Madsen's view of home as "an incommensurable place, a place of safety and security that cannot be replicated. For migrants, refugees, and seekers of asylum, the difficulties of locating such a space, a place like home, are insurmountable. For the deterritorialised or deracinated subject, there can be no place like 'home.'" See Deborah L. Madsen, "'No Place Like Home': The Ambivalent Rhetoric of Hospitality in

displaced is to be *uprooted* (detached, disconnected) from one's place; to become homeless.

The *manava,* besides being a place of origin, is also a *place of departure;* once departed from (as in the event of giving birth) there is no going back. Any attempt to return to an originary place is futile, because it has either been altered or ceased to exist. Similarly, any nostalgic attempt to re-enact such a place in an already *ceased space* poses the risk of displacing those who occupy that space.[200] Nobody can step into the same place twice. Here *fonua* implies *routedness*; one's place can only be negotiated *on the move*.[201]

Second, *fonua* includes the *tangata* (people). There is a Tongan saying, *fonua pe tangata,* which literally means "the people *are* the *fonua.*" Where there are people, there is the *fonua*! One cannot speak of one without the other. The *fonua* and the *tangata* are mutually connected.[202] What affects one also affects the other. In this sense, no *fonua* is empty; to think otherwise is an illusion.

Third, *fonua* also includes the *moana* (ocean). The *moana* does not stand apart from the *fonua*; it *is* the *fonua*. One cannot limit the

---

the Work of Simone Lazaroo, Arlene Chai, and Hsu-Ming Teo," *Journal of Intercultural Studies* 27, no. 1/2 (2006): 118.

[200]Such a risk is evident in the colonial perceptions of place in Oceania. Inhabitants of our islands constantly face the issue of displacement because colonizers view some of our places as deserted islands, hence used as nuclear testing and waste dumping grounds. See Jeffrey Sasha Davis, "Representing Place: 'Deserted Isles' and the Reproduction of Bikini Atoll," *Annals of the Association of American Geographers* 95, no. 3 (2005): 607–625.

[201]Literature on diaspora also provides some perspectives. Avtar Brah speaks of the idea of home as "a mythic place of desire in the diasporic imagination"—A. Brah, *Cartographies of Diaspora: Contesting Identities* (London: Routledge, 1996), 192. Jon Austin also points to the irony that is involved in the constructing or imagining of such a place that we call home. While the notion of home indicates those who belong on the one hand, it also casts up the foreigner and outsider. Belongingness always goes hand in hand with foreignness and/or otherness. The implication therefore is that the notion of home should be constructed in a manner that would include, not exclude, others. Home should be imagined as a hybridized space, a place of plurality and difference, rather than a purist space, which is limited and limiting. See Jon Austin, "Space, Place & Home," in *Culture and Identity* (ed. Jon Austin; Frenchs Forest, NSW: Pearson, 2005), 111. Another perspective is from S. Nair who speaks of home as "a shifting point of origin and deferred site of return, as a multiple layer of exiles makes it a complicated task to lay categorical claim either to a homeland or to a nation." See Supriya Nair, "Diasporic Roots: Imagining a Nation in Earl Lovelace's *Salt*," *The South Atlantic Quarterly* 100, no. 1 (2001): 260.

[202]Other concepts are derived from, and coined around, this relation: for example, *tangata-e-fonua* (people of the land), *tala-e-fonua* (tradition/ways of the land/people), and *tupu'ifonua* (indigenous people).

notion of *fonua* to land-space; *fonua* includes ocean-space.[203] As the *moana* is an open and fluid space, so is the idea of place theorized with *fonua*: it is a shared heritage, bordered by nothing, and opens to all. To think otherwise is to give legitimacy, on the one hand, to the colonial/continental mentality that defines places into "continents" (big lands) and "islands" (small lands)—which accentuates the sense of smallness, inferiority and peripherality in the mind of those who are identified with the latter—and subscribes, on the other hand, to the *myth of boundary*.[204] Boundary is only erected, physically or mentally, upon an assumption that place can be defined, owned and controlled.

Fourth, and finally, *fonua* (as a gift of the gods) has *mana* (life-giving power) and is therefore regarded as *tapu* (sacred). To share in the *mana* of the *fonua*, one has to treat both peoples and places with respect. To act otherwise is to violate what *fonua* stands for.

Some concepts are formed in relation to *fonua*: *tala-e-fonua* (ways of the land), *hiki-fonua* (leaving, or departing from, one's land), *tau-fonua* (arriving and settling in an-other land), and *langa-fonua* (building place/land). But there are two that are integral to my reading of texts: *tangata-e-fonua* and *kumi-fonua*. *Tangata-e-fonua* (variant: *kakai-e-fonua*) signifies the native inhabitants of a place/land; those who grew out of the land (*tupu'ifonua*). In contrast, *kumi-fonua* refers to those who have departed from a supposedly originary homeland, and are constantly seeking to negotiate a place of arrival and settlement—sometimes they face oppositions; in other cases, they negotiate their place violently (as with colonizers). In the process of negotiation, some (in most cases the natives, *kakai-e-fonua*) face the harsh reality of dis-place-ment.

As a *tu'a* seeks to negotiate such a place, so *tu'a* reading accounts for displaced subjects in biblical texts. Through the category of *fonua*, *tu'a* reading regards displacement as driven by certain perceptions of place. With displaced subjects, *tu'a* reading takes seriously the perception of place/space in the Hebrew Bible, examines the effect of place perceptions on the construction of displaced subjects, and locates

---

[203]The Tongan anthropologist and author, 'Epeli Hau'ofa, had a similar concern when defining the concept of Oceania: "Oceania is vast, Oceania is expanding, Oceania is hospitable and generous, Oceania is humanity rising from the depths of the brine and regions of fire deeper still, Ocean is us. We are the sea, we are the Ocean, we must wake up to this ancient truth and together use it to overturn all hegemonic views that aim ultimately to confine us again, physically and psychologically, in the tiny spaces which we resisted accepting as our sole appointed place, and from which we have recently liberated ourselves. We must not allow anyone to belittle us again, and take away our freedom" (Hau'ofa et al., eds. *A New Oceania: Rediscovering Our Sea of Islands*, 16.).

[204]This island notion of boundary is discussed in Havea, "The Future Stands Between Here and There: Towards an Island(ic) Hermeneutics," 61–68.

the ideologies behind any claim to an originary place and/or the myth behind any event of return. *Tu'a* reading also regards the *idea of an empty land* and any *notion of boundary* in biblical texts as an illusion that disguises a demand for power and a need to control.

These senses of *fonua* provide a general impression of how the notion of place is perceived in this work. That is, *fonua* is a place of origin and departure but no return. *Fonua* is not empty because it is home to people. *Fonua* is fluid and open, because there is no boundary. Such a place is essential for displaced subjects like *tu'a*. It gives the *tu'a* a chance to re-claim a new sense of place that is not bordered and territorialized, but open and free. A place that is not excluding, but inviting; not colonizing, but liberating. Moreover, *fonua* offers a dynamic identity that is at once *rooted* and *routed*; *indigenous* and *diasporic*.[205]

The following questions guide a reading of biblical texts through the lens of *fonua*: What is the dominant perception of place? What are the drivers/bases of that perception? How is that perception constructed in biblical texts? Who owns that perception? Who is going to benefit from that perception? Who is likely to be displaced by that perception? Are there ignored perceptions? How would this ignored perception affect the current interpretations of the texts?

CATEGORY 2: *TĀKANGA*

A *tu'a* is not a *subject-in-isolation*; s/he is always a *subject-in-tākanga*! A *tu'a* does not preoccupy with his/her own being as the Heideggerian *da-sein*; a *tu'a* prefers *being-with-others*. *Tu'a* reading is therefore theorized with a sense of community derived from the concept of *tākanga*.

Tākanga is Tongan for "community" and it presupposes plurality, hybridity, solidarity, and reciprocity. Plurality because a *tākanga* is constituted of different peoples, cultures, values, beliefs, and interests. Hybridity because everything, human and non-human, is a fusion of different elements. Nothing is pure. Solidarity because "no man is an island"; one **is not** without others. Reciprocity because no one has the ability and resources to do everything; we always need the assistance

---

[205] A similar understanding is discussed in Vicente M. Diaz and J. Kehaulani Kauanui, "Native Pacific Cultural Studies on the Edge," *The Contemporary Pacific* 13, no. 2 (2001): 319. Clifford also made this important remark: "We find ourselves occupying the sometimes fraught borderland . . . between "indigenous" and "diasporic" affiliations and identities" (Clifford, "Indigenous Articulations," 471.).

of others as they need ours. In a *tākanga*, individualism is a heresy; there is no "I-I" or "I-It" (to use Buber's terminology); *tākanga* is all about "I-Thou."[206]

The word *tākanga* has two variants: (i) the first is *taka-'anga*; (ii) the second is *tā-ka'anga*. Let me discuss the first combination. The word *taka* indicates something or someone that is not stable but constantly changing, drifting, and travelling from one place to another. The Tongan word *matangi taka* refers to the wind when it continually shifts and blows from various directions. This diasporic orientation of *taka* becomes static when the term *'anga* is attached. The latter carries a specific reference, pointing to a particular person, way, thing or place. When combined with *taka*, they form the word *taka'anga*, which indicates a particular location as *the place to be* or a group of people as *those to be with*. In this sense, *tākanga* refers to a group of people or otherwise that share certain things in common—such as experiences, visions, interests, beliefs, and so on.[207]

The second variant, *tā-ka'anga*, offers another alternative. The word *tā* refers to the acts of beating/striking (of something or someone), cutting (of something), or playing (of a musical instrument). Combined with the term *ka'anga*, which signifies total destruction of something or someone, they give *tākanga* brutal and violent overtones. That is, whereas *taka-'anga* envisions a community that is free, *tā-ka'anga* entails a community that tends to abuse and brutalize.

These two variants of *tākanga* portray the dual tendencies of any community. On the one hand, it offers a fertile breeding ground for freedom and justice. On the other hand, it cannot prevent the unwanted seeds of violence and injustice from growing. As a *tu'a* reader engages the Bible with the notion of *tākanga*, s/he seeks to identify visions of society that are inscribed in biblical texts. S/he also realises that certain visions validate claims to power and drive the displacement of people from their places. Envisioning a sense of community through *tākanga* gives *tu'a* reading another agenda: to expose any biblical vision of society that is based on a *myth of purity*, because such a vision is not only unreal but exclusivist and threatening. When confronted with such a vision, *tu'a* reading seeks transformation. Transformation, however, does have costs. To transform for the sake of the displaced requires radical changes in society, which may be experienced by some as a violent change to the way they live even if not negotiated violently.

---

[206]Martin Buber, *I and Thou* (New York: Charles Scribner's Sons, 1970), 28.

[207]*Tākanga* requires solidarity, harmony, difference, equal opportunity, as well as freedom and justice. When one of these is lacked, a *tākanga* is jeopardised.

The following questions guide a *tu'a* reading of biblical texts through the lens of *tākanga*: What is the dominant vision of society? What kind of society does it seek to establish? What is at stake in such a vision? What is the basis of that vision? For whom is such a society? What kind of value- and belief-systems does the vision endorse? Is there an alternative vision that is being ignored or suppressed? What implications does it have for interpretation?

CATEGORY 3: *TĀLANGA*

Tālanga is a Tongan *way of talanoa* (dialogue, verbal interaction, conversation) and it always presupposes orality, multivoicedness, and alternatives. It involves the acts of speaking and listening; *tālanga* is lost when one of the two is not practiced. *Tālanga* is initiated by several things: an issue that needs to be solved, a protocol that has been overlooked or an idea that needs to be developed. If the Western notion of dialogue requires a consensus, *tālanga* does not, and neither does it expect a final word. It is always an open-ended forum that invites multiple perspectives, options, solutions and/or meanings. It involves critical engagements and critique rather than mere agreements and acceptance. In *tālanga*, the horizons of participants are extended and enriched.

A *tu'a*, as a subject-in-*tākanga*, is also a subject-in-*tālanga*. S/he is capable of speaking because s/he has a voice of her/his own. S/he also has the ability to understand because s/he can create knowledge and make meanings. Displacement however accompanies the suppression and manipulation of voices. To give voices to the voiceless, *tu'a* reading is theorized with the notion of *tālanga*.

Like *tākanga*, *tālanga* has two variants: (i) *tala-'anga*; (ii) *tā-langa*. The word *tala* means either *to tell, to inform,* or *to expose*. Its nature varies according to the many words affixed to it. *Tala-noa* is chatting or talking in a free and informal manner (*noa*), as in the act of story-telling. In *talanoa*, there is no agenda to dictate conversation; at times *talanoa* can be done without the participation or presence of a second party, hence, *talanoa-mo e-loto* (to converse with one's heart). Another word is *pō-tatala* (literally, "night-talking") which conveys an informal sense of talking, but signifies particularly talking into/out of the night. In some cases, it refers to conversation amongst friends, or parties who are in love. Two other words are hermeneutically significant: *fakamatala* and *talatalaifale*. *Faka-matala* denotes an act of explanation, clarification or sense-making. *Talatala-i-fale* signifies the imparting of advice or wisdom within the *fale* (family or household). The *fale* serves as the context of utterance, and implies the speaker's genuine concerns for the well-being of the addressee. When affixed with *'anga* (as defined above), *tala* brings along with it the various nuances alluded to above. By definition, *tālanga* (as a combination of *tala* and *'anga*) is a mode of discourse that presupposes community and otherness, the kind espoused by the notion of *tākanga*.

The other variant is a combination of *tā* and *langa*. The *tā* in *tālanga* is akin to *tā* in the notion of *tākanga*. The second word, *langa*, carries both positive and negative connotations. Positively, it means "to build" or "to construct"; negatively, *langa* means "pain," the kind of pain caused by "beating" and "striking" (as *tā* of *tākanga* signifies). These two connotations give *tālanga* (*tā* and *langa*) a dual tendency: it can be a powerful tool of community construction, and/or a violent means of repression and displacement. To avoid the violent tendency of *tālanga*, *tu'a* reading seeks through the process of interpretation not only to scrutinise dominant voices, but also to recover repressed and unheard voices in biblical texts. Moreover, *tu'a* reading examines the function of language (what language *does*) to expose rhetoric of domination. It suspects that discourse of any form is ideologically driven and tends to silence other voices.[208]

The following questions guide a *tu'a* reading of the Bible through the lens of *tālanga*: How are voices represented in biblical texts? Whose voices are dominant? How is language employed to serve these dominant voices? What are the rhetorics of domination? Whose voices are repressed? How is language manipulated to maintain repression? Are there echoes of resistance? What is the rhetoric of resistance? How does the intersection of voices affect the meaning of texts and the interpretive task?

These three categories of analysis offer alternative lenses for reading the Bible. Each category focuses on different aspects of the text,

---

[208]There are other meanings of *tālanga* derived from its nature as a cultural practice. In Tonga, as in other Oceanic islands, we learn more by talking to each other than reading books. Orality expresses the knowledge people possess. See Subramani, "The Oceanic Imaginary," *The Contemporary Pacific* 13, no. 1 (2001): 151. By talking to each other we find solutions to our problems, and meanings for our lives. *Tālanga* is also a pedagogical instrument; a mode of learning. We are able to move forward by listening to the wisdom of our ancestors, and the instructions of our elders. Unlike the undemocratic and restrictive space of Western education, *tālanga* is open and non-restrictive. *Tālanga* (orality) is possible only within the *tākanga* (community). Without *being* together, it is impossible to *talk* together. Without talking to each other, community is meaningless

and requires different methods of analysis (which will be discussed in the next chapter). The three combined demand a reconsideration of key interpretive principles, which I will now turn to.

KEY PRINCIPLES RECONSIDERED *TU'A*-WISE

Lau faka-tu'a (*tu'a* reading) takes three key interpretive principles very seriously: context, text, and interpretation. Each of these principles is defined from a Tongan standpoint, rather than their usual meanings in biblical scholarship.

PRINCIPLE 1: IDEA OF CONTEXT

The term "context" designates a surrounding, background, framework, situation or perspective. In biblical studies, it indicates the following: the social and historical situation in which a text was written (the world behind the text or the author's world);[209] the literary setting of a text (the preceding and succeeding materials);[210] and the situation in which biblical texts are read and applied (world in front of the text or the reader's world).[211] Each notion of context corresponds to the threefold idea of meanings discussed in the previous chapter. In a sense, context is the meaning-shaping environment.

The idea of "context" in Tongan is derived from the word '*ātakai* (literally, '*ā* fence, *takai* around), which indicates that which surrounds

---

[209] See Gordon D. Fee, "History as Context for Interpretation," in *The Act of Bible Reading: A Multi-disciplinary Approach to Biblical Interpretation* (ed. Elmer Dyck; Downers Grove: InterVarsity, 1996), 10–32. M. Daniel Carroll R., "Introduction: Issues of 'Context' Within Social Science Approaches to Biblical Studies," in *Rethinking Contexts, Rereading Texts: Contributions from the Social Sciences to Biblical Interpretation* (ed. M Daniel Carroll R; Sheffield: Sheffield Academic Press, 2000), 13–21.

[210] See Elmer Dyck, "Canon as Context for Interpretation," in *The Act of Bible Reading* (ed. Elmer Dyck; Downers Grove: InterVarsity, 1996), 33–64.

[211] As promoted in publications such as Bailey, ed. *Yet With A Steady Beat: Contemporary U. S. Afrocentric Biblical Interpretation*, Dietrich and Luz, eds. *The Bible in a World Context: An Experiment in Contextual Hermeneutics*, Segovia, ed. *Interpreting Beyond Borders*, Segovia and Tolbert, eds. *Reading from this Place: Social Location and Biblical Interpretation in Global Perspective*, *Reading from this Place: Social Location and Biblical Interpretation in the United States*, Sugirtharajah, *Asian Biblical Hermeneutics and Postcolonialism: Contesting the Interpretations*, *Postcolonial Reconfigurations: An Alternative Way of Reading the Bible and Doing Theology*, West and Dube, *The Bible in Africa: transactions, trajectories, and trends*.

something or somebody. Every '*ātakai* has two sides: '*ā-ki-tu'a* (outer '*ā*) and '*ā-ki-loto* (inner '*ā*). The '*ā-ki-loto* defines each object of investigation on its own, its constitutive parts and characteristic features. The '*ā-ki-tu'a* examines the object in contradistinction to objects in its surrounding. The '*ā-ki-loto* holds the unique and non-iterative aspects of the object; the '*ā-ki-tu'a* encompasses the shared and interrelated elements. Both the '*ā-ki-loto* and '*ā-ki-tu'a* are two sides of the same '*ātakai*, and are therefore linked despite holding different aspects of the investigated object. Without the '*ā-ki-tu'a* it is impossible to speak of the '*ā-ki-loto*, and vice versa. The '*ātakai* is definable when the two sides are located. *Tu'a* reading perceives every biblical text as having its own '*ātakai* (limit), defined by its '*ā-ki-loto* and '*ā-ki-tu'a*. When the term is used in *tu'a* reading, it points to the context (environment or surrounding) of a particular book or pericope.[212] *Tu'a* reading takes account of the contexts of texts and contexts of readers. Contexts of texts do not refer here to historical contexts behind the texts (or contexts of production) but to the location of biblical texts in relation to other texts (biblical and extra-biblical). The contexts of readers are where the Bible is received and read; it is where readers can create a world in front of texts. The contexts of readers signify the various locations that shape the ways readers interpret the Bible. Whereas the contexts of texts indicate the *situatedness* of texts, the contexts of readers point to the *locatedness* of readers, and the *circumstantiality* of reading. The contexts of readers condition and define the way *tu'a* readers make meaning.

Between the contexts of texts and contexts of readers lies the process of *faka'uhinga* (interpretation), where readers seek to negotiate what is relevant (*'uhinga mālie*) for the well-being of the reading community. Negotiation is an inevitable task since there are gaps (cultural, social, religious, ideological, political, economic, etc.) that need to be connected between the contexts of texts and the contexts of readers. It is an inevitable responsibility of a *tu'a* reader to do so in order to avoid dehumanizing mechanisms woven into texts from affecting the well-being of the reading community. *Tu'a* reading in this case needs every tool available to make sure that forces of domination and mechanisms of displacement are exposed and avoided.

---

[212]In the historical sense, a text's '*ā-ki-tu'a* refers to the *world behind the text* (contexts of production) and the world before the text (contexts of reception). The '*ā-ki-loto* refers to the *world within the text* (contexts of texts).

PRINCIPLE 2: IDEA OF TEXT

There is no direct equivalent in Tongan language for "text" as a literary document.[213] The closest terms are *lea* and *tohi*. The term *lea* means "words, speech, language or speaking"; *tohi* means "to write or draw." The influence of Western literary culture gives *tohi* another meaning: a book or a letter. What is significant about *lea* and *tohi* is the fact that their meanings put emphasis on *action* rather than on something written. In that sense, a "text" indicates an *event* not a product;[214] a practice not a theory.

Before the introduction of literary culture, our stories were not "frozen" with ink on papers. Rather, they were orally *tala* (told, re-told) with words of mouth in the forms of *tala-e-fonua* (myths)[215] and *ta'anga* (poetry)[216]; they were *lalanga* (woven) onto our *fala* (mats), *tohi* (drawn) onto our *ngatu* (tapa), *lalava*[217] onto our *fale* (house), expressed with our *haka* (dance movements),[218] and worn around our bodies as *ta'ovala* (waist mat).[219] Our texts were, and still are, parts of our lives, and we live with them. These "texts" share the following characteristics:

a) They are works of art produced from existing "texts"; none comes out of nothing; none is original. Our *talanoa* (stories) and *ta'anga* (poetry) are revised forms of previous versions, and are open to revisions. Our *fala* are woven from different *fe'unu*

---

[213] The reason for this is that Tongan culture is very much oral, not literary.

[214] As an event, this Tongan idea of "text" presupposes "organizers" (who initiate the text–event) and "participants" (who take part in the text–event); it emphasises the collective rather than the individual; sharing not ownership.

[215] Some English versions of Tongan myths and tales are recorded in works such as Gifford, *Tongan Myths and Tales*. See also Collocott, "Tongan Myths and Legends, III," 275–283.

[216] The best written record of Tongan *ta'anga* thus far is the work edited by Elizabeth Wood–Ellem, ed. *Songs & Poems of Queen Sālote* (Nuku'alofa: Vava'u, 2004).

[217] *Lalava* is the Tongan art "lashing coconut fiber ropes (*kafa*) to bind Tongan house beams together." See Ka'ili, "*Tauhi vā*: Nurturing Tongan Sociospatial Ties in Maui and Beyond," 97. The term is also defined as the "art of lineal and spatial intersection." See 'Okusitino Māhina, "*Tufunga Lalava*: The Tongan Art of Lineal and Spatial Intersection," in *Genealogy of Lines Hohoko e Tohitohi: Filipe Tohi* (ed. Simon Rees; New Plymouth: Govett–Brewster Art Gallery, 2002), 5–9, 29–30.

[218] For information on Tongan dance, see 'I. F. Helu, "Aesthetics of Tongan Dance: A Comparative Approach," in *Critical Essays: Cultural Perspectives from the South Seas* (Canberra: The Journal of Pacific History, 1999), 261–269.

[219] "Tongan Dress," in *Critical Essays: Cultural Perspectives from the South Seas* (Canberra: The Journal of Pacific History, 1999), 288–292.

(fabrics) and always expect new *fe'unu* when they are torn or damaged. Our *faiva* (dances) incorporates different bodily movements (*haka*) that differ from one place to another. In that sense, each "text" is an intersection of other "texts"; each is plural and inter-text-ual. No text is an island.

b) They are produced to serve various social functions, and in anticipation of different situations. For example, our *ta'ovala* (waist mat) are not merely woven and worn as an emblem of respect, but are designed differently to indicate differences in social status, and differences between occasions (as between celebration and mourning). A "text," in this sense, is socially-oriented and contextually-defined. It is a reflection of society; its norms, values, and world-views.

c) Their significance lies in their appropriateness to the occasions they are designed for and their aesthetic quality. They may reflect the competency of their *tufunga* (creator, author), but the question of relevance/quality supersedes the question of production. A "text," in this sense, requires no author to determine what it means.

d) To ensure their relevance, they all give in to change as society and community evolve and develop. In diaspora, new *haka*s are introduced into our *faiva*, new words into our *talanoa*, and new material for our *tapa*. Most importantly, they assume new functions and yield new meanings. The relevance of a "text," in this sense, is always negotiated in each new context.

These notions of textuality influence to a certain degree my perception of the Bible and the methods charted for *tu'a* reading. First, biblical texts are not empty and static documents; they speak of events and are themselves "events"—they make things happen. Second, each biblical text is intertextual; it incorporates previous texts, and relates to other texts. Third, each biblical text is socially located and contextually defined, and therefore contains visions of peoples in their places. Fourth, meanings of biblical texts are not owned by authors; they are negotiated by real readers who are situated in various contexts of reception. This leads the discussion to the last principle: idea of interpretation.

PRINCIPLE 3: IDEA OF INTERPRETATION

Meaning is the central concern of the interpretive task. To interpret is to make meaning. Knowing how to make meaning is supposedly the determining factor for a valid interpretation. In the development of hermeneutical theory over the past century, three main locations of meaning have been identified: behind the text as *property of authors* (Schleiermacher, Dilthey),[220] within the text as textual properties (Genette[221]), and in front of the text as *property of readers* (Barthes,[222] Iser[223] and Fish[224]).

---

[220]This represents the romanticist stance on interpretation which finds its ground on the works of F. Schleiermacher and W. Dilthey. Hermeneutics, according to Schleiermacher, is "the art of understanding," its principles must be universal, and thus "equally applicable to all texts without exception"—David E. Klemm, "Hermeneutics," in *Dictionary of Biblical Interpretation* (ed. John H. Hayes, et al.; Nashville: Abingdon, 1999), 499. Schleiermacher divides hermeneutics into two major areas: one is *grammatical*; the other *psychological*. Within the former, the interpreter "strives to remove obscurities in the text by means of philological analysis"—Manfred Oeming, *Contemporary Biblical Hermeneutics: An Introduction* (trans. Joachim F. Vette; England: Ashgate, 2006), 16. This requires knowledge and certain skills. Within the latter, the interpreter deals with the "interplay between the reader and the text"—David Jasper, *A Short Introduction to Hermeneutics* (Louisville: Westminster John Knox, 2004), 85. This "requires the ability to empathise with the author—Oeming, *Contemporary Biblical Hermeneutics: An Introduction*, 16.

Romanticist hermeneutics also privileged *the world of the author* (behind the text) as the locus of meaning, and thus the utmost goal of interpretation. Wilhelm Dilthey, in his famous article "The Development of Hermeneutics" sums up this romanticist stance very clearly: "The final goal of the hermeneutics procedure is to understand the author better than he understood himself"—Wilhelm Dilthey, "he Development of Hermeneutics," in *Hermeneutical Inquiry* (ed. David E. Klemm; Atlanta: Scholars Press, 1986), 104. In other words, readerly prejudices and presuppositions must be avoided as one pursues the *objective meaning* of the text; that is, the intention of the original author(s).

[221]For examples: Gerard Genette, *Palimpsests: Literature in the Second Degree* (trans. Channa Newman and Claude Doubinsky; vol. 8; Nebraska: University of Nebraska Press, 1997), *Paratexts: Thresholds of Interpretation* (trans. Jane E. Lewin; Cambridge: Cambridge University Press, 1997).

[222]Roland Barthes, "The Death of the Author," in *Literature in the Modern World: Critical Essays and Documents* (ed. Dennis Walder; Oxford: Oxford University Press, 2004), 259–263.

[223]Wolfgang Iser, *The Act of Reading: A Theory of Aesthetic Response* (Baltimore: John Hopkins University Press, 1978).

[224]Stanley Fish, *Is There a Text in this Class?: The Authority of Interpretive Communities* (Cambridge: Harvard University Press, 1980). The major turning points in this development began with the *ontological turn* empowered by the works of Martin Heidegger and Hans-Georg Gadamer, which marked a departure from romanticist

As authorial property, meaning is identified with an author's intention, and the agenda for interpretation therefore is to reconstruct the authorial intention that lies *behind the text*.[225] That is facilitated by employing methods from the historical-critical methodology (such as source, redaction, tradition, and form criticisms). As a property of texts, interpretation shifts from the world *behind the text* to that *within the text*. The role of readers is to retrieve meaning from the text by using literary critical methods (such as literary and rhetorical criticisms).[226] As a

---

hermeneutics; the *critical turn* that grounded in the works of Jürgen Habermas and the critical theorists of the Frankfurt School in Germany; the *Post-structuralist turn* founded in the works of French philosophers such as Michel Foucault, Roland Barthes and Jacques Derrida, as well as the *postcolonial turn* that was effected by the works of Edward Said, Gayatri Spivak, Frantz Fanon and Homi Bhabha. Each of these turns pointed to the need for interpreters to be aware of their presuppositions and prejudices, and how they affect the meaning-making task. But the postcolonial turn, as discussed in Chapter 2, played the major role in allowing the real reader to emerge from obscurity and become a key factor in the process of interpretation. This provides a strong foundation for doing contextual hermeneutics in biblical studies; hence, this whole work. For more insights into these turns see, at least, the following works: Barthes, "The Death of the Author," *The Pleasure of the Text* (trans. Richard Miller; New York: Hill and Wang, 1975), Bhabha, *The Location of Culture*, Jacques Derrida, *Writing and Difference* (Chicago: University of Chicago Press, 1978), Frantz Fanon, *The wretched of the earth* (New York: Grove, 1968), James Gordon Finlayson, *Habermas: A Very Short Introduction* (Oxford: Oxford University Press, 2005), Michel Foucault, "What Is an Author?," in *The Death and Resurrection of the Author?* (ed. William Irwin; Westport: Greenwood, 2002), Hans-Georg Gadamer, *Truth and Method* (New York: Continuum, 1994), Martin Heidegger, *Being and Time: A Translation of Sein und Zeit* (trans. Joan Stambaugh; Albany: SUNY Press, 1996), Paul Ricoeur, *The Conflict of Interpretations: Essays in Hermeneutics* (Evanston: Northwestern University Press, 1974), *Interpretation Theory: Discourse and the Surplus of Meanings* (Fort Worth, Texas: The Texas Christian University Press, 1976), Paul Ricœur and Lewis Seymour Mudge, *Essays on Biblical Interpretation* (Philadelphia: Fortress, 1980), Said, "Opponents, Audiences, Constituencies, and Community," *Orientalism, The World, The Text and The Critic*, Spivak, *Death of a Discipline*. See also Barthes, *The Death of the Author* (1977 [cited 29 March 2007]); available from http://social.chass.ncsu.edu/wyrick/debcllass/whais.htm, Jacques Derrida, *Structure, Sign, and Play in the Discourse of the Human Sciences* (2007 [cited 19 April 2007]); available from http://www.hydra.umn.edu/derrida/sign-play.html.

[225] An ardent proponent of this stance in biblical studies is E. D. Hirsch Jr. See E. D. Hirsch Jr., *The Aims of Interpretation* (Chicago: University of Chicago Press, 1976), *Validity in Interpretation* (New Haven: Yale Divinity Press, 1967).

[226] Danna Nolan Fewell and David M. Gunn, *Reading Between Texts: Intertextuality and the Hebrew Bible* (Louisville: Westminster John Knox, 1992), Norman C. Habel, *Literary Criticism of the Old Testament* (Philadelphia: Fortress, 1971), Edgar V. McKnight, *The Bible and the Reader: An Introduction to Literary Criticism* (Philadephia: Fortress, 1985), Stephen D. Moore, *Literary Criticism and the Gospels: The Theoretical Challenge* (New Haven: Yale University Press, 1989), Vernon K. Robbins, *Exploring the Texture of Texts: A Guide to Socio-Rhetorical Interpretation* (Valley Forge: Trinity,

property of readers, meaning is understood to be a created in the context of reception, the *world in front of the text*.[227] Interpretation therefore proceeds in the light of the reader's social locations, using reader-response criticism,[228] ideological criticism,[229] and other modes of reading that are shaped by cultures and contexts.

Various attempts have been made to provide an integrated approach that would give equal privileges to the various locations of meaning and the various methods of interpretation.[230] Providing a balanced and "politically correct" approach to interpretation, from a *tu'a* standpoint, is not the issue. What is at stake here is whether or not the traditional understanding of meaning and interpretation (in continental philosophy and biblical studies) should be universally accepted. If that is to be the case then interpreters from non-Western and non-continental contexts would have no other option but to subscribe to ideas that are alien to them, on the one hand, and abandon their own familiar thought world, on the other hand. My position in this regard is that the two concepts, like all others, have different connotations and emphases in different cultures. The task of every interpreter therefore is, firstly, to critically interrogate the assumptions that have determined the goals of interpretation for centuries. Secondly, there is an urgency to re-define the goal of interpretation. Questions such as the following need to be asked: Is the pursuit of meaning really the goal of interpretation? If so, what is

---

1996), Dennis L. Stamps and Stanley E. Porter, *The Rhetorical Interpretation of Scripture: Essays from the 1996 Malibu Conference* (Sheffield: Sheffield Academic Press, 1999), Phyllis Trible, *Rhetorical Criticism: Context, Method, and the Book of Jonah* (Gene M. Tucker; Minneapolis: Fortress, 1994), Kevin J. Vanhoozer, *Is There a Meaning in This Text?: The Bible, The Reader, and the Morality of Literary Knowledge* (Grand Rapids: Zondervan, 1998), Hugh C. White, *Speech Act Theory and Biblical Criticism* (Atlanta: Scholars Press, 1988).

[227]For more insights on this idea of "the world in front of the text" see Ricoeur, *The Conflict of Interpretations: Essays in Hermeneutics, From Text To Action: Essays in Hermeneutics, II* (trans. Kathleen Blamey and John B. Thompson; Evanston: Northwestern University Press, 1991), *Interpretation Theory: Discourse and the Surplus of Meanings*, Ricœur and Mudge, *Essays on Biblical Interpretation*.

[228]For further reading on this method see Robert Detweiler, *Reader response approaches to Biblical and secular texts* (Atlanta: Scholars Press, 1985), Iser, *The Act of Reading: A Theory of Aesthetic Response*.

[229]For example, T. Pippin, "Ideology, Ideological Criticism, and the Bible," *Currents in Research: Biblical Studies* 4 (1996): 51–78.

[230]As discussed in W. Randolph Tate, *Biblical Interpretation: An Integrated Approach* (Peabody: Hendrickson, 1997), Anthony C. Thiselton, *New Horizons in Hermeneutics: The Theory and Practice of Transforming Biblical Reading* (Grand Rapids: Zondervan, 1992), Vanhoozer, *Is There a Meaning in This Text?: The Bible, The Reader, and the Morality of Literary Knowledge*.

meaning? What does it mean to interpret? What are the tools required by the task? The answers to such questions would certainly re-focus the direction of interpretation in each new context and yield new insights.

Tu'a reading agrees that interpretation is about meaning. Yet "meaning" in this work is not seen as a property of an author, a text, or a reader. "Meaning" is *'uhinga*. The term *'uhinga*, commonly translated as "meaning" or "purpose," is a derivative of the root *'uhi* (relation).[231] Its longer form, *'uhi'anga*, refers to "a point of intersection" or "a space of relation." In that sense, *'uhinga* denotes a "connection" or a "link." When a connection is fitting, relevant, matched and related, Tongans call it *'uhinga mālie*.[232] Otherwise, it is *ta'e'uhinga*—non-sense, irrelevant, or unrelated.

'Uhinga mālie requires the task of *faka'uhinga*; a causative term that aims "to make *'uhinga*" or "to connect or to link." The aim of *faka'uhinga* is to make a link that is *mālie*—fitting or relevant. When *mālie* is not achieved, interpretation (*faka'uhinga*) is irrelevant. To make the connection, *faka-'uhinga* involves, at least, two tasks: *lau* and *vete*. The term *lau* means "to read or to count";[233] *vete* means "to unbind or to set free."[234] These tasks provide *faka-'uhinga* with a mandate: to set free the meanings of texts and readers of texts through the process of interpretation. Any *faka-'uhinga* (interpretation/reading) that ignores that mandate is devoid of any *mālie*, hence irrelevant.

---

[231]From this root we have verbs of relation such as *fe'uhi'aki* (to relate to one another) and *fefa'uhi* (to struggle with one another). Additional elements determine the kind of relation (*'uhi*).

[232]*Mālie* is a congratulatory term that is usually heard when a speech or song is well-delivered; or when a *faiva* (dance) is well-performed. The word is uttered to let a speaker, singer, or performer knows that s/he is connected well with his or her audience.

[233]Both acts are not limited to written texts, because the idea of texts as written, published and copyrighted is alien. Tongan texts are drawn (*tapa*), woven (*lalanga/lalava*), composed (*ta'anga*), spoken (*tala*), performed (*haka/vaa'ihaka*), and embodied (*teunga/vala*). All of these modes of textuality are collectively done and shared. Each text comes in different forms and styles, serves different purposes and uses on different occasions. Each text reflects the lives and aspirations of those who made it; it also ties to the tradition of a particular place; it contains place–specific jargons and imageries. Meaning of each text is expressed in designs, patterns, melodies, genres, and choreographies/movements—each expression serves a particular function. The aesthetic quality of each text is more important than their creators. The latter may no longer be known, but that does not diminish the meaning and purposes of their creations. Some texts are often intertwined—e.g. songs, performances, costumes—when they matched, they become harmonious and symmetrical. A *tu'a* can read/count waves, stars, places, faces, movements, and so forth.

[234]*Vete* gives *tu'a* reading a liberating orientation: to set free the meanings of texts and subjects of texts from any form of control (bind, tie). Tying and binding are the stuff of domination.

As a *tu'a* reader attempts to find *'uhinga mālie*, so *tu'a* reading seeks to unbind and set free displaced and neglected subjects in biblical texts. *Tu'a* reading is not obsessed with the colonial/continental notion of meaning as something that is located behind, within or in front of texts. Meaning, in the sense of *'uhinga*, is always in the *context of reception*; the space where connection can be made, and *mālie* is realized. After all, meaning for a *tu'a* is what answers his/her questions. That which does not provide answers is meaningless. Meaning (*'uhinga*), moreover, is neither a sole proprietorship of a *tu'a* reader nor a property of texts. *'Uhinga* lies in-between texts and readers; readers and reading communities. It is a communal property because it is communally defined. *Faka'uhinga* (interpretation) therefore is an interactive task.

THEORISING *TU'A*-WISE

To sum up this chapter, certain points need to be re-emphasized. First, *lau faka-tu'a* (*tu'a* reading) is constituted of three categories of analysis: *fonua, tākanga,* and *tālanga*. *Fonua* offers a reading of place; *tākanga* provides an alternative vision of society, and *tālanga* deals with aspects of orality, voices and silences. Second, *lau faka-tu'a* also holds certain ideas of contexts, texts, and interpretation. These categories and principles provide the theoretical underpinning for the various methods of analysis that I will discuss in the next chapter.

CHAPTER 4
CHARTING *LAU FAKA-TU'A*

As soon as I desire I am asking to be considered. I am not merely here-and-now, sealed into nothingness. I am for somewhere else and for something else. I demand that notice be taken of my negating activity insofar as I pursue something other than life; insofar as I do battle for the creation of a human world—that is a world of reciprocal recognitions.

Homi K. Bhabha[235]

[C]riticism must think of itself as life-enhancing and constitutively opposed to every form of tyranny, domination, and abuse; its social goals are noncoercive knowledge produced in the interests of human freedom.

Edward Said[236]

The text is in-between; it is intertext. The text is a fabric, woven (Latin *texere/textus*) from many threads . . . Every reading is gathering-in of older threads into a new tissue; an interweaving of the particular life of the reader with the tissue of the tradition.

David R. Blumenthal[237]

Lau faka-tu'a is more than just a theory; it is a practice. Without practice, a theory lacks value. *Lau faka-tu'a* shifts from what Houston Wood called a *discipline-based* to a *practice-based* approach.[238] Whereas a discipline-based approach relies on discipline-based concepts, theories, and methods, a practice-based approach focuses on concrete activities of

---

[235]Bhabha, *The Location of Culture*, 12.
[236]Said, *The World, The Text and The Critic*, 29.
[237]David R. Blumenthal, *Facing the Abusing God: A Theology of Protest* (Louisville: Westminster John Knox, 1993), 60–61.
[238]The distinction between the two approaches is discussed in Houston Wood, "Three Competing Research Perspectives for Oceania," *The Contemporary Pacific* 18, no. 1 (2006): 33–55.

a particular people within a particular culture.[239] A discipline-based approach seeks to answer disciplinary questions; it is a form of *homogenization*.[240] A practice-based approach, on the other hand, seeks to answer practical questions that people face in their everyday life. It counters the myth that real people live within self-organizing "systems" of beliefs, values, norms and symbols by focusing on concrete activities.[241] It is a form of *decolonization*.

In Chapter 3, I discussed three categories of analysis that constitute the theoretical framework of *lau faka-tu'a* (namely, *fonua*, *tākanga*, and *tālanga*). This chapter seeks to chart a practice-based methodology[242] within that framework, and thus departs from the existing discipline-based methods that dominate biblical interpretation.[243]

---

[239] Ibid, 33.

[240] Houston writes: "Disciplines are part of the homogenization of the world. In asserting the ability to know, disciplines encourage their practitioners to form opinions about how others should live. Discipline-based research undermines place-based decision making about local cultural, economic, and political matters. Because expert researchers tend to believe their theories, concepts, and methods provide universally appropriate knowledge, they often feel an ethical obligation to guide local peoples when these people confront issues that researchers believe they know much about. Discipline–based researchers also tend to subscribe to the view that educated elites generally know what is best for a people . . ." (37).

[241] Ibid, 33. Wood also argues that "[t]hinking of people as defined by their practices also has the advantage of making it easier to think about similarities and differences between diasporic Oceanic groups and those who have remained nearer to their ancestral islands. Place of residence can have greater or lesser impact on a person's available ensemble of practices" (46).

[242] The idea of methodology encompasses two Tongan concepts: *founga* and *angafai*. *Founga* designates a point of entry, a pathway, or a direction; *angafai* indicates how things ought to be done. In that sense, methodology designates, on the one hand, the points through which the interpreters shall enter the text; on the other hand, it provides the guidelines and tools for engaging texts.

[243] Methods that are subjects of many publications such as the following: A. K. M. Adam, *Faithful Interpretation: Reading the Bible in a Postmodern World* (Minneapolis: Fortress, 2006), *Handbook of Postmodern Biblical Interpretation* (St. Louis: Chalice, 2000), *What Is Postmodern Biblical Criticism?* (Minneapolis: Fortress, 1995), Roland Barthes, *Structural Analysis and Biblical Exegesis: Interpretational Essays* (Pittsburgh: Pickwick, 1974), Carl Joachim Classen, *Rhetorical criticism of the New Testament* (Tübingen: Mohr Siebeck, 2000), Charles H. Cosgrove, ed. *The Meanings We Choose: Hermeneutical Ethics, Indeterminacy and the Conflict of Interpretations* (London: T&T Clark, 2004), John M. Court, *Biblical Interpretation: The Meanings of Scripture—Past and Present* (London: T&T Clark, 2003), Laura E. Donaldson and R. S. Sugirtharajah, *Postcolonialism and Scriptural Reading* (Atlanta: Scholars Press, 1996), Johann August Ernesti and Moses Stuart, *Elements of Interpretation* (Andover: Flagg and Gould, 1824), Fewell and Gunn, *Reading Between Texts: Intertextuality and the Hebrew Bible*, Klaus Koch, *The Growth of the Biblical Tradition: The Form-Critical Method* (trans. S. M. Cupitt; New York: Scribner's, 1969), Hindy Najman et al., *The Idea of Biblical*

This is not an exercise for the sake of being different. It is however a deliberate move that is based on the following reasons.

First, a practice-based methodology is informed by views and practices that are familiar to real Tongan *tu'a*. That is what this work is all about: to develop an alter-native way of reading the Bible, but one that takes into account the experience, struggles, and longings of *tu'a* in Tongan society.

Second, there is an urgent need to construct new *ways of reading* that are enlightened by the richness of our own cultures. Tongan culture, like other Oceanic cultures, offers a wealth of knowledge and perspectives that are yet to be seriously considered in academia. These knowledge and perspectives have been submerged for a long time under the aggressive waves of Western and colonial scholarships. Likewise, the globalisation of Western/colonial cultures dominates academic disciplines and impacted island cultures to a great extent. This resulted in the creation of a strange mindset amongst Oceanic islanders that regard their own cultures inferior and unfit to be part of academic discourses. Oceanic cultures are mentioned only in such discourses when they are objects of investigation. There is still a long way to go to convince the restricted space of Western scholarship that island cultures have a lot to offer in terms of theories and methodologies.

Third, developing a practice-based methodology does not endorse a rejection of Western biblical scholarship; rather it is to make a statement: *biblical scholarship needs more than just Western, continental, and colonial knowledge and perspectives. Oceania cultures have their own ways of thinking and knowing that should be taken into account.* This may echo what Homi Bhabha calls "a desire to be

---

Interpretation: Essays in Honor of James L. Kugel (Leiden: Brill, 2004), *Methods of biblical interpretation: excerpted from the Dictionary of biblical interpretation,* (Nashville: Abingdon, 2004), Stephen D. Moore and Fernando F. Segovia, *Postcolonial Biblical Criticism: Interdisciplinary Intersections* (London: T&T Clark, 2005), Norman Perrin, *What is Redaction Criticism?* (Philadelphia: Fortress, 1969), Phillips and Duran, *Reading Communities, Reading Scripture,* Robert Polzin, *Biblical Structuralism: Method and Subjectivity in the Study of Ancient Texts* (Philadelphia: Fortress, 1977), Priscilla Pope-Levison and John R. Levison, *Return to Babel: Global Perspectives on the Bible* (Louisville: Westminster John Knox, 1999), Mark Allan Powell, *What is Narrative Criticism?* (Minneapolis: Fortress, 1990), Richard N. Soulen and R. Kendall Soulen, *Handbook for Biblical Criticism* (Louisville: Westminster John Knox, 2001), Stamps and Porter, *The Rhetorical Interpretation of Scripture: Essays from the 1996 Malibu Conference,* Sugirtharajah, *Postcolonial Criticism and Biblical Interpretation,* Trible, *Rhetorical Criticism: Context, Method, and the Book of Jonah,* Gene M. Tucker, *Form Criticism of the Old Testament* (Philadelphia: Fortress, 1971), Francis Watson, *The Open Text: New Directions for Biblical Studies?* (London: SCM, 1993), White, *Speech Act Theory and Biblical Criticism.*

considered,"[244] but it is strongly linked to what Edward Said sees as a need to oppose "every form of tyranny, domination, and abuse ... in the interests of human freedom."[245]

I have divided this chapter into two sections. The first section charts the methods of analysis that comprise *lau faka-tu'a* as a methodology. These methods are for the most part based on the three categories of analysis discussed in Chapter 3, which reflect the way Tongans (especially *tu'a*) live, think and relate in real life. The second section discusses four rationale of analysis: *un-weaving, relocating, re-stor[y]ing, and re-vis[ion]ing*. The use of hyphens and parentheses indicate that words are used hereinafter with meanings that are different from the usual. Without hyphens and parentheses, words assume their conventional meanings.

METHODS OF ANALYSIS

Tu'a reading (*lau faka-tu'a*) is charted as a methodology that encompasses four methods: *lau fe'unu, lau lea, lau vā,* and *lau tu'unga* (see Figure 3).[246] The names given to these methods are intended to

---

[244]Bhabha, *The Location of Culture*, 12.

[245]Said, *The World, The Text and The Critic*, 29.

[246]The inspiration for constructing these methods came from works of two scholars: Vernon Robbins' works on *socio-rhetorical interpretation* and Elaine M. Wainwright's development of that method from a feminist perspective. For some of Robbins' works see Robbins, *Exploring the Texture of Texts: A Guide to Socio-Rhetorical Interpretation, Jesus the Teacher: A Socio-rhetorical Interpretation of Mark* (Philadelphia: Fortress, 1984), *The Tapestry of Early Christian Discourse: Rhetoric, Society, and Ideology* (London: Routledge, 1996), Vernon K. Robbins et al., *Fabrics of Discourse: Essays in Honor of Vernon K. Robbins* (Harrisburg: Trinity, 2003). See also the latest publication from Elaine M. Wainwright, *Women Healing/Healing Women: The Genderization of Healing in Early Christianity* (London: Equinox, 2006). In *Exploring the Texture of Texts*, Robbins offers five areas of focus when reading biblical texts using the socio-rhetorical method of interpretation, namely, inner texture, intertexture, social and cultural texture, ideological texture and sacred texture. Each area focuses on particular aspects of the text, allowing the reader to engage the text very closely. For example, the inner texture of the text directs the attention of the reader to literary features of the text; the way it is being woven, whereas the social and cultural texture calls for a close examination of aspects of the text that reflect the era in which it was written. To read a text socio-rhetorically is to engage it from different angles. Wainwright, in *Women Healing/Healing Women*, also provides a multi-dimensional approach to interpretation that weaves together different lenses of reading, namely, feminist, postcolonial, ecological, and socio-rhetorical. Each dimension scrutinizes the text in a different manner, and thus brings out transformative insights that take account of feminist, postcolonial, and ecological interests. Whereas in Robbins' approach, the reader is invited into the inner world of the text and its social, cultural, ideological and sacred

avoid being mistaken with traditional methods of literary, rhetorical, social and ideological criticisms. Each name designates the scope of each method and its application. All is designed for the simple purpose of guiding the reader through texts in the meaning-making process. Texts are viewed not as repository of meanings, but as *points of entry* or *pathways* to meanings. The methods developed herein are for the purpose of guiding *tu'a* readers as they engage with texts. Each method bears some marks of existing methods in biblical studies, and that shows the fact that although I am charting new and indigenous ones, they are not pure. Categories are Tongan organized within a Western framework.

METHOD 1: *LAU FE'UNU*[247]

The word *lau* as defined above can mean "to read" or "to count": *fe'unu* is Tongan for the dried material made from pandanus leaves for mat weaving. The name *lau fe'unu* literally means "to count the woven *fe'unu*," but in this work, it refers to the art of reading the design and arrangement of a text. It gives the reader an opportunity to read the text closely by focusing on the various strands that make up the text, their organization, and the function each plays vis-à-vis the text and its immediate and larger literary contexts. In short, *lau fe'unu* is the *unweaving of the text*.

This method visualizes any biblical text as a *fala* (mat) woven with different *fe'unu* (strands).[248] Each *fala* has five important elements: *fatunga* (type of fabrics), *fa'unga* (structure), *fōtunga* (form), *tu'unga* (place, status) and *tūkunga* (occasion, setting). The *fatunga* is defined by the value of the *fe'unu* that makes up a *fala*.[249] Types of *fe'unu* designate

---

surrounding, Wainwright provides a framework that allows not only what Robbins seek to achieve in interpretation, but also a dialogue with that challenges that are posed by feminist, postcolonial, and ecological hermeneutics. Here the world of the text comes face to face with the issues that confront the real reader. Like Robbins' and Wainwright's approaches, I have developed an approach with four methods of analysis based on Tongan cultural concepts and practices.

[247]This method, though based on Tongan concepts, shares the assumptions of literary criticism. See Jeanine Parisier Plottel and Hanna Kurz Charney, *Intertextuality: New Perspectives in Criticism* (New York: New York Literary Forum, 1978). Daniel Patte, "One text: Several structures," *Semeia*, no. 18 (1980): 3–22. McKnight, *The Bible and the Reader: An Introduction to Literary Criticism*. Fewell and Gunn, *Reading Between Texts: Intertextuality and the Hebrew Bible*.

[248]Knowledge of mat-making belongs to Tongan women. Each *fala* reflects the skills, imaginations and visions of those who weave it.

[249]*Fe'unu* are made from pandanus leaves; some are considered superior to others.

the category where each *fala* belong. The *fa'unga* signifies how a *fala* is woven together; each *fa'unga* reflects the skills and imaginations behind the weaving. The *fōtunga* refers to the outward appearance (*mata*) of the *fala*; the finer the *mata*, the higher the value.

The *fatunga, fa'unga,* and *fōtunga* determine the *tu'unga* and *tūkunga* for each *fala*. Each *fala* is woven for a social occasion, and therefore given a place and a function.[250] Each is socially situated in a certain time and space. These elements determine not only the aesthetic quality of each *fala*, but also reflect the purpose behind its making. To analyse these elements requires an act of "un-weaving."

As with a *fala*, so *tu'a* reading seeks to "un-weave" each biblical text to unfold its *fatunga* ([intra/inter]textures), *fa'unga* (structure), *fōtunga* (design, pattern), *tu'unga* (place, function) and *tūkunga* (occasion, setting). These aspects of texts direct the attention of *lau fe'unu* to the literary dimension of texts, and it operates as follows. First, each text will be read as an *intersection* of many texts (intra-texts), and also *in relation to* other texts (inter-texts). *Intra-texts* refer to texts that are present within the text that is under investigation. *Inter-texts* indicate texts outside the text of concern that echo similar subject matter, motif, belief, value, and so on. These aspects render every text as both *intersectional/intratextual* and *relational/intertextual* at once. The significance of this lies in the fact that each text stands on the "shoulders" of, and relates in some ways to, other texts. Reading texts as such is a "cross-textual" (intra-/inter-)[251] endeavour, and it therefore sheds light on the *fatunga* of each text.

Second, *lau fe'unu* analyses the *fa'unga* of texts by identifying the literary units, the way they are arranged and woven together as self-contained pericopes. The *fa'unga* expresses the organization of thoughts and structure of arguments woven into each text. This will determine whether or not a text is consistent, coherent and logical. As a *fala* has loopholes between its *fe'unu*, so does each text. *Tu'a* reading also

---

[250] Some mats are reserved for special occasions, and cannot be used in ordinary places and activities.

[251] The term "cross-textual" is used by Archie Lee to indicate a method of biblical interpretation that reads the Bible alongside other religious texts, especially those that belong to ancient Asian religions, such as Hinduism, Buddhism, Islam and so forth. See Archie C. C. Lee, "Exile and Return in the Perspective of 1997," in *Reading from this Place: Social Location and Biblical Interpretation in Global Perspective* (ed. Fernando F. Segovia and Mary Ann Tolbert; Minneapolis: Fortress, 1995), 97–108. Also "The Bible in Asia: Contextualizing and Contesting" (paper presented at the Society of Asian Biblical Studies, Seoul, South Korea, 14–16 July 2008), 30–42. In this work, the term refers simply to the relationships of texts within and outside the text under investigation, religious or otherwise.

accounts for the loopholes (ignored aspects) between the lines that challenge the supposed stability of texts. The *fa'unga* provides the basis for the analysis of the *fōtunga*.

Third, *lau fe'unu* un-weaves the *fōtunga* of texts by examining patterns and designs revealed by their *fa'unga*. Patterns and designs differ amongst texts, but they all serve as cultural devices employed to heighten the effect of texts on readers.

Fourth, *lau fe'unu* analyses the *tu'unga* of texts by examining their literary placement and function. By *placement*, I am referring to the location of each text vis-à-vis the immediate context. By *function*, I am referring to the role each text plays within the context where it is placed. Texts, however, do not always connect to the immediate context, and are therefore considered misplaced. The role of a *tu'a* reader in this case is not to attempt to harmonize texts, but to locate the significance of that misplacement for the text and its interpretation.

Finally, the *tūkunga* of each text is viewed in the light of the previous aspects, and will be determined by asking the following questions: *What is the typical occasion/setting for such a text? To what end is such a text? Whose interest is served by the text? How does the tūkunga of the text relate to its fatunga, fa'unga, fōtunga and tu'unga?* *Lau fe'unu* seeks to provide a close reading of texts in their literary contexts (*'ātakai*), and to allow the reader to identify the flow of the text. This provides the platform for the next mode of analysis, the *lau lea* method.

METHOD 2: *LAU LEA*

The second method of analysis is *lau lea*. The word *lea* is Tongan for "speech, language, word" or the "act of speaking."[252] This method is influenced by insights from rhetorical criticism. The term "rhetoric," according to Aristotle, is "the faculty of observing in any given case the available means of persuasion."[253] In other words, rhetorical criticism is about seeking to understand the means used by an author in a text to capture the interest of his or her audience. Phyllis Trible follows in the tradition of classical rhetoric by putting emphasis on the language of the

---

[252]Language is understood herein as a tool of representation and construction. It embodies certain viewpoints, ideas, and attitudes; it is the vehicle for constructing voices, characters, and spaces.

[253]P. K. Tull, "Rhetorical Criticism and Intertextuality," in *To Each Its Own Meaning. An Introduction to Biblical Criticisms and Their Application* (ed. Steven L. McKenzie and Stephen R. Haynes; Louisville: Westminster John Knox, 1999), 160.

text, their arrangement and design, among other stylistic aspects.[254] The definition by Vernon Robbins however provides the basis for the method designed herein (*lau lea*). Robbins defines "rhetorical" as "the way language in a text is a means of communication among people," and "rhetorical criticism" as an analysis "that give[s] special attention to the subjects and topics a text uses to present thought, speech, stories, and arguments."[255] The point of difference between Robbins' concern and the concerns of *lau lea* lies in the categories of analysis and aspects of the text to be investigated.

To analyse *lea* in texts, *lau lea* focuses on two aspects of the texts: *tufunga lea* and *tō'onga lea*. The word *tufunga lea* can be used both as a verb and a noun; it designates an act and signifies a person at once. As a verb it indicates the act of composing a speech or "weaving" speeches together. As a noun, it refers to an artist; the *tufunga* (composer, creator) of *lea*.[256] In Tongan culture, *tufunga lea* is a selective event. It includes as much *lea* as it excludes, and thus depends on what serves the interest of the *tufunga*. The way *lea* is woven is also determined likewise. *Lau lea* views texts as a work of a *tufunga* who weaves together different fabrics that fit his or her purpose, and excludes those which do not.[257] *Lau lea* therefore does not only allow one to read what is being woven or written in the text, but also that which is being ignored and unwritten.

The second aspect, *tō'onga lea*, can mean "ways of speaking." Each *lea*, on the one hand, is uttered in a way to have an effect on the hearers, and to drive home a message. When *tō'onga lea* are analysed, they tend, on the other hand, to say something about the speakers, revealing in most cases the kinds of intention that shape the utterances. The *lau lea* method examines different ways of speaking that are woven together in the text, the way they portray speaking subjects, and the significant contribution they make to the meaning of the text as a whole. I will deal particularly with three Tongan ways of speaking to demonstrate how this method works, namely, *lea hualela, lea akonaki*, and *lea faka-punake*.

---

[254] See Trible, *Rhetorical Criticism: Context, Method, and the Book of Jonah*.
[255] Robbins, *Exploring the Texture of Texts: A Guide to Socio-Rhetorical Interpretation*, 1.
[256] The skills for *tufunga lea* are different from those of *faiva lea*. The latter refers to the one delivering the speech or poem. Here the act of speaking is to be distinguished from the act of composing. The one who does both is referred to in Tongan as the *punake*.
[257] This is an aspect that could exclude and my reading would want to be alert to and expose any such exclusion.

The *hualela* way of speaking is characteristically direct, plain, and in some cases, judgmental. It includes the following categories: *lea lau*, *lea vale* (*fieme'a/fiepoto*) and *lea tuki* (*valoki*). *Lea lau* refers to a way of speaking that concerns somebody who is not present in the context of utterance. *Lea vale* (*fieme'a/fiepoto*) is a way of speaking that precedes thinking (where the mouth deviates from one's mind), and it tends to offer a false idea of oneself as socially and intellectually superior while reality points otherwise. This way of speaking often uses stereotypic references, and has the propensity to demoralize, vilify and humiliate the hearers. *Lea tuki* or *lea valoki* is a judgmental type which in most cases offers a hypocritical evaluation of others while the speaker tends to be behaving in a similar, or worse, manner.

The *akonaki* way of speaking differs from the *lea hualela* in the sense that it takes the interest of others into account and presupposes a special relation between the speaker and hearer. This *tō'onga lea* imparts advice and instruction, and is usually uttered by a person with experience and wisdom.

The *faka-punake* way of speaking is characteristically poetic, figurative, persuasive, and in some cases, parodic, confrontational and argumentative. Various manners of speaking belong to this category: *fakalangilangi, lau'aitu, fakahekeheke, hua, fetau,* and *heliaki*. *Lea fakalangilangi* uses symbols and imageries to exalt a person or an event. This is aimed to highlight a person's status or achievement, and thus installs a sense of respect and awe on the hearers. *Lea lau'aitu* like *fakalangilangi*, uses figures of speech, but has a different aim and situation. *Lau'aitu* is Tongan equivalent of laments and funeral dirges. It is found only in situations of mourning, and it serves to comfort those who have lost a loved one or who have experienced an unexpected crisis. *Lea fakahekeheke* is a *tō'onga lea* that utters more lies than truth, and it tends to exaggerate. It is *aimed solely to flatter or gain the favour of somebody else*. Such a type can be found when those of lower status address those in the upper stratum. *Lea hua* uses figurative languages to mock and ridicule others. It has a dual tendency to evoke laughter or provoke anger.

Lea fetau is a persuasive, confrontational and argumentative type. Unlike the other *tō'onga lea*, this one requires special skills to convince the hearers to agree with one's view on an important subject, to challenge existing views, and to offer alternative perspectives. The primary aim of this *tō'onga lea* is to counter any claim of domination. *Fetau* is political in orientation. It is the stuff of any rhetoric of resistance. *Lea heliaki* is the master of verbal disguise. It is a way of speaking where speech and deed never match; where the meaning of any utterance lies otherwise. *Heliaki* is the epitome of *lea faka-punake*; it resists determinacy and dis-closure. It tends to (mis)guide (*hē*) the hearers from the point, and abandon (*li'aki*) them in another (I will discuss *heliaki* more below).

These ways of speaking are Tongan, and therefore context-specific. They will be employed in the reading of Ezra 9–10 in forthcoming chapters to see if they shed some new light on the meanings of the text. This attempt will not be the first of its kind, because other methods (such as form and rhetorical criticisms) also operate in the same manner. Genres and categories are chosen and employed as lenses of reading, rather than something natural to the text. They are culturally specific ideas selected to assist the reader in the meaning-making process. Texts do not come with genres; readers create them.[258] Likewise, texts do not define different ways of speaking; these ways belong to the reader. In that case, each reader may perceive speeches within a text differently, depending on how words and speeches are understood in different cultural contexts.

METHOD 3: *LAU VĀ*

With the first two methods, attentions are directed at the literary aspects of the text. This third method, *lau vā*, probes into a text's *socio-spatial* dimension. I use the term "socio-spatial" to indicate the distinction of *lau vā* method from the social-scientific reading of the Bible. Whereas social-scientific criticism attempts to investigate the original social and cultural setting of a text,[259] the *lau vā* method seeks to read the social and

---

[258] With regard to the nature of text, Gerard Genette emphasises that texts are ignorant of their generic quality. A text neither knows itself to be a novel nor a poem, prose nor narrative. To determine "the generic status of a text is not the business of the text but that of the reader, or the critic, or the public." This generic openness gives the reader the freedom to read texts across and around genres despite their imagined generic boundaries. Generic perceptions guide and determined the reader's expectations in the process of interpretation. See Genette, *Palimpsests: Literature in the Second Degree*, 4, 5.

[259] For more information on the method see Dale B. Martin, "Social–Scientific Criticism," in *To Each Its Own Meaning: Biblical Criticisms and Their Application* (ed. Steven L. McKenzie and Stephen R. Haynes; Louisville: Westminster John Knox, 1999), 125–141. Charles E. Carter, "Opening Windows onto Biblical Worlds: Applying the Social Sciences to Hebrew Scripture," in *The Face of Old Testament Studies: A Survey of Contemporary Approaches* (ed. David W. Baker and Bill T. Arnold; Grand Rapids: Baker Books, 1999), 421–451. David J. Chalcraft, ed. *Social-scientific Old Testament Criticism* (Sheffield: Sheffield Academic Press, 1997), John H. Elliott, *What is Socia-*

cultural codes and practices inscribed in the text in the light of the reader's own social and cultural world. *Lau vā* method is more interested in the effect of the social orientation of the text on the reader's culture than seeking to know the social world behind the text. The social and cultural context of the reader takes precedence over the social and cultural setting of the text. Hence, the use of the Tongan term "*vā*."

The term *vā* refers to *(imaginary) spaces* that define relations, social or otherwise.[260] Such spaces are required to be observed and respected in order to maintain right relations in Tongan society. *Lau vā* can therefore mean "to read spaces or relations." *Vā* has two dimensions: vertical and horizontal. Vertically, it encompasses the sacred spaces between the *'otua* (gods) and their adherents, and between *tu'a* (commoners) and *'eiki* (chiefs). Horizontally, *vā* indicates the spaces amongst people within different classes, between males (*tangata*) and females (*fafine*), and between parents (*mātu'a*) and children (*fānau*). These *vā* (both vertical and horizontal) are considered sacred (*tapu*) and are therefore prohibited (*tapu*) to be transgressed.[261]

The *tapu* of *vā* is maintained by practicing the key fundamental (pre-Christian) value of *faka'apa'apa* (unreserved respect) which is expressed through *fetauhi'aki* (reciprocity). The absence of *faka'apa'apa* puts the *tapu* of *vā* at risk of being violated, and will therefore hinder the goals envisioned through *tākanga*. These dimensions of *vā* offer the agenda for *lau vā* method.

The *lau vā* method scrutinizes texts as follows. First, it seeks to identify *fa'ahinga* (social groups) that the text constructs, and examines the social visions they advocate.[262] This task involves a critical assessment of four social aspects: *tu'unga, fa'unga, lōlenga* and *ākenga*. The word *tu'unga* indicates one's position, location or status. Analysis of the *tu'unga* focuses on how the text positions and locates each *fa'ahinga*

Scientific Criticism? (Minneapolis: Augsburg Fortress, 1993), Robert A. Wortham, *Social-scientific Approaches in Biblical Literature* (Lewiston: E. Mellen, 1999).

[260] Other nuances of *vā* are discussed in Ka'ili, "*Tauhi vā*: Nurturing Tongan Sociospatial Ties in Maui and Beyond," 83–114.

[261] There is no distinction between political and religious *vā*, because in Tonga *what is political is religious*, and vice versa.

[262] Analysing the *fa'ahinga* is significant for several reasons: it brings to light, on the one hand, the reality that every *tākanga* (community) is diversely constituted; it exposes, on the other hand, the illusion of a homogeneous society. The presence of various *fa'ahinga* also highlights that there is always interplay of different roles and often conflicting values in the space of the text; texts also position *fa'ahinga* to protect the interests of those it favours against those it does not. In most cases, the favourites turn out to be those with power and privilege, and texts are often (if not always) written from their perspectives, and for their own interests.

in relation to others. The word *fa'unga* encompasses the way a *fa'ahinga* is constituted and structured. Analysis of the *fa'unga* focuses on factors like class, gender, ethnicity, and roles. The term *lōlenga* refers to the way a group behaves, thinks, and conducts itself in any given circumstances; it is a group's way of being and way of thing.[263] The *lōlenga* also points to the way a group defines itself in relation to others, the social ideals it endorses, as well as the values it seeks to live by. Analysis of the *lōlenga* focuses on how a *fa'ahinga* behaves in certain circumstances, and takes account of both their action and/or non-action in regard to issues that confront them. It also deals with a group's attitudes, emotions, ideas, and visions.

Second, *lau vā* evaluates how the dimensions of *vā* are maintained and/or transgressed in and by the text. The need for this evaluation is to see if there are internal and external tensions in and amongst the *fa'ahinga*. This second task of *lau vā* is based on the insights provided by the first. Third, and finally, *lau vā* assesses the insights from the preceding tasks to determine whether or not the social visions inscribed in the text foster or impede the goals envisioned through the analytical category of *tākanga*.

The underlying assumption of *lau vā* method is that *every text is social*. By this I mean, first all, that every text is socially produced and preserved (within a social setting); second, every text is an intersection of different, and often conflicting, visions of society. The primary goal of *lau vā* is therefore to reveal social visions that have been "woven" into the "fabrics" of the text. To analyse these visions, *lau vā* focuses on the social aspects *fa'ahinga* (social groups), and thus examines their *tu'unga* (position, status), *fa'unga* (social structure), *lōlenga* (way of being), and *ākenga* (way of thinking).

METHOD 4: *LAU TU'UNGA*

The name I have given to the final method of analysis is *lau tu'unga*. The word *tu'unga* can mean "where one stands," "the basis upon which something is built," or "a stepping stone." It also indicates a person's status or position as above-mentioned. When dealing with literary texts, *tu'unga* encompasses beliefs, ideologies and/or worldviews that shape

---

[263]Tongans usually refer to the way of people from small islands as *lōlenga faka-motu* (island way). The *'eiki* class also defines the way the *tu'a* class conduct themselves as *lōlenga faka-tu'a*. *Lōlenga* applies only to groups, and it refers generally to behaviour and attitude that are characteristics of that group.

the text and the perspectives therein. These are expressed not only in the way texts are arranged and woven, but also through myths, folklores, and genealogies that are inserted into texts to validate certain truth-claims.

Tu'unga shapes the weaving of texts, determines the representation of voices and the employment of language, as well as validates the kind of social setup it portrays. Tongan society is constructed upon a belief that one social class descends from the gods, while others are of earthly origin. The divine-descendants are therefore destined to rule, while their earthly counterparts are there to serve. As such it validates the status quo, and thereby legitimizes the power and privilege of a minority over the subjugation and suffering of the majority.

This orientation of *lau tu'unga* links itself to ideological criticism, and is in fact influenced by insights from that method. By definition, "ideology" refers to "the complex system of ideas, values, and perceptions held by a particular group that provides a framework for the group members to understand their place in the social order."[264] This system creates a reality for people, "making the bewildering and often brutal world intelligible and tolerable . . . [it also m]otivates people to behave in specific ways and to accept their social position as natural, inevitable, and necessary."[265] Ideological criticism in that sense seeks to uncover the production and consumption of ideologies in any given text, and it involves intrinsic and extrinsic analyses. The latter deals with historical conditions in which a text was produced, whereas the former pays attention to how the text inscribes such conditions to recreate a particular ideology. Extrinsic analysis requires some knowledge of the world behind the text; intrinsic analysis focuses on the text. The *lau tu'unga* method, like the latter, has the text and its content as its major concern. Moreover, *lau tu'unga* does not look for ideologies that drove the creation of the text, but the one that is expressed within the text vis-à-vis the ideologies that shaped the reader's culture.

In Tongan culture, ideologies are expressed in different ways and forms such as *talatupu'a* (origin myths, etiological narratives), *lea* (language), *ta'anga* (compositions), *tohi hohoko* (genealogies),[266] and *lotu* (belief-system, religion). Most of our *talatupu'a* provide the rationale for the status quo. They describe why things are the way they are. They also aim to create awe and respect for the *'eiki* class. Likewise, *lea* is categorized into three tiers where vocabulary for the *'eiki* resemble

---

[264]Gale A. Yee, *Judges and Method: New Approaches in Biblical Studies* (Minneapolis: Fortress, 2007), 345.
[265]Ibid.
[266]See Wood-Ellem, *Queen Salote of Tonga: The Story of an Era 1900–1965*, 24–47.

those for gods, and words for the *tu'a* are those used for animals as was laid out in chapter one. Many of our classical *ta'anga* are composed for the same purpose, so too our *tohi hohoko*. The *'eiki* class is always traced back to the gods, while the *tu'a* is linked to a maggot or an animal. The strongest force of legitimation is *lotu*. Ancient Tongan religion was polytheistic;[267] each *ha'a* (tribe) worshipped a tribal god. The *'eiki* of each *ha'a* was seen as representative of the god, and thus deserved reverence. These forms provide a strong basis upon which the belief that shaped them is sanctioned and legitimized. As a result, the powerful continue to enjoy the privilege they have, and the oppressed accept their situation as the way life should be.

The *lau tu'unga* method is therefore devised to look for charters in biblical texts that legitimize dominant ideologies and/or beliefs. In the act of *faka-'uhinga*, a *tu'a* reader seeks to engage with any myth, tradition, and genealogy constructed or invoked by texts. S/he asks: *What kind of "reality" does the Bible constructs to validate domination and injustice? What is the likely impact of such a reality upon the context of reception and the reading community? What is the new world in front of the text that the tu'a reader will create?*

These four methods constitute *lau faka-tu'a* as a methodology for biblical interpretation. Each method is influenced to an extent by existing methods, yet unique in terms of the concepts employed and questions asked.

Charting *Tu'a*-wise

The methodology of *lau faka-tu'a* has been charted with the following rationale: *un-weaving, re-locating, re-stor[y]ing,* and *re-vis[ion]ing*.

Lau faka-tu'a seeks to *un-weave* texts in the reading process. This is based on the assumption that texts are woven with different linguistic, social, ideological and cultural *fe'unu*. Un-weaving aims to reveal how texts are woven and arranged, as well as the factors that shape the textual arrangement.

Lau faka-tu'a also seeks to *rel[oc]ate* (i.e. locate and relate) displaced subjects of texts. This is based on the assumption that texts contain mechanisms of displacement, and thus contribute to the dis-

---

[267]See E. E. Collocott, "Notes on Tongan Religion I," *The Journal of the Polynesian Society* 30, no. 119 (1921): 152–163, "Notes on Tongan Religion II," *The Journal of the Polynesian Society* 30, no. 120 (1921): 227–240.

placement of subjects in real life. Re-locating aims to re-claim a space for those subjects.

Lau faka-tu'a is an event in *re-stor[y]ing*. It is an attempt both to *re-story* and *re-store*. This is based on the assumption that texts are written from a position of power, and tend to ignore subjects, voices, and perspectives that do not serve the interests of their authors. What we have in the Bible, in its final form, are re-storied traditions. They serve as tools for re-storing and re-establishing different faith communities from time to time. In that sense, biblical authors were re-stor[y]ing writers. Likewise, the many readings of the Bible reflect various ways of re-stor[y]ing the written texts from different perspectives and world-views. Each reader therefore is a re-stor[y]ing reader. Re-stor[y]ing is a form of resistance; it resists not for resistance's sake, but to retrieve alternative voices and to re-store ignored perspectives.

The fourth, and final, rationale for *lau faka-tu'a* is re-vis[ion]ing; it involves *re-vision* and *revision*. This rationale is based on the assumption that texts contain visions of society that give privilege to some at the expense of others. Re-visioning in that sense seeks alternative visions, and thereby a revising of the existing ones.[268]

The methods and rationales discussed above indicate that *lau faka-tu'a* is a multidimensional methodology: the *lau fe'unu* method unweaves texts to reveal its structure, design and emphasis; the *lau lea* method directs the attention of *lau faka-tu'a* to the linguistic and rhetorical aspects of texts; the *lau vā* method focuses on the social and sacred aspects of texts; the *lau tu'unga* method, finally, scrutinizes texts to expose the beliefs and ideologies that shape visions and claims. These methods provide tools for reading texts through the lenses of *fonua*, *tākanga* and *tālanga*. The ultimate goal is to negotiate a sense of place for displaced subjects through the process of interpretation. Each rationale corresponds to either one of the methods, and thus shapes the four readings of Ezra 9–10 in the forthcoming chapters.

---

[268]It is also a movement in time; between past and present. In Tongan culture, the past lies ahead (*kuonga-kimu'a*), whereas the future lies behind (*kuonga-kimui*). *Lau faka-tu'a* envisions the future by *moving forward to the past*. It *revises* the past by *moving backward to the future*. The past, on the one hand, is where Tongan culture and values are *rooted*. The past also holds painful experiences caused by both colonial and local regimes. *Lau faka-tu'a* finds comfort neither in idealizing nor in retrieving the past; the past needs *revision*.

The future, on the other hand, offers possibilities and welcomes new visions. It presents a liberating space for Tongan *tu'a*. The future however is full of uncertainties. Any vision thus requires checks and balances. To envision otherwise is to leap into "a frightening utopia." *Revising* the past and re-*visioning* the future are inseparable obligations; hence, *re-vis[ion]ing*!

PART 3: *ANGAFAI*

CHAPTER 5
UN-WEAVING EZRA

The Bible, of all books, is the most dangerous one, the one that has been endowed with the power to kill.

Mieke Bal[269]

The Bible does not demystify or demythologize itself. But neither does it claim that the stories it tells are paradigms for human action in all times and places ... Perhaps the most constructive thing a biblical critic can do toward lessening the contribution of the Bible to violence in the world, is to show that certitude is an illusion.

John J. Collins[270]

In the preceding chapters, I have developed *lau faka-tu'a* as an alternative way of reading. That involved the formulation of a theoretical framework and methodology to guide biblical interpretation. In this chapter, and those that follow, I will read Ezra 9–10 *tu'a*-wise.

The first step in *lau faka-tu'a* is to locate and define the *'ātakai* of texts. As defined in chapter 3, the term *'ātakai* indicates a well-defined location or a designated space. The significance of *'ātakai* lies in the relationship between its two sides: *'ā-ki-loto* (inner *'ā*) and *'ā-ki-tu'a* (outer *'ā*). To examine the *'ā-ki-loto* involves defining every object on its

---

[269]Mieke Bal, *Anti-Covenant: Counter Reading Women's Lives in the Hebrew Bible* (Sheffield: Almond, 1989), 8.
[270]John J. Collins, "The Zeal of Phinehas: The Bible and the Legitimation of Violence," *Journal of Biblical Literature* 122, no. 1 (2003): 20, 21.

own, and investigating its constitutive parts and characteristic features. To analyse the *'ā-ki-tu'a* requires examining an object in contradistinction to its surrounding. Whereas the *'ā-ki-loto* holds the unique and non-iterative aspects of the object, the *'ā-ki-tu'a* encompasses shared and interrelated elements. Both the *'ā-ki-loto* and *'ā-ki-tu'a* are two sides of the same *'ātakai*, and are therefore linked despite holding different aspects of the investigated object. Without the *'ā-ki-tu'a* it is impossible to speak of the *'ā-ki-loto*, and vice versa.

Lau faka-tu'a perceives every biblical text as having its own *'ātakai* (context, limit), defined by its *'ā-ki-loto* and *'ā-ki-tu'a*. This chapter locates Ezra 9:1–10:17 in its *'ātakai*, focusing on its *'ā-ki-loto* and *'ā-ki-tu'a*. This is the groundwork for the various readings of the text in the chapters that follow.

'ĀTAKAI

To define the *'ātakai* of texts is not to erect an *'ā* (fence, boundary) that prohibits their intertextual orientations. The *'ātakai* indicates, rather, that despite this web of relations, texts do have (and need) limits.[271] Setting the limit however is a responsibility of readers, because texts do not admit having one. This part seeks to define the *'ātakai* of Ezra 9:1–10:17 by marking the *'ā* (limit) where the *'ā-ki-loto* and *'ā-ki-tu'a* intersect.

The *'ātakai* of Ezra 9:1–10:17 opens with an accusation made by one group against another (9:1–2):

> *When these were done, the chiefs approached me, saying, "The people of Israel, the priests and the Levites have not separated themselves from the peoples of the lands; their abominations are likened to the Canaanites, the Hittites, the Jebusites, the Ammonites, the Moabites, the Egyptians, and the Amorites,*[272] *because they have taken their daughters for themselves and for their sons, and they have mingled the holy seed with the peoples of*

---

[271]These limits make intertextuality possible. This is true of texts as with human beings. We speak of human relationships because there are individual human beings. Each individual has limits, yet they do not obstruct human interactions. Relationship is possible only amongst individuals. To understand the individuals is to study each one of them individually and then in relation to each other.

[272]One Greek manuscript (Aquila's) reads "and the Edomites" instead of "Amorites."

the lands, and the hand of the chiefs and the prefects are foremost in this unfaithful act."[273]

According to the chiefs (שרים *šrym*),[274] to marry outside their own social and ethnic boundaries is a very serious problem, since it exposes the "holy seed" (זרע הקדש *zr' hqdš*) to the abominations of the "peoples of the lands" (עמי הארצות *'mmy h'rswt*), which are comparable only to those of the named ethnic groups. What the people, priests and Levites have done is an unfaithful act.

The *'ātakai* logically ends in 10:17 with the impression that the problem may have been solved:

> *By the first day of the first month, they put an end to all the men who have married*[275] *foreign women.*

The word ויכלו (imperfect 3rd masculine plural form of the root כלה) is rendered differently in various English : "they made an end" (KJV), "they had passed judgment" (NAB), "they finished dealing" (NIV), "they had come to the end" (NRSV), or "they were done" (JPS). The meaning of the root כלה is ambiguous, since it refers to completion of a task (e.g. 1 Kgs 6:38) or a period of time (e.g. Gen 41:53), on the one hand, and denotes complete destruction and annihilation (e.g. Ezek 13:13), on the other hand. My translation, "put an end to," seeks to take advantage of that ambiguity and thus allows readers the freedom to read either way. The phrase could mean either *the end of the questioning process* or the *final execution of justice* upon those men who married "foreign women."

The latter reading seems to be more plausible, since in 9:1 the report is about male members of the returning exiles taking "foreign women" for their wives. The ending in 10:17 is proper since it offers the duly disciplinary action against those men, and not the women. To extend the *'ātakai* of the text to 10:44, as the majority of scholars do,[276]

---

[273]Translation of the text is mine unless otherwise indicated.
[274]Hebrew texts are from the *Biblia Hebraica Stuttgartensia*, (Stuttgart: Deutsche Bibelgesellschaft, 1967/77).
[275]This is a translation of the verb ההשיבו—a Hiphil perfect form (3ms) of the root ישב (to dwell). It can also be rendered as "to give a dwelling to." Meanings of Hebrew terms are mostly from Francis Brown et al., *The Brown-Driver-Briggs Hebrew and English Lexicon* (Peabody: Hendrickson, 2003).
[276]For examples: Tamara Cohn Eskenazi and Eleanore P. Judd, "Married to a Stranger in Ezra 9–10," in *Second Temple Studies: 2. Temple and Community in the Persian Period* (ed. David J. A. Clines and Philip R. Davies; Sheffield: JSOT, 1994), 266–285. Daniel Smith-Christopher, "The Mixed Marriage Crisis in Ezra 9–10 and

is to shift the responsibility for the problem from the offenders to their wives and children. That transference of blame, however, is exactly what the text would like the readers to accept, and most readers unfortunately do so.[277]

Within the confinement of the '*ātakai* lies a claim that those who returned from "exile" (בני הגולה, *bny hgwlh*) are a special group, the "holy seed"; they have an exclusive right to all of God's promises, particularly the inheritance of land and its wealth (9:11–12). Their responsibility therefore is to protect the *purity* of their identity by *separating* (בדל *bdl*) themselves from "the peoples of the lands." This claim sets the whole story in motion, and thus invites its readers to the kind of world it projects.

The offenders are identified as the people (of Israel), the priests (כהנים *khnym*), and the Levites (לויים *lwyym*). Some of them have taken their wives from "the peoples of the lands", and thereby jeopardized the "holy seed." *Intermarriage* becomes the key issue in the text. That highlights the xenophobic tendency of those who supposedly returned from exile towards foreign women who married Israelite men. Interesting to note is the absence of any reference to intermarriage between the daughters of Israel and the sons of "the peoples of the lands." There are two possible explanations for this: it is either an intentional decision on the part of the author-editor to exclude it or it was not considered a problem at all. In her introduction to Ezra-Nehemiah in the *Women's Bible Commentary*, Eskenazi argues that

> [w]omen in the postexilic community possessed more power than the fleeting references to them in the canonical literature indicate at first glance.[278]

Nehemiah 13: A Study of the Sociology of Post-Exilic Judaean Community," in *Second Temple Studies: 2. Temple and Community in the Persian Period* (ed. Tamara Cohn Eskenazi and Kent H. Richards; Sheffield: JSOT, 1994), 243–265. Willa Mathis Johnson, "The Holy Seed Has Been Defiled: The Interethnic Marriage Dilemma in Ezra 9–10" (Ph.D., Vanderbilt University, 1999). A. Philip Brown II, "The Problem of Mixed Marriages in Ezra 9–10," *Bibliotheca Sacra* 162 (October–December 2005): 437–458.

[277]The NRSV renders 10:44 as if the women and their children were actually expelled, whereas the MT reads otherwise. NRSV reads: "All these had married foreign women, and they sent them away with their children." The JPS version which follows the MT reads: "All these had married foreign women, among whom were some women who had borne children."

[278]Tamara Cohn Eskenazi, "Ezra-Nehemiah," in *Women's Bible Commentary* (ed. Carol A. Newsom and Sharon H. Ringe; Louisville: Westminster John Knox, 1998), 125.

She uses extra-biblical sources from Elephantine to corroborate her argument. Those sources show Jewish women in diaspora initiating divorce, buying and selling property, and inheriting property "even when there were male siblings."[279] If that was the case, then Israelite women who may have married "foreign" men would not be considered a loss but a gain for the returnees, since they can inherit properties.

The *'ātakai* I have set shows that Ezra 9:1–10:17 is a definable text which can be read on its own apart from the preceding and succeeding material. A look at the *'ā-ki-loto* and *'ā-ki-tu'a* will provide further support.

'A-KI-LOTO

The analysis of the *'ā-ki-loto* focuses on the text and its *fa'unga*. The *fa'unga* refers to the various *fe'unu* (strands) that are woven together to make up the text. To examine the *fa'unga* requires *un-weaving*; its goal is to know how and why a text is woven in such a manner. The *fa'unga* of Ezra 9:1–10:17 is an admixture of different *fe'unu* woven together. Some are direct speeches (D); others are narrations (N). These features of the *fa'unga* are evident in the outline below:

9:1a N^1 (first person)

9:1b–2 D^1 (Officers)

9:3–6a N^2 (first person)

6:6b–15 D^2 (Ezra)

10:1–2a N^3 (third person)

10:2b–4   X (Shecaniah)

10:5–10a N^4 (third person)

10:10b–11 D^{2a} (Ezra)

10:12a N^5 (third person)

10:12b–14 D^{1a} (People)

10:15–17 N^6 (third person)

---

[279] Ibid.

The narrator's voice (N) dominates, and shifts from first person in chapter 9 to third person in chapter 10. The progression of narration is as follows. N^1 identifies those who bring the allegation of mixed marriages to Ezra as "the chiefs" (השרים *hsrym*). In N^2, the readers are informed of Ezra's response to that allegation. The first person narration ends there. From N^3 to N^6, events are narrated in the third person. N^3 picks up from where N^2 ends but with a change to the location of events, people involved, and those who were speaking. N^4, like N^2, reports another reaction and response by Ezra to somebody else's (Shecaniah's) words, and N^5 introduces another word, now for the first time, by the people accused of mixed marriages. N^6 closes the narrative by *doing away* with the men who married foreign women.

The progression of direct speeches (D) forms a chiastic structure. In D^1, the officers bring to Ezra's attention the prevalence of mixed marriages amongst the returnees, whereas in D^{1a} the people accused of mixed marriages pledge to go along with what Shecaniah recommends in X: to expel their foreign wives.[280] D^2 and D^{2a} are Ezra's responses, first, to the officer's allegation, and second, to Shecaniah's recommendation. The alleged problem and proposed solution are given to Ezra; he is not aware of the problem despite being in Jerusalem for some time, and has no clue to a solution despite being portrayed as הוא־ספר מהיר בתורת משה ("a scribe skilled in the law of Moses" [7:6]).

This *fa'unga* supports the *'ātakai* set for the text in the preceding section. It witnesses to the natural flow of the text from 9:1 to 10:17, which thus leaves out 10:18–44 as in Mark A. Throntveit's outline of Ezra 9–10:

    A   Reporting (9:1-2)
         B   Mourning (9:3-4)
            C   Praying (9:5-15)
                X   Confession and Request (10:1-4)
            C'   Exhortation and Oath (10:5)
         B'   Mourning (10:6)
    A'   Resolution (10:7-17)
(Appendix: List of men with expelled wives [10:18-44])[281]

---

[280] The NRSV adopts the harmonization made in 1 Esdras 9:36, which brings the resolution to pass while the MT reads otherwise. This politics of translation imposes alien "text" upon the story, and thus actualizes the very act the story resists.
[281] Mark A. Throntveit, *Ezra-Nehemiah* (Louisville: John Knox, 1992), 49.

Unit A' (10:7–17) provides the resolution (i.e. expulsion[282]) to the so-called problem of mixed marriage reported in unit A (9:1–2). What links the resolution and report is the confession and recommendation in unit X (10:1–4). Because mixed marriage has been problematized and prohibited by the community, a representative (silent about any consultation with men who married foreign women) acknowledges their responsibility, and volitionally recommends what should be done. That creates a symmetrical pattern for a rather asymmetrical event. While Throntveit's construction sheds light on the text, he finds no place in his structure for the last unit (10:18–44). As I have argued above, that part belongs to the *'ā-ki-tu'a* not the *'a-ki-loto* of the text.

'A-KI-TU'A

The *'ā-ki-tu'a* deals with two aspects: *tūkunga* and *tu'unga*. The *tūkunga* directs the reader to explore the outer limit of the *'ātakai*; the material surrounding the limit of the *'ā-ki-loto*. The *tu'unga* refers to location and function of the text in its *tūkunga*. These two elements provide support for defining the *'ātakai* of the text, on the one hand, and show aspects that link the *'ā-ki-loto* to the *'ā-ki-tu'a*, on the other hand.

Ezra 9:1–10:17 is traditionally located within the wider *tūkunga* of Ezra and Nehemiah.[283] These two books combined are perceived to have woven together three different events of return of the Judaean exiles

---

[282] The root (יצא) from which the word "to expel" (להוציא) is derived here conveys, on the one hand, a sense of condemnation, and carries, on the other hand, a sense of release or emancipation (for examples: Gen 40:14; Exod 6:3; Isa 42:7; Jer 20:3). In the forthcoming readings of Ezra 9–10, I will argue that Shecaniah's word in 10:2–4 is not as straightforward as it seems.

[283] I am using the phrase "Ezra and Nehemiah" to reflect the way they are in the final form of the Hebrew canon, as two separate books, rather than the usual "Ezra-Nehemiah," which is based on the arguments that they were counted as one in ancient Jewish tradition and manuscripts. Scholars who read Ezra and Nehemiah together based their view on these evidences: (1) Josephus counted the two books as one; (2) Melito, Bishop of Sardis, refers to the whole work as "Ezra"; (3) the Talmud includes the activities of Nehemiah in the book of Ezra; (4) the Masoretes regard the books as one, (5) the medieval Jewish commentators move from Ezra to Nehemiah without interruption, and (6) in the earliest Hebrew manuscripts the books are also treated as one. Williamson points out that the separation of the two books was first attested by Origen, followed by Jerome in the Vulgate, and adopted into Jewish tradition in the Middle Ages, which was attested in the early printed editions of the Hebrew Bible. See H. G. M. Williamson, *Ezra, Nehemiah* (Waco: Word Books, 1985), xxi.

from Babylon to Judah under Persian rule.[284] Each event is authorized by a Persian king, is led by a different individual, projects its own distinct vision of restoration, and encounters different sorts of oppositions. The events are arranged as follows:

    A   First Return (Ezra 1:1–6:22)
- King: Cyrus
- Leader: Zerubbabel
- Vision: To Rebuild the Temple
- Opposition: Enemies of Judah and Benjamin

    B   Second Return (Ezra 7:1–10:44)
- King: Artaxerxes
- Leader: Ezra
- Vision: To Reconstitute the Community
- Opposition: Zerubbabel-Group and Peoples of the lands

    C   Third Return (Neh 1:1–13:31) Under Nehemiah
- King: Artaxerxes
- Leader: Nehemiah
- Vision: To Restore the City Wall
- Opposition: Government and Religious Officials

The first return (Ezra 1:1–6:22) begins with a royal decree that offers a vision for those who are willing to return. The decree (1:2–4) reads:

> *Thus Cyrus, the king of Persia, said, "The Lord God of heaven has given me all the kingdoms of the earth, and has appointed me to build for Him a house in Jerusalem, which is in Judah. Anyone of you from all His people – may his God be with him, and let him ascend to Jerusalem which is in Judah and build the house of the Lord God of Israel, the God who is in Jerusalem. And all who remain, wherever he may be living, let the people of his place assist him with silver, gold, goods, and livestock, besides the freewill offering to the House of God that is in Jerusalem."*

The decree opens with an acknowledgment of divine favour and the charge that comes with it: to build a house in Jerusalem for the God of

---
[284]See Throntveit, *Ezra-Nehemiah*, 2.

Heaven. This charge serves as the primary goal of restoration for the first group. Membership in this group is open to whoever wills to join the restoration task. Following the edict of Cyrus, people prepare to leave for Jerusalem with gifts from their neighbours and the king, for the temple (1:5–11). Names of those who leave to rebuild the temple are listed in 2:1–72.[285] In 3:1–13, Jeshua ben Jozadak, Zerubbabel ben Shealtiel, and their brothers lead the people in building an altar, offering sacrifices, and the celebration of the Feast of the Tabernacles, according to the Teaching of Moses and in fear of "the peoples of the lands". Moreover, they pay builders, Sidonians and Tyrians to bring cedars from Lebanon for the temple. From 1:1 to 4:2, the rebuilding of the temple was unopposed.

Opposition, however, begins from 4:3 up to 5:17. In 4:1–2, a group identified by the narrator as "adversaries of Benjamin and Judah" offer their help in the rebuilding project. The identity of this group is not clear, except that their request is rejected by Zerubbabel (4:3). The rebuilding project from here onward faces opposition that calls for the intervention of Persian authorities on two occasions. In 4:4–24, the "adversaries" oppose the work and then request that the project be stopped. This request is granted by Artaxerxes in 4:17–22. The project was put on hold. Zerubbabel restarts the project without permission (5:1–2) to which Tattenai, "governor of the province of Beyond the River, Shethar-bozenai" and colleagues again oppose (5:3–4). The returnees take their concern to the Persian authority (5:5–17) and King Darius decided in their favour (6:1–12). From this point, the building of the temple progresses until its completion and dedication (6:13–22). The ultimate goal for the first group of returnees is now realized and celebrated.

The second return begins in 7:1, authorized by king Artaxerxes and led by Ezra. This group consists of temple servants who bring vessels for the temple. The primary goal of this group is for Ezra to teach the law of God to the people, presumably, in the completed temple (7:1–28). As in 2:1–72, names of those who returned with Ezra are listed in 8:1–36. Prior to their arrival, they fasted at the Ahava River, where twelve priests are selected to carry the temple vessels to the house of God in Jerusalem. It is in the house of God that the event in 9:1–15 (the problem of mixed marriage) are narrated. Ezra 10:1–44 (the solution to mixed marriage), however, moves the action out of that place to the square outside the temple. In short, events in Ezra move towards the

---

[285]For further information on names listed in Ezra, see Jacob Liver, *Chapters in the History of the Priests and Levites: Studies in the Lists of Chronicles and Ezra and Nehemiah* (Jerusalem: Magnes, 1968).

temple, occur within the temple, and move away from the temple. Unlike the first return which was realized and celebrated, it is unclear whether or not this group fulfills its mission due to oppositions from those who are already in the land, which includes members of the Zerubbabel group.

The third return is narrated in Neh 2. Nehemiah negotiates with king Artaxerxes another opportunity to return to Jerusalem to rebuild its wall. Like the first two returns, Nehemiah's request is granted and authorized with a royal letter (2:7–8). When Nehemiah and his wall-building group arrived in Judah, they faced oppositions from parties whom the text repeatedly identifies as Sanballat the Horonite, Tobiah the Ammonite, Geshem the Arab, Noadiah the prophetess, and others. Despite the oppositions, the restoration of the wall was completed (6:15). Neh 13:1–31 wraps up the narrative by portraying Nehemiah as a leader according to the Torah, after overseeing with Ezra the reconstruction of the community, in the form of marriage reform (Ezra 7:1–10:44), the rebuilding of the city wall and socio-political reform (Neh 1:1–7:72a), the renewal of the covenant (7:72b–10:40), and the repopulation of Jerusalem (11:1–12:43).[286]

This traditional reading of Ezra and Nehemiah as the *tūkunga* for Ezra 9:1–10:17 implies that readers should:

1. abandon the final form and arrangement of the narratives in favour of earlier traditions and manuscripts;

2. rearrange the material in both narratives to harmonize the somewhat incoherent and misplaced portions;[287] and

3. acknowledge that both narratives would be unintelligible and incomplete if treated separately. The underlying assumption is that Ezra and Nehemiah were originally works of a single author.

What if Ezra and Nehemiah do not belong together? James C. VanderKam provides some convincing evidence for a separation of Ezra from Nehemiah as independent works.[288] He argues that Ezra and

---

[286]See Michael W. Duggan, *The Covenant Renewal in Ezra-Nehemiah (Neh 7:72b–10:40): An Exegetical, Literary, and Theological Study* (Atlanta: SBL, 2001), 60.

[287]See Charles C. Torrey, *Ezra studies* (Chicago: University of Chicago Press, 1910), 252–284.

[288]James C. VanderKam, "Ezra-Nehemiah or Ezra and Nehemiah?," in *Priests, Prophets and Scribes* (ed. Eugene Ulrich, et al.; Sheffield: JSOT, 1992), 55–75. His claim also separates Ezra and Nehemiah from Chronicles, rejecting the theory promoted

Nehemiah are works of two different authors, rather than one (as traditionally held), who "wrote about different points in Ezra's career, as was to happen later with the NT Gospels."[289] Supporting this argument are three kinds of evidence: language, source, and theme. With the linguistic evidence, VanderKam lists five differences between Ezra and Nehemiah:

1. Both Ezra and Nehemiah refer to the temple by its common name בית האלהים (Ezra 3.8, 9; Neh. 12.40), but Ezra alone calls it בית יהוה (3.8, 11; cf. 7.27 [8.29]).

2. Persian monarchs: (a) Although Ezra and Nehemiah mention Persian kings often, Ezra alone refers to one as מלך אשור (6.22). Neh. 9.32 ... does have the phrase מלכי אשור, but the ones intended are the actual Assyrian monarchs who had played parts in Israel's past. (b) In editorial and source passages Ezra calls the monarch מלך פרס (2.7; 7.1; cf. 1.1, 2, 8; 4.3, 5, 7, 24; 6.14; 9.9 [plural]). In Nehemiah, however, although one finds the phrase פרס מלכות דריוש הפרסי in 12.22 [non-editorial], the noun פרס is never used with מלך.

3. Ezra, both in source and redactional passages, employs the divine title אלהי ישראל (1.3; 3.2; 4.1, 3, 6, 21; 5.1; 6.14, 22; 7.6, 15; 8.25; 9:4, 15). It is not attested in Nehemiah.

---

by Blenkinsopp and others that the three books belong to one single author. See Joseph Blenkinsopp, *Ezra-Nehemiah* (Peter Ackroyd, et al.; Philadelphia: Westminster, 1988), 47–54. This view is based on four arguments: (1) The presence of the first verses of Ezra at the end of Chronicles; (2) the evidence of 1 Esdras, which begins with II Chronicles 35–36 and continues through Ezra; (3) linguistic similarities between Chronicles and Ezra-Nehemiah; (4) the similarity of theological conception in both works. See Throntveit, *Ezra-Nehemiah*, 9. For other works that relate to this view, see Peter R. Ackroyd, *I & II Chronicles, Ezra, Nehemiah* (London: SCM, 1973), Rebecca Corwin, *The verb and the sentence in Chronicles, Ezra and Nehemiah* (Borna: Noske, 1909), Matt Patrick Graham, *The Chronicler as Historian* (Sheffield: Sheffield Academic Press, 1997), *The Chronicler as Theologian: Essays in Honor of Ralph W. Klein* (London: T&T Clark, 2003), Liver, *Chapters in the History of the Priests and Levites: Studies in the Lists of Chronicles and Ezra and Nehemiah*, Céline Mangan, *1–2 Chronicles, Ezra, Nehemiah* (Wilmington: Michael Glazier, 1982). Edward Sell, *Chronicles, Ezra, Nehemiah* (Madras: SPCK, 1924).

[289] VanderKam, "Ezra-Nehemiah or Ezra and Nehemiah?," 61.

4. Both books offer a phrase that seems to have the same meaning in a similar context but is worded slightly differently in them: Ezra 3.13 הקול נשמע למרחוק; Neh. 12.43 ותשמע שמחת ירושלם מרחוק.

5. If Ezra's prayer in 9.6–15 and the historical survey with confession in Neh. 9:6–37 are included among the editorial contributions, other differences emerge: for examples, (a) although both texts make regular reference to sins of sundry kinds, Ezra uses forms of אשמה four times (9.6, 7, 13, 15; cf. 10.10, 19); in Nehemiah this word never appears, here or elsewhere in the book. (b) Ezra refers to himself and the other returnees as פליטה (9.8, 13, 14, 15); the word does not occur in Nehemiah 9. (c) The word יתד in Ezra 9.8 is not found in Nehemiah.[290]

The second type of evidence is the ways in which each book employs sources. Both books depend heavily on sources; if subtracted very little would remain. The list of those who return with Zerubbabel and Joshua appear in both books (Ezra 2 and Neh 7), but serve different purpose. Whereas in Ezra the list is used to identify those who returned in the time of Cyrus, in Nehemiah it is employed for Nehemiah's effort to repopulate Jerusalem (7.4–5).[291]

The third type of evidence, which VanderKam considered to be the most important, is the themes of the book of Ezra. He argues that

> If one pays close attention to the central thematic statement in Ezra, it becomes evident that it embraces all of the material in Ezra and leaves no room for the contents of the book of Nehemiah which has other fundamental concerns. Ezra in its entirety focuses on the restoration of the temple and people, while Nehemiah centers more on rewalling and repopulating Jerusalem.[292]

From this stance, he calls for a rejection of Eskenazi's position in *In An Age of Prose*.[293] The main point of contention is Eskenazi's claim that the restoration of the city wall in Nehemiah extends the space of the

---

[290]See ibid, 65.
[291]Ibid, 66, 67.
[292]Ibid, 69–70.
[293]Tamara Cohn Eskenazi, *In An Age of Prose: A Literary Approach to Ezra-Nehemiah* (Atlanta: Scholars Press, 1988).

house of God to the entire city.²⁹⁴ To VanderKam, the house of God refers to the temple but not the entire city as Eskenazi claims. Jerusalem is never called the house of God, and "sanctifying something like a part of a city wall does not transform it into a temple."²⁹⁵ He continues,

> She [Eskenazi] is correct in seeing that the themes of Ezra are executed in three movements, but all of them are within one book. Its two principal entities—temple and people—are restored within the confines of Ezra's 10 chapters.²⁹⁶

The three movements VanderKam identifies begin with Sheshbazzar who despite the uncertainty of his identity brought the vessels to Jerusalem (1.8–11). This is followed by the movement led by Zerubbabel and Joshua, and the last movement points to Ezra and his group (Ezra 7). In this sense, the themes of Ezra do not have a space for the contents of Nehemiah. The narrative in the book of Ezra can certainly be read apart from Nehemiah. In short, Ezra alone will serve as the *tūkunga* for the reading of Ezra 9:1–10:17.

In the light of the *tūkunga*, the *tu'unga* of Ezra 9:1–10:17 is within the third movement under Ezra (7:1–10:44). This *tu'unga* begins in 7:1–10 with an introduction of Ezra as a priest and scribe of the Torah, and closes in 10:18–44 with the list of men who were found to have married "foreign women." Enclosed between these two limits are the account of Ezra's return and the series of meetings that problematized intermarriage. The restoration of the temple by the Zerubbabel group in Ezra 1:1–6:22 indicates the Ezra narrative intends the temple to be the designated place for the story it unfolds, and nothing to do with the restoration of the wall by the Nehemiah group in Neh 1:1–6:15.²⁹⁷

---

²⁹⁴VanderKam is not alone in critiquing Eskenazi's work. Two other scholars find Eskenazi's work problematic in different ways. See Havea, "Shifting the Boundaries: house of God and politics of reading," 55–71, Roland C. Boer, "No Road: On the Absence of Feminist Criticism of Ezra-Nehemiah," in *Her Master's Tools? Feminist and Postcolonial Engagements of Historical-Critical Discourse* (ed. Caroline Vander Stichele and Todd C. Penner; Atlanta: SBL, 2005), 233–252.
²⁹⁵VanderKam, "Ezra-Nehemiah or Ezra and Nehemiah?" 73.
²⁹⁶Ibid, 74.
²⁹⁷The question of unity and disunity of the books of Ezra and Nehemiah is still open for more discussion. I based my reading however on VanderKam's view presented above. For more insights on the issue, see the collection of papers in Mark J. Boda and Paul L. Redditt, eds. *Unity and Diversity in Ezra-Nehemiah: Redaction, Rhetoric, and Reader* (Sheffield: Sheffield Phoenix Press, 2008).

Un-weaving *Tu'a*-wise

Probing into the '*ātakai* of Ezra 9:1–10:17 offers insights into its *fa'unga* (structure), *tūkunga* (context) and *tu'unga* (location/placement). The *fa'unga* reveals the different *fe'unu* that had been woven into the text. Whereas the text portrays Ezra and his group as dominating the narrative, the *fa'unga* reveals that all the events that occur revolve around Shecaniah not Ezra. A *tu'a* reading of Ezra 9:1–10:17 will put more emphasis on Shecaniah's words vis-à-vis Ezra's words. The focus on Shecaniah will not only change the direction that the text would like the readers to go, but it will also provide alternative insights as to the meaning of the text.

The *tūkunga* of the text also departs from its traditional domain: Ezra-Nehemiah. Instead, the text is located, and will be read, only in the light of the Ezra narrative, which I have argued does not require Nehemiah to give it closure, but is instead intended to be an open-ended story that invites readerly participations. As such, Ezra 9:1–10:17 is read only with reference to Zerubbabel's temple restoration scheme, rather than the wall restoration programme of Nehemiah.

The above analysis also raises some significant issues that concern *lau faka-tu'a* (*tu'a* reading). The first issue arises from the way the text constructs peoples and places. The negative attitude of the text to the land and its peoples resonates with the experience of *tu'a* readers and natives of Oceania. Because of this tendency, I will give the text a reading based on the notion of *fonua* to expose its perception of place and people, and to glean any transformative elements it has.

The second issue is the kind of world projected by the text and into which the reader is invited. Since a *tu'a* reader belongs to a community, I am also interested in the kind of society endorsed and promoted by the text, and seek to retrieve any alternative vision it suppressed. In other words, I will give Ezra 9:1–10:17 a reading through the analytical category of *tākanga*.

The third issue revolves around the demeaning rhetoric employed by the text to characterize peoples it hates and/or condemns: peoples of the lands. I, as a *tu'a* reader, am sensitive to such characterization since *tu'a* are victims of colonial construction and misrepresentation. In that case, I will give Ezra 9:1–10:17 a reading through the analytical category of *tālanga*.²⁹⁸ The next three chapters deal with each issue respectively.

---

²⁹⁸Another reading option revolves around the question of *exile* and *return*. The text is woven together to give legitimacy to the claim that some of those who were deported by the Babylonians did return to Jerusalem. Such a claim has influenced biblical scholarship to such an extent that biblical literature is divided into pre-exilic, exilic, and post-exilic categories. Numerous works in the Second Temple Studies series attempt to shed light on the events of exile and return. See Charles E. Carter, *The Emergence of Yehud in the Persian Period: A Social and Demographic Study* (Sheffield: Sheffield Academic Press, 1999), Philip R. Davies and John M. Halligan, eds. *Second Temple Studies III: Studies in Politics, Class and Material Culture* (Sheffield: Sheffield Academic Press, 2002), Diana Vikander Edelman, *The Origins of the 'Second' Temple: Persian Imperial Policy and the Rebuilding of Jerusalem* (London: Equinox, 2005), Tamara Cohn Eskenazi and Kent H. Richards, eds. *Second Temple Studies 2: Temple and Community in the Persian Period* (Sheffield: JSOT, 1994), Lester L. Grabbe, *A History of the Jews and Judaism in the Second Temple Period* (London: T&T Clark, 2004), Oded Lipschitz and Manfred Oeming, *Judah and the Judeans in the Persian period* (Winona Lake: Eisenbrauns, 2006), David J. Reimer and John Barton, eds. *After the Exile: Essays in Honour of Rex Mason* (Macon: Mercer University Press, 1996), Eugene Ulrich et al., eds. *Priests, Prophets and Scribes: Essays on the Formation and Heritage of Second Temple Judaism in Honour of Joseph Blenkinsopp* (Sheffield: JSOT, 1992), Joel Weinberg, *The Citizen-Temple Community* (trans. Daniel L. Smith-Christopher; Sheffield: JSOT, 1992). This tendency faces a challenge from scholars who question the historicity of exile and return. Robert C. Carroll argues that exile is "a biblical trope . . . a fundamental element in the cultural poetics of biblical discourses."—Robert P. Carroll, "Exile! What Exile?" in *Leading Captivity Captive: 'The Exile' as History and Ideology* (ed. Lester L. Grabbe; Sheffield: Sheffield Academic Press, 1998), 64. In that sense, "to use the term 'exile' in a book title is to connive at, conspire or collaborate with the biblical text in furthering the myth represented by the ideological shaping of biblical history" (67).

CHAPTER 6
REL[OC]ATING EZRA

> From one culture to another, or within a given culture, land is a social symbol with a range of meanings. We invest the concept of land with a selection of these meanings, some more profound or elusive than others. We create the land we experience; we construct the meanings of land for ourselves.
>
> Norman C. Habel[299]
>
> For the deterritorialised or deracinated subject, there can be no place like 'home.'
>
> Deborah L. Madsen[300]

One of the key issues highlighted in the previous chapter ('*ātakai* reading) is the xenophobic attitude of a group within "the *golah* community" (בני הגולה) to "the peoples of the lands" (עמי הארצות). According to "the *golah* community," the "peoples of the lands" in general have polluted the land. For that reason, they should not mingle with them, nor should they be allowed a place in the land. I, as a *tu'a* reader, am interested in this aspect of the text because it invokes historical realities I have experienced; two of which have affected to a great extent the lives of Oceanic islanders and Tongan commoners (*tu'a*): (i) perception of place, and (ii) construction of identity. These two processes depicted our islands and their inhabitants negatively to validate the superimposition of Western cultures, beliefs, and values.[301] Likewise,

---

[299]Norman C. Habel, *The Land Is Mine: Six Biblical Land Ideologies* (Minneapolis: Fortress, 1995), 1.

[300]Madsen, "'No Place Like Home': The Ambivalent Rhetoric of Hospitality in the Work of Simone Lazaroo, Arlene Chai, and Hsu-Ming Teo," 118.

[301]Our islands were given names they did not ask for; names that lead to the desecration of places and peoples. To the colonizers, our islands are uncivilized—as if

the inventors of Tongan culture employed similar strategies to justify the continuing subjugation of *tu'a* to their *'eiki* counterparts. From this text-context intersection, I will reread Ezra 9–10 using *fonua*[302] as a category of analysis.

CATEGORY OF ANALYSIS

As discussed in Chapter 4, *fonua* denotes, first of all, a place of origin (*manava*) which in turn provides a sense of rootedness; as also a place of departure it entails routedness and no return. Second, *fonua* is not just about place; it includes people (hence the saying, *fonua-pe-tangata* [the people is the *fonua*]). Without the *tangata*, the *fonua* makes no sense. To exclude people (*tangata*) from the *fonua* or to speak of the *fonua* as empty is antithetical to what *fonua* signifies. Third, *fonua* (as it includes the *moana* [ocean]) promotes an idea of place that is open and fluid; a shared heritage without border. To erect a boundary or to claim ownership of a particular place/land is the stuff of colonization. Fourth, and finally, *fonua* as a gift of the gods has *mana* (life-giving power) and is considered *tapu* (sacred). These aspects of *fonua* inform the reading offered in this chapter. A *fonua* reading will not only look for dominant

---

civilization belongs only to the West—and thus required civilization. Our islands are "empty"—as if the native inhabitants never exist—and are therefore suitable sites for nuclear experiments (as in Bikini Atoll and Mururoa). To missionaries, inhabitants of our islands are savages, hence treated as objects of Christianization. Like the view of the "golah community," they considered our cultures as unclean and should therefore be deracinated in order to give way to the "pure" or "clean." What is best for the islands was mostly determined, without any consultation with its inhabitants, miles away in imperial sanctuaries. The results of such perceptions (of places and peoples) had been the annexations of our islands, the desecration of native sacred sites (as in Hawaii and Aotearoa), the loss of native languages, the suppression of native belief systems and symbols, the disintegration of societies due to imported values, the degradation of our natural environment, and the continuing disadvantage in many areas due to the association of our islands with global institutions (WTO, UN, and others) that are controlled not only by the rich and the powerful, but by people who have neither been to our places nor have any knowledge that our places do exist.

[302] Such a reading is significant since locating Ezra 9–10 in its *'ātakai*, as discussed in Chapter 5, brings to the fore a perception of place and peoples that is threatening to the *tu'a* (as displaced Tongans and as native inhabitants of Oceania). From the standpoint of exiles, their hosts ("the peoples of the lands") are impure, and they have polluted the land with their impurity. To restore the purity of the land, the impure (peoples of the lands) has to be separated from the pure (holy seed). Here the question of (im)purity serves as a linguistic guise for the non-linguistic realities of reclaiming land rights, ethnic and religious discrimination, as well as social exclusion.

perceptions, but will also read through gaps in the *fe'unu* (fabrics) of the text to bring out alternative insights.

METHODS OF ANALYSIS

The need for a *fonua* reading is based on the fact that perceptions about place are not abstract ideas; they are rooted in worldviews and values that are potentially liberating or oppressive when taken for granted as the truth without considering the interests of others. To expose such perceptions, a *fonua* reading employs two methods of *tu'a* reading: *lau lea* and *lau tu'unga*.[303] The *lau lea* method focuses on the ways *lea* (rhetoric, language) is used in biblical texts to construct peoples and places.[304] Questions such as these guide this method: What kind of *lea* is used to express perception of place and to portray peoples? Whose interests do those *lea* serve? What is the likely effect of those *lea*? The *lau tu'unga* method seeks to locate the beliefs and/or worldviews that shape the perceptions of place and constructions of identity. It asks: what kind of reality does the text construct? What justifies that construction? Is the *mana* and *tapu* of the *fonua* respected? What mechanisms of displacement, and transformative forces, are involved? What is the likely impact of place perception on a *tu'a* reader?

RELOCATING EZRA 9–10

Reading Ezra 9–10 through the category of *fonua* reveals two contradictory perceptions: the first comes from "the *golah* community"; the second from "the peoples of the lands." In the analysis below, I will refer to the former as *kumifonua*, and to the latter as *kakai-e-fonua*. The name *kumifonua*, on the one hand, literally means "to look for a place" or "*place*-seeker(s); it is applied to a routed person (or group) that seeks to

---

[303] For a more detail discussion of these methods, please refer back to Chapter 5.

[304] This method resonates with some aspects of literary and rhetorical criticisms, but it uses distinctive Tongan categories rather than those proposed by the proponents of the named methods, such as Stanley E. Porter and Dennis L. Stamps, *Rhetorical criticism and the Bible* (London: Sheffield Academic Press, 2002), Robbins, *Exploring the Texture of Texts: A Guide to Socio-Rhetorical Interpretation*, Stamps and Porter, *The Rhetorical Interpretation of Scripture: Essays from the 1996 Malibu Conference*, Trible, *Rhetorical Criticism: Context, Method, and the Book of Jonah*.

taufonua (arrive and settle). The name *kakai-e-fonua*, on the other hand, is an inclusive variant of the Tongan term *tangata'ifonua*, which designates the first inhabitants of a place; the natives or indigenes. Whereas a *kumifonua* group seeks to negotiate a place, the *kakai-e-fonua* is a rooted group.

MYTH OF (IM)PURITY AND THE *KAKAI-E-FONUA*

> The colonizers' most significant ideological achievement was the invention of the Native, a category embracing all non-Europeans. The Native—singular and masculine—lacked European virtues such as application and foresight. His mind—the Native Mind—worked in mysterious ways.[305]

Ezra 9–10 is narrated with a gaze that does not merely seek to identify the *other*, as if the other can really be identified, but also to vilify and victimize. Those who bring the allegation of mixed marriages to Ezra's attention fix their censorious eyes on subjects they view as threats to their social, religious, economic and political well-being:

(i) "the peoples of the land(s)" (עמי הארצות, 9:1, 11[306]; עמי הארץ, 10:2, 11);[307] and

(ii) "foreign women" (נשים נכריות 10:2, 14).

I refer to these two groups as *tu'a* subjects because, like Tongan commoners, they are portrayed by the text in contrast to *'eiki* subjects labelled as "people of Israel" or "holy seed." Mingling of the two subjects is considered in the text as a *tapu* (prohibited) practice; as an offense against Yhwh.

Who are the "peoples of the lands"? Scholarly readings of Ezra 9–10 offer three views.[308] First, the "peoples of the lands" are read as

---

[305]Firth, "Colonial Administration and the Invention of the Native," 262.

[306]This plural form is also attested in the following texts: Neh 10:29; 2 Chr 13:9; 15:5; 32:13, 17.

[307]The form also appears in Ezra 10:2, 11; Est 8:17; Deut 28:10, Josh 4:24, 1 Kgs 8:43, 53, 60; 1 Chr 5:25; 2 Chr 6:33, 32:19; Ezek 31:12; Zeph 3:20. Another variant is עם הארץ (singular) which occurs in the following: Gen 23:12, 13; 42:6; Exod 5:5; Lev 20:2, 4; Num 14:9; 2 Kgs 11:14, 18, 19, 20; 15:5; 16:15; 21:24 (2); 23:30, 35; 24:14; 25:19; 2 Ch 23:13. 20, 21; 26:21; 33:25 (2); 36:1; Ezra 4:4; Job 12:24; Isa 24:4; Jer 34:19; 52:25; Ezek 7:27; 12:19; 22:29; 33:2; 39:13; 45:22; 46:3, 9; Dan 9:6; Hag 2:4; Zech 7:5.

non-Judean inhabitants of Judah during the exile.[309] The basis for this view is the comparison made between the practice of this group and the practices of eight groups of different ethnic origins in 9:1b:

> [t]he Canaanites, the Hittites, the Perizzites, the Jebusites, the Ammonites, the Moabites, the Egyptians, and the Amorites.

Within this reading perspective "peoples of the lands" are defined in terms of ethnicity. The problem however is that these groups no longer existed in the Persian Yehud.[310] The listed nations may have been used by Ezra "to pattern his own return to Israel after the Exodus and the Conquest."[311]

Second, "peoples of the lands" are read as non-exiled Judaean inhabitants.[312] This is based on the insight that only a portion (approximately 10%)[313] of the Judaean population (mostly members of the ruling class and skilled members of society) was deported by the Babylonians. The majority—consisting mainly of the working class, the elderly, and residents in rural areas—remained in Judah. This group may have become owners of the land and properties left behind by the deportees, and upon the return of the latter, there may have been struggles to regain the ownership of their ancestral land from those who

---

[308]See a summary of these views in Brown II, "The Problem of Mixed Marriages in Ezra 9–10," 437–458.

[309]See Karl Friedrich Keil and Sophia Taylor, *The Books of Ezra, Nehemiah, and Esther* (Karl Friedrich Keil; Edinburgh: T&T Clark, 1873), 73–74. George Rawlinson, *Ezra and Nehemiah: Their Lives and Times* (New York: A. D. F. Randolph, 1890), 139. Derek Kidner, *Ezra and Nehemiah: An Introduction and Commentary* (Downers Grove: Inter-Varsity, 1979), 71. J. G. McConville, *Ezra, Nehemiah, and Esther* (Philadelphia: Westminster, 1985), 60. Mervin Breneman, *Ezra, Nehemiah, Esther* (vol. 10; Nashville: Broadman & Holman, 1993), 148–149.

[310]Harold C. Washington, "The Strange Woman (אשה זרה/נכריות) of Proverbs 1–9 and Post-Exilic Judaean Society," in *Second Temple Studies 2. Temple and Community in the Persian Period* (ed. Tamara Cohn Eskenazi and Kent H. Richards; Sheffield: JSOT, 1994), 238. See also David J. A. Clines, *Ezra, Nehemiah, Esther* (Grand Rapids: Eerdmans, 1984), 119.

[311]Brown II, "The Problem of Mixed Marriages in Ezra 9–10," 439. See also Walter F. Adeney, *Ezra, Nehemiah, and Esther* (New York: A. C. Armstrong, 1893), 132. Ackroyd, *I & II Chronicles, Ezra, Nehemiah*, 252. Throntveit, *Ezra-Nehemiah*, 50.

[312]See Smith-Christopher, "The Mixed Marriage Crisis in Ezra 9–10 and Nehemiah 13: A Study of the Sociology of Post-Exilic Judaean Community," 243–265. Eskenazi and Judd, "Married to a Stranger in Ezra 9–10," 266–285.

[313]Weinberg, *The Citizen-Temple Community*, 37.

remained (the remainees). In that sense, peoples of the lands are defined in terms of their non-exiled status not ethnicity.

Third, and finally, "peoples of the lands" are read to include both non-Judaean and non-exiled Judaean inhabitants of Judah during the Babylonian exile.[314] Since the returning exiles regard themselves as the true continuation of pre-exilic Israel and true worshippers of Yhwh, the non-exiled and non-Judaean inhabitants are both filed under one group who, in the eyes of the returnees, are impure and should therefore be excluded from the community of the exiles. This reading defines "the peoples of the lands" in terms of their alleged religious orientation: syncretistic.[315] "Ezra's [marriage] reform was therefore intended to purge these syncretistic influences from the community, thereby restoring it to a condition of holiness or purity."[316] Such a condition is to be achieved at the cost of community solidarity.

Joel Weinberg reads various forms of the phrase in Hebrew, and their uses in the sixth to fourth century B.C.E. to offer some perspectives on the issue. He sees the phrase עמי הארצות as more than just the plural form of עם הארץ.[317] The latter was used as a self-designation for pre-exilic Israel, but changes in the socio-political situation gave the term new meanings. In the sixth century B.C.E., עם הארץ was used not only for the Israelite community, but also for the adversaries. The fifth century B.C.E. however limited the meaning of the term as a designation of a Yahwistic community, whereas the plural עמי הארץ/הארצות refers to "totally strange and non-Yahwistic communities." [318] Despite these perspectives, it is still unclear which meaning fits the group in Ezra 9:1–10:17. If one locates the text in the fifth century B.C.E. or later, then the "peoples of the lands" would refer to the non-Judaean population of Judah. My problem with Weinberg's analysis is twofold: (i) those referred to in Ezra 9:1–10:17 as "peoples of the lands" may have included Judaeans, though probably those belonging to a different faction of Judaism; and (ii) the singular form עם הארץ refers also to enemies of Judah (4:4). Both terms are used interchangeably rather than pointing to distinct groups. These views indicate that to ascertain the identity of the "peoples of the lands" is an illusion. The text mentioned this group as if

---

[314]See Brown II, "The Problem of Mixed Marriages in Ezra 9–10," 444.

[315]Becking views the underlying problem as one of religious struggle amongst competing forms of Judaism. See Bob Becking, "Ezra's Re-enactment of the Exile," in *Leading Captivity Captive: 'The Exile' as History and Ideology* (ed. Lester L. Grabbe; Sheffield: Sheffield Academic Press, 1998), 53.

[316]Brown II, "The Problem of Mixed Marriages in Ezra 9–10," 445.

[317]Weinberg, *The Citizen-Temple Community*, 70.

[318]Ibid, 73.

they can be identified; readers also attempt to define this group. Both efforts are fruitless as the identity of the group continues to shift, resisting any form of control and characterization.

Within a *tu'a* reading, the phrase "peoples of the lands" can be read differently from the above perspectives. In Tongan, "peoples of the lands" is rendered *kakai 'o e fonua*.[319] It carries no connotation that may refer to such a group as aliens or pagans. *Kakai 'o e fonua* is an inclusive concept that combines men and women together, and designates those "who grew out of the land" (*tupu'ifonua*) or rightful residents of the land (*tangata'ifonua* "men of the land" *or fefine 'ifonua* "women of the land"); *tupu'ifonua* and *tangata'ifonua* are not necessarily defined by ethnicity, although certain ethnicity is presupposed. Every person belongs to the *kakai e fonua* either by birth or by law. In that sense, "peoples of the lands," to a *tu'a* reader, encompasses both the natives and citizens of a particular place. As I have mentioned in Chapter 4, the *kakai* and *fonua* belong to each other. Anybody who does not want to be identified as such is a real alien, and therefore has no right to claim ownership of any place.

The phrase *kakai-e-fonua* includes the following aspects. First, it does not presuppose ethnic purity, simply because *purity is a myth*. One can only speak of hybridity. Second, *kakai-e-fonua* indicates connectedness of people to place, rather than people owning place. In Tonga, as in Oceania, people belong to the land, but not vice versa. Nobody has a right to claim ownership. Third, it requires respect to be given to natives and citizens in their places. Here lies the irony of the claim made by the returning exiles: those they considered unsuitable to mingle with are not at all aliens but natives of the land, the *kakai e fonua*; the returnees are in fact the outsiders. Yet in their words, "the peoples of the lands" are abominable (תועבה *tw'bh*, 9:1, 11, 14), impure (נדה *ndh*, 9:11), and unclean (טמאה *tum'h* 9:11). These terms depict "the peoples of the lands" as an untouchable group, and therefore not worthy to be mingled with nor married to.

A closer look at each term will reveal what the phrase עמי הארצות really means to the *'eiki* subjects, and the reason behind their indifference to them. The first is תועבה *tw'bh* which is a feminine noun (appearing in 9:1, 11, 14 in the plural construct form) and it occurs 117 times in the Hebrew Bible indicating abominable practices. Its verbal

---

[319]In J. E. Moulton's Tongan translation of the Bible, עמי הארצות is rendered "ngaahi kakai 'o e ngaahi fonua" (9:1 "peoples of the lands"), and עמי הארץ as "ngaahi kakai 'o e fonua" (10:2 "peoples of the land"). Both Tongan renditions do not designate two different groups.

counterparts are derivatives of the noun, and they occur in other stems (e.g. Niphal in 1 Chron 21:6; Piel in Ps 106:40; Hiphil in Ezek 16:52) but not Qal. Each form, nominal and verbal, carries two senses: ritual and ethical. In the ritual sense, *tw'bh* is used with references to sacrifices (e.g. Exod 8:22 [MT]) or physical unattractiveness as in Ps 88:9 [MT]). It refers also to unclean food (Deut 14:3), worshipper of idols (Is 41:24), objectionable acts (Deut 24:4), idolatrous practices (Deut 13:15; 17:4), and in Ezra 9–10 to intermarriage with "foreign women" (*nšym nkrywt*). In the ethical sense, *tw'bh* is used with reference to what a person ought not to do, such as wickedness (e.g. Prov 8:7) and evil deeds (e.g. Lev 18:22–30; 1 Kgs 14:23ff.; Prov 16:12).

The second term, נדה (*ndh*), like תועבה (*tw'bh*) appears in the feminine form denoting impurity or filthiness. In many instances it refers to ceremonial impurity, such as sleeping with the wife of one's brother (e.g. Lev 20:21), contact with a corpse (Num 19:13), and female menstrual discharges (e.g. Lev 15:19; 18:19). Ezekiel 36:17 used *nddh* metaphorically in the latter sense to describe Israel's sin (cf. also Zech 13:1; 2 Chron 29:5). A cognate term (*nydh*) which occurs only in Lamentation 1:8 derives itself from the root *ndh*, which means "to exclude" (Is 66:5) and "refuse to think of" (Am 6:3). Ezra 9:11 speaks of such impurity as polluting the land, and those responsible for such pollution are no other than "the peoples of the lands". For that reason they have to be excluded (*ndh*) from the community.

The third term, טמאה, *tm'h* appears like the other two in the feminine, and indicates sexual, ritual, ethical and geographical uncleanness. Sexually, a man is unclean through having intercourse with a woman during her menstruation period (Lev 15:24). Ritually, a person is rendered unclean by way of idolatry, contact with carcasses of unclean animals, or having leprosy (see Lev 11–15). In the ethical and religious sense, it refers to unclean spirit (Zech 13:2). Ezra 9:11 identifies "the peoples of the lands" as filling the land from *end to end* (literally, "from mouth to mouth") with their טמאה *tm'h*. Placing טמאה *tm'h* in the mouth stirs in "the reader an irresistible urge to expel, a nauseous desire to vomit; in a word, what Kristeva calls "the abject."[320]

These three terms have been loaded by the "chiefs" (Ezra 9:1–2), the *'eiki* subjects, onto the phrase "peoples of the lands," providing therefore a strong basis for their objection to inter-marriage between the so-called returning male exiles and the daughters of "the peoples of the lands," whom they identified as "foreign women" (נשים נכריות *nšym*

---

[320] Harold C. Washington, "Israel's Holy Seed and the Foreign Women of Ezra-Nehemiah: A Kristevan Reading," *Biblical Interpretation* 11 (2003): 433.

nkrywt). Since "the peoples of the lands" are abominable, impure and unclean in all aspects of life, marrying their daughters would indeed violate their own purity as זרע הקדש (*zr' hqds* "the holy race/seed").

The above analysis shows how *lea* (rhetoric/language) is used by the *'eiki* subjects as a tool to degrade. The types of *lea* employed to characterize "the peoples of the lands" is *lea hualela*, and particularly the sub-type of *lea vale*. As discussed in Chapter 5, *lea vale* (lit. silly talk) is a senseless utterance that offers a false idea of oneself as superior to others while the reality points otherwise. Here it functions to portray the עמי הארצות as impure, in contrast to the עם ישראל as the *tapu* (holy/sacred) seed, while the text itself provides the opposite. The confessional aspects of Ezra's prayer in 9:6–15 reveal the impurity of the returning exiles, rather than the *kakai-e-fonua*. This is first mentioned in vv.6–7:

> and I said, My God, I am ashamed and horrified to lift my face to You, my God, because our iniquities have become higher than our head, and our wrong-doing has grown as high as heaven.
>
> From the days of our fathers we have been in great sin to this very day, and with our iniquities, we, our kings, and our priests have been handed over to foreign kings, to the sword, to captivity, to booty, and to shame of face, as it is today.

In v.6, Israel's guilt is described in hyperbolic terms to highlight its enormity: "higher than our head" and "as high as heaven." This guilt was not caused by the offense being described (intermarriage), but has been their mark since the time of their foreparents. To blame the *kakai-e-fonua* for their own sinful tendency is an injudicious act. The second reference to Israel's impurity is again mentioned in vv.10–12, but with the blame shifted. Whereas in vv.6–7 Ezra acknowledged their guilt, in vv.10–12 that guilt is identified as inter-marriage with inhabitants of the land, which is a reference to the Canaanites and other peoples who were in the land at the time of the Exodus (cf. Deut 7:1–7). As above-mentioned, it is doubtful whether the same groups of people existed in the time of Ezra. The reference however invokes a past tradition to justify the claim they are making in a distantly different context. The third, and final, aspect of Ezra's prayer that mentioned Israel's guilt is v.15b, which reads: "Behold, we are before you with our sins" (הננו לפניך באשמתינו). Again, Ezra acknowledged their guilt and the likely consequences. The portrayal of the *kakai-e-fonua* as impure has no basis except sheer hatred of others.

This is further stressed in the portrayal of the female members of the *kakai-e-fonua*.

An interesting aspect of identity construction in Ezra 9–10 is the gendering of *lea*.[321] The phrase *peoples of the lands* and the words that describe it are feminine. In contrast, the returnees refer to themselves in the masculine: עם ישראל (people of Israel) and זרע הקדש (holy seed). It is not surprising therefore that they put a group of women (נשים נכריות) as the target of their gaze, and as the ones at whom they shoot their ideological arrows of dislike. In other words, the despised feminine subjects should bear the responsibility for the feminine abomination (impure and unclean) of the feminine other (peoples of the lands). This aspect needs further exploration since the identities of the subjects that the returnees have an aversion to are all expressed in feminine forms.

The identity of the "foreign women" is as blurred as that of ""the peoples of the lands." The only description provided by the text is that they are wives (to some male members of the exiled community; 9:2), and are also mothers with children (10:3, 44). As with the "peoples of the lands," these women may either have been (1) non-Judaean women, (2) daughters of the non-exiled inhabitants of Judah, or (3) a combination of both groups. Given the multiethnic composition of the Yehud,[322] it is likely that these so-called foreign women have different ethnic origins, with perhaps Judaean majority. Despite their ethnicity, all had been in the land prior to the arrival of Ezra and his group, and are therefore rightful residents not "foreigners." On what basis are they being considered "foreign"? What does the term "foreign" mean and imply? What risks do these "foreign women" pose to Ezra and his group?

The occurrences of the phrase "foreign women" and its cognates in other texts offer some perspectives. In Gen 31:15, the term נכריות indicates an outsider, whereas in 1 Kgs 11:1, it refers to women of gentile descent (Moabite, Ammonite, Edomite, Phoenician, Hittite, Egyptian) who had been the desire of Solomon's heart (despite Yhwh's prohibition), and whom the Deuteronomists accused of luring Solomon to apostasy (1 Kgs 11:4). To the Deuteronomists, they are the reason for the fall of Judah (cf. 1 Kgs 11:11–13). That is also the reason for the attitude towards the "foreign women" in Ezra 9–10. Both Ezra and Nehemiah fear the influence of "foreign women" (see Neh 13). From the returnees' standpoint, they have experienced the consequences of such a

---

[321]The role of language in negotiating identity is discussed in Daniel I. Block, "The Role of Language in Ancient Israelite Perceptions of National Identity," *Journal of Biblical Literature* 103, no. 3 (1984): 321–340.

[322]See Johnson, "The Holy Seed Has Been Defiled: The Interethnic Marriage Dilemma in Ezra 9–10."

mistake, and they will not allow it to happen again. The reality of the situation however points otherwise. Those who have returned from exile have married daughters of "the peoples of the lands." Women whom they identified as "foreign" are not from the same descent as those women whom Solomon married, and whose influence Yhwh feared. The attitude of the returnees in Ezra is a parodic version of the attitudes of their pre-exilic counterparts. Here even their own women are regarded as foreigners.

The use of the singular form נכריה exposes other nuances.[323] In Ruth 2:10, the term is used by Ruth with reference to herself as a Moabite, a foreigner. In Isa 28:21 it is a description of the work of Yhwh (נכריה עבדתו "Strange is His Work" [JPS]), whereas in Jer 2:21 the prophet uses the term with reference to Israel's sin:

ואנכי נטעתיך שרק כלה זרע אמת ואיך נהפכת לי סורי הגפן נכריה

I have planted you with choice vines, all with seed of truth; how then did you turn aside and become a strange vine?[324]

The most significant use of the term comes from the book of Proverbs, where the foreign woman is constructed as the "negative antitype of Wisdom, against whom the young man is warned in lurid terms."[325] In Prov 2:16, the נכריה (foreign woman; "adulteress" [NRSV], "seductress" [NKJV], "alien" [JPS]) is associated with the זרה (strange woman; "loose woman" [NRSV], "immoral" [NKJV], "forbidden" [JPS]). Such a woman disregards the covenant of her God (v.17). A similar association is mentioned in 5:20, again with caution against their influence. In 6:24, נכריה is associated with the adjective רע (bad, evil). The strange/forbidden woman is seen as evil, and one should therefore avoid being lured by her smooth voice. Proverbs 23:26–28 (cf. 27:13) utters this warning:

---

[323]See Ludwig Koehler and Walter Baumgartner, *Hebrew and Aramaic Lexicon of the Old Testament* (trans. M. E. J. Richardson; 5 vols.; vol. 2; Leiden: Brill, 1995), 700. Also David J. A. Clines, ed. *The Dictionary of Classical Hebrew* (Sheffield: Sheffield Academic Press, 2001), 694.

[324]That the same term is used for both Yhwh's act and Israel's sinful practices is interesting. Does the strangeness of Yhwh's work mean that Yhwh has sinned? Or does the strangeness of Israel's practices mean that the planter may have planted a strange seed instead of the choice ones?

[325]Washington, "The Strange Woman (אשה זרה/נכריות) of Proverbs 1–9 and Post-Exilic Judaean Society," 217.

תנה־בני לבך לי ועיניך דרכי (תרצנה) [תצרנה]

Give, my son, your heart to me, and your eyes [to] my ways

כי־שׁחה עמקה זונה ובאר צרה נכריה

A harlot is a deep pit; a strange woman is a narrow well

אף־היא כחתף תארב ובוגדים באדם תוסף

She too lies in wait as if for prey, and destroys the unfaithful among men.

Here נכריה (narrow well) is associated with זנה (harlot) which thus implies that the strange woman is also a harlot. Being a harlot means not only to have improper sexual intercourse, but it also symbolizes religious apostasy. To worship other gods beside Yhwh is to whore oneself like the harlot does (e.g. Exod 34:15; 34:16; Deut 31:16). Such a perception portrays the foreign woman as the symbol of evil *par excellence*. Together such women are threats to society and its supposedly moral order.

This perception may have been the basis for the treatment of "foreign women" in Ezra 9–10. The "foreign women," as daughters of "the peoples of the lands," and as far as the text is concerned, epitomize the impurity, uncleanness and abomination of their peoples. As נכריות they are "total foreigners"[326] without protection in the host community. Assumed to have worshipped other deities, they are the *out-group* of the Yahweh-alone *in-group*.[327]

The Mosaic laws make Israel's responsibility to foreigners clear. For examples, Deut 10:19 enjoins,

ואהבתם את־הגר כי־גרים הייתם בארץ מצרים

You must love the stranger, for you were strangers in the land of Egypt.

Exodus 23:9 reads,

---

[326]Harold V. Bennett, *Injustice Made Legal: Deuteronomic Law and the Plight of Widows, Strangers and Orphans in Ancient Israel* (Grand Rapids: Eerdmans, 2002), 39.
[327]Ibid, 43.

וגר לא תלחץ ואתם ידעתם את־נפש הגר כי־גרים הייתם בארץ מצרים

You shall not oppress a stranger; you know the heart of the stranger, for you were strangers in the land of Egypt.

The legal obligation to the גר/גרים (*gr/grym*) is to be motivated by the fact that as they themselves were גרים, they should understand the את־נפש הגר ("what being a stranger is like"). In both texts, גר is used instead of נכריה/נכריות. As such, the foreign women of Ezra 9–10 are identified beyond the boundary of legal protection. They, like their peoples have no rights under the laws that bound the "returnees" and they do not deserve any sympathy, as far as the "returnees" are concerned.

The depiction of "the peoples of the lands" and "foreign women" in Ezra 9–10 clearly files them under the category of exclusion. That is particularly evident in the returnees' (some of their leaders, to be precise) attitude to inter-marriage. Any foreign woman who married a male member of the returnees is to be sent away (10:3). Washington raises a concern with regard to judging Ezra 9–10 under exclusion, since it

> [r]epresents a Protestant, anti-cultic bias that hearkens back to Wellhausen's disparagement of the postexilic era as a decline into arid and legalistic separatism, thus in continuity with Luther's theological attack on the Jews, the anti-Judaism of medieval Christianity, and the *adversus Judaeos* tradition of the early Church.[328]

This concern reflects a need not to foster any spirit of anti-Semitism. But to cower away from the judgment that is encoded in the text would be utterly unfair to "the peoples of the lands", foreign women, and to readers who are identified with those subjects. The fact of the matter is: exclusion in any form is alienating and cruel. There is really no euphemism for the exclusivist stance perpetuated in Ezra 9–10.[329]

---

[328] Washington, "Israel's Holy Seed and the Foreign Women of Ezra-Nehemiah: A Kristevan Reading," 428.

[329] Such a stance reflects a vision that is closed, inward–oriented, ethnocentric, and territorialized; it offers no space for otherness, and tends to regard difference not as a fact of life, but as anomaly. A community that is built on such a vision is threatening, because it would require serving the interest of a powerful minority at the cost of the underprivileged majority.

ILLUSION OF HOME AND THE *KUMIFONUA*

Kumifonua, as defined above, refers to those who seek a place of arrival and settlement; they are routed and rootless. Their perception of place is often contrary to the perception of those who are in their own place (the *kakai-e-fonua*). In Ezra 9–10, the *kumifonua* are the exile community (בני הגולה). This group is defined as such because despite the claim that they were uprooted by force from an originary homeland to which they have now returned, they really do not belong to any place and are also yet to settle. Their routedness however gives them the urge to negotiate their place by imposing upon others a view that is alienating and displacing. Believing they are "returning residents," they regard everyone else in the land as pagans who have defiled the land with their impurity. To restore that purity, the pagans have to be excluded from the community, and not to be mingled with in any way or form. They also view the land as a divine gift to Yahweh's chosen people, Israel; non-Israelites have no right to inherit it.

The *kumifonua* view of place is reflected in their preoccupation with the House of God (בית אלהים).[330] Its reconstruction, according to the text, is the initial purpose for allowing the exiles to return, as described in the edict of Cyrus (cf. Ezra 1:3). The House also becomes a space of contention when the returnees reject the request of the so-called צרי יהודה ובנימן "adversaries of Judah and Benjamin" (4:1–5) to assist in its reconstruction. The rest of the events narrated in Ezra are situated either inside or outside the House.[331] In that sense, the House serves as a significant hermeneutical key for any reading of Ezra.[332]

---

[330] Referred to as "the House" hereafter.

[331] Tamara C. Eskenazi views the "house of God" as the binding factor of Ezra-Nehemiah, since it is the point of focus from the start to the end, with its boundary being *extended* to the city as a whole by means of the city wall. See Eskenazi, *In An Age of Prose: A Literary Approach to Ezra-Nehemiah*, 53. What might be the rationale behind this extension? There are two possible answers: (i) it is an attempt to make the city as a whole a sacred space, or (ii) it is a political means of pushing out subjects not just from the house of God *per se*, but from the community in general. By extending the boundary of the house of God, its ideology and claims are also extended. That is, those excluded from the house of God also have no place in the land/community.

[332] In Ezra 9, the house is the centre of power and place of the privileged and powerful. That is where officials and priests are gathered; that is where they assert their power over "the peoples of the lands." Events *in the house* feature power and authority, and display forces of domination. The house, as a sacred space/place, serves as the

Ezra 9–10 opens within the House (cf. 8:35–36). Here Ezra and the *kumifonua* (especially those with whom he returned) present the gifts for the temple from the Persian king, and offer burnt offerings to the God of Israel. That event is linked to what follows by the clause in 9:1a (אלה וככלות "and after completing these"),[333] which conveys immediacy, and thus leaves no gaps between the preceding and succeeding events. In the House certain שרים ("chiefs")[334] approach the new Persian-sent priest, Ezra (9:1), and there they meet. In the tranquillity of the House they bring an allegation, initially, against three groups of people: העם ישראל והכהנים והלויים ("the people of Israel, the priests, and the Levites"); two other groups are later added (9:2b): השרים והסגנים ("chiefs and leaders"). These groups, obviously without their knowledge, are accused of committing an offense which is described in the following terms:

(i) they have not *separated* (בדל *bdl*) themselves from the עמי הארצות("peoples of the lands"; 9:1b),

(ii) they have taken some of their daughters as wives (9:2a)

(iii) therefore they have polluted the זרע הקדש ("the holy seed") by engaging with "the peoples of the lands" (9:2b)

All this amounts to what the accusers called מעל ("abomination or faithlessness" in 9:2c). To put the description of the case otherwise, faithfulness requires ethnic purity. Whereas in 8:31–36 Ezra and the *kumifonua* (בני הגולה) bring ornaments for the House, 9:1–4 portrays a different picture; an allegation of unfaithfulness is brought into the same place. The two events intersect in this religious space. Within that bordered space, the *kumifonua* perception of place becomes evident in Ezra's prayer in 9:6–15. The prayer is woven into the narrative as a response to the problem of mixed marriage (9:1–5), albeit the lack of clarity as to the sort of mix that is implied. Its content is dominated by

---

symbol for purifying the unclean land; land that has been polluted by unclean people and their beliefs and practices.

[333] Clines sees this phrase as characteristic of the Chronicler's (e.g. 2 Chron 7:1, 20:23, 24:10) attempt "to bridge the gap left by the omission of the law–reading narrative that is now to be found in Neh. 8." See Clines, *Ezra, Nehemiah, Esther*, 119. I however prefer to read Ezra as a self-contained narrative which is intelligible in itself.

[334] The term שרים is rendered in the Tongan translation as *hou'eiki* (plural form of *'eiki*). This translation is significant because it gives this group the status, power, authority and rights accorded to Tongan chiefs; they are *'eiki* subjects and their place, words, and all that are in relation to them are *tapu*—sacred and prohibited to be questioned, challenged, or transgressed.

confessions of guilt (9:6–7, 10–12, 15) interspersed with acknowledgments of God's merciful acts toward Israel (9:8–9, 13–14). The emphasis however falls on a belief that the exiles (the *kumifonua*) are a remnant (להשאיר, 9:8) preserved by God to return and restore the land (9:9e). The opportunity to return comes with the responsibility to protect the land according to the instruction given in the past to their forefathers (9:11–13 [JPS]; cf. Deut 7:1–6):

> The land that you are about to possess is a land unclean through the uncleanness of the peoples of the land, through their abhorrent practices with which they, in their impurity, have filled it from one end to the other. Now then, do not give your daughters in marriage to their sons or let their daughters marry your sons; do nothing for their well-being or advantage, then you will be strong and enjoy the bounty of the land and bequeath it to your children forever.

By invoking this ancient instruction, the *kumifonua* perception of place becomes clear. First, the land (claimed as a divine gift from Yhwh to his people) is something *to possess* (ירש), and not to be shared. Such a view is threatening since possession always goes hand in hand with its antithesis: dispossession![335] In that sense, it does not merely contradict what *fonua* symbolizes; it also gives legitimacy to colonial domination in Oceania, and the displacement of peoples in their own (is)lands. Second, the *land is unclean* (נדה) because the uncleanness (טמאה) of its occupants has filled it *from end to end* (מפה אל־פה, literally "from mouth to mouth").

Third, to restore the purity of the land requires the separation of the *kumifonua* from those already in the land, and to avoid any activity that might promote their well-being (שלמם וטובתם, literally "peace of them and good of them"). Separation (בדל) is here viewed as the only *means for gaining strength and enjoying the bounty of the land*. A failure to separate, as far as the narrator is concerned, would deprive them of strength and joy. Separation from the residents of the land guarantees the land as *an eternal inheritance* for the *kumifonua* and their children. In other words, to return to the land requires the dispossession, exclusion and displacement of those who regarded that place as their home.

---

[335] The root ירש is rendered in Qal form "to possess," whereas in Niphal it means "to be dispossessed." Here lies the irony of Yhwh's promise to Israel. To possess the land is also to dispossess those who are already in the land. The very land that binds Yhwh and the chosen people together is also the place where other peoples are to be displaced.

Such a mindset is deeply rooted in various biblical traditions, like the covenant and the exodus. In any covenant between God and God's people in the Hebrew Bible, promise of land is one of the most vital elements. To Abraham, a promise of land and offspring was given; the *land is granted to be possessed* (Gen 12:1-2; 15:1-7). The exodus event, and the Sinai covenant, is also narrated with the expectation of a promised land;[336] again, it is *a land to be possessed* (Deut 1:8),

> See, I place the land at your disposal. Go, take possession of the land that the LORD swore to your fathers, Abraham, Isaac, and Jacob, to assign to them and to their heirs after them [JPS].

As the Israelites are about to enter the land, a further instruction is also given in regard to what they should do when they possessed the land (Deut 7:1-6). First, they must *doom* those (i.e. seven nations dislodged by Yhwh [v.1]) who already occupied the land *to destruction*, and "grant them no terms and give them no quarter" (v.2 [JPS]). Second, there shall not be any intermarriage with them: *"do not give your daughters to their sons or take their daughters for your sons"* (v.3). The reason is: *"For they will turn your children away from me* [Yhwh] *to worship other gods"* (v.4a); an offense that will provoke God's anger leading to their annihilation (v.4b). Third, they shall *tear down* those people's altars, "smash [נתץ] their pillars, cut down (שבר) their sacred posts, and consign (גדע) their images to the fire" (v.5). These three verbs combined indicate utter destruction of religious sites and symbols of those in the land.[337] As far as the Deuteronomists are concerned, that is how Yhwh's chosen people should think and act (v.6). This is also what the narrative in Ezra

---

[336]This perception of land as promise, according to Walter Brueggemann, "binds Israel in new ways to the giver [Yhwh]. Israel was clear that it did not take the land either by power or stratagem, but because Yahweh had spoken a word and had acted to keep his word. The central memories of Israel were told and retold to recall this very point." See Walter Brueggemann, *The Land: Place as Gift, Promise, and Challenge in Biblical Faith* (Minneapolis: Fortress, 2002), 45. While this insight helps to clarify the general perception of place in the Hebrew Bible, it provides no consolation to those who have been dispossessed and dislodged from their lands due to the myth of promise the Hebrew Bible validates and enforces.

[337]The religious orientation of the acts to be taken against the occupants of the land reaffirms in a sense the argument by Bob Becking that the text is narrated to give legitimacy to one form of Judaism at the expense of others. As such the reader is expected "to believe that the belief system of the Ezra-group is the only acceptable, divinely willed continuation of pre-exilic Yahwism." See Becking, "Ezra's Re-enactment of the Exile," 61. Becking's argument rests on the assumption that the "Ezra-group" is characterised by their strict observance of the Torah and the need to reinstitute the celebration of the Passover; hence *the need to rebuild the temple.*

9–10, in the form of Ezra's prayer, would like the readers to believe: *the land is unclean*, because "the peoples of the lands" *are unclean*. To purify the land requires the maintenance of ethnic purity by setting the holy seed apart from "the peoples of the lands."

Other aspects of Ezra's prayer require further consideration. First, if Deut 7:1–6 is the text invoked in Ezra's prayer, then he would have probably viewed the return of the exiles from Babylon as another exodus: to re-possess the land by dispossessing and destroying its occupants and their religion. In thinking so, Ezra is characterized as imposing a tradition that has long exceeded its relevance into a context so different from that into which the exodus generation entered.

Second, if the *kumifonua* group thought of Judah as their homeland and place of origin, that place has long gone.[338] The Judah they knew was ruled by their own kings; the one that they now return to is a small province (Yehud) of a foreign empire (Persia). The hope of returning is typical of dispersed people, but according to S. Hall such a hope is "more precarious than usually thought."[339] This is due to the fact that the place called homeland will have transformed beyond recognition, and "there is no going 'home' again."[340] There can be detour but no return. The notion of home therefore is much more complex than approaches to diasporas premised on the power of nostalgia would want us believe.[341] In that sense, the problem with the returnees is they are looking for a place that exists only in their memory and imagination.

Third, the notion of the *unclean land* and *people* is in a sense ironic. While it is used as a reference to others, it is more of a self-designation. As Ezra's prayer points out, the very reason for Judah's captivity was their own sin not the sin of others. Here the *kumifonua* are probably trying to shift the blame to those who remained in Judah.

Fourth, Judah has always been a home to peoples from diverse ethnic origins with different religions[342] and values. Its boundary has

---

[338]Such a place, in the words of A. Brah, is "a mythic place of desire in the diasporic imagination. In this sense it is a place of no return." In Brah's view, home in diaspora is neither the place of departure nor the place of arrival, but a hyphenated space *in–between* reality and imagination. See Brah, *Cartographies of Diaspora: Contesting Identities*, 192.

[339]Stuart Hall, "Culture, Community, Nation," *Cultural Studies* 7, no. 3 (1993): 355.

[340]Ibid.

[341]Roza Tsagarousianou, "Rethinking the concept of diaspora: mobility, connectivity and communication in a globalised world," *Westminster Papers in Communication and Culture* 1, no. 1 (2004): 57.

[342]Yahwism is just one belief system in the diverse religious landscape of Israel. For more insights see Stephen L. Cook, *The Social Roots of Yahwism* (Atlanta: SBL, 2004), 11. "Biblical Yahwism did not evolve out of earlier forms but existed as a religious option alongside of such other forms of religion in ancient Israel as Canaanite religious

always been shifting due to interactions with foreign powers throughout the centuries.[343] Ezra and his group are therefore not returning to the same place twice.

The idea of an *unclean land* is a myth fabricated by the *kumifonua* to advance their need for settlement. I am using the phrase "unclean land" to indicate my departure from Robert P. Carroll's view that the essential stories of the Hebrew Bible are framed and constructed upon the myth of "empty land." While Carroll's view may be true of the Chronicler's "sabbathization" of the exile, I contend that it is not applicable to the perception of place in Ezra 9–10.[344]

The House (built with divine initiative, royal edict and imperial support) is constructed to be the locus of authority with its border protected and controlled. Within the bordered space of the House, nothing in the land deserves respect; all are subject to be (dis)possessed. In the House, the land has no *tapu* because it is unclean. To purify the land is to extend the boundary of the House as a *tapu* space to make the land a *tapu* place, and thereby be inhabited by the returnees as a *tapu* race. Such a perception degrades the life-giving *mana* of the land, imposes a boundary that excludes, which therefore shatters the mutual connection between the people and their place, and offers no sense of security to those who count that place home, the *kakai-e-fonua*.

Kakai-e-fonua, as defined above, is Tongan for native inhabitants of a place. These peoples have roots, and are strongly connected to their places. Their perception of place is dominated by the *kumifonua* perspective. Whereas the latter views the *fonua* as something to be exclusively possessed and owned, the *kakai-e-fonua* perceives otherwise. This is evident in their preferred space of dwelling, which is mentioned in Ezra 10 as the square (רחוב).

Chapter 10 shifts from the bordered space of the House in chapter 9 into the borderless space of the square, the open (רחוב). This space is located לבני בית אלהים ("in front of the house of God," 10:1, 6). From the House, Ezra and his cohort have now found themselves in the midst of "the peoples of the lands," in the unbounded space of the square. This openness of the square poses a problem for those who

---

practices, syncretic forms of religion, popular or folk practices, and official, state religion."

[343] See Charles E. Carter, "The Province of Yehud in the Post-exilic Period: Soundings in Site Distribution and Demography," in *Second Temple Studies: 2. Temple and Community in the Persian Period* (ed. Tamara Cohn Eskenazi and Kent H. Richards; Sheffield: Sheffield Academic Press, 1994), 115.

[344] See Carroll, "Exile! What Exile?," 63. See also "The Myth of the Empty Land," *Semeia* 59 (1992): 79–93.

would like to read Ezra together with Nehemiah. If one reads Ezra as such, then the wall built by Nehemiah would serve as a closed boundary for both the House and the square. To read Ezra as a self-contained narrative, the square indicates there really is no boundary.

Whether or not this shift from inside the House to the square was intentional is unclear. Only one thing is certain: the square becomes the centre of power; here the community decentred the power-claim of *kumifonua* group, and ridiculed their aggressive programme of restoration. Even their self-proclaimed purity is now "polluted" in the open by mingling with peoples of the lands. If that is the sin they are concerned with, they are now as guilty and abominable as the *kakai-e-fonua* (peoples of the lands).

A valuable study by John Wright on the development of the square complements my *tu'a* reading at this point. Wright traces the development of the square in Israel in three distinct periods: Iron Age II, Neo-Babylonian, and Achaemenid. During the Iron Age II, membership of the city was defined in terms of access to the gate. The gate was an ordered-space, the locus of power, and gathering place for the elites, mainly males. In the gate, justice was expected to be upheld and served. In contrast, the square was an anonymous space; it was a "public realm outside the regulating control of the societal forces. The square [was] a "no-man's land" in the midst of the city."[345] A transformation of society came in the Neo-Babylonian era. Membership in the community was defined in terms of access to the temple, the new locus of power, since the old locus (the gate) disappeared with the destruction of its location (the wall). The square remained anonymous and un-ordered, and became a symbol of danger and adultery in prophetic discourse (e.g. Ezek 16:24, 31).[346] In the Achaemenid period, a reconfiguration of power took place which saw access to the square as the defining criterion of membership in the society. Wright says,

> The square defines national citizenship, a place where those of proper patrimony may gather. In gathering in the square, the citizenry is subjected to the gaze of the royal/imperial power.[347]

---

[345]John W. Wright, "A Tale of Three Cities: Urban Gates, Squares and Power in Iron Age II, Neo-Babylonian and Achaemenid Judah," in *Second Temple Studies III: Studies in Politics, Class and Material Culture* (ed. Philip R. Davies and John M. Halligan; Sheffield: Sheffield Academic Press, 2002), 28.
[346]Ibid, 39.
[347]Ibid, 49.

If readers follow Wright's final analysis, the square in Ezra 9–10 would be seen as an ordered space, where Ezra and his officers maintain their authority and control over "the peoples of the lands." Wright's view of the square however is very much dictated by the dominant portrayal of the square in texts attributed to each period he investigates. He also assumes that the functions of the square can be strictly defined into temporal slots. If Wright had read texts on the square from a non-dominant standpoint, a standpoint like that adopted in my *tu'a* reading, he would have come up with different answers. Likewise, the development of an idea does not mean abandoning its previous meanings; rather, it carries them along. The square should also be understood in like manner. The Achaemenid administration may have imposed some new functions on the square, but it does not take away the understanding of the square held by "the peoples of the lands": open and borderless.[348]

A rereading of texts Wright referred to in his analyses provides different insights on the square. The square is a preferred place for the un-homed and the displaced (outsiders, strangers, prostitutes, etc.), despite being negatively portrayed by the homed and the well-placed as a place of danger. In Gen 19, the square is where the two angels who visit Sodom prefer to spend the night. After Lot invites them into his house, they respond: לא כי ברחוב נלין ("No, for in the square we will spend the night," v.2). Upon Lot's insistence, they finally comply. I wonder what would have happened if they decided to spend the night in the square. There are two possibilities: (1) the people of Sodom would have the chance to "know" them, and (2) Sodom may have never been destroyed because the people would not have dared to force their way into the bounded space of Lot's house.[349]

---

[348] Those who were not deported to Babylonia are likely to have a different of view of the square from those deported. The events in Ezra 9–10, where others apart from Ezra dominate the scene, are evident. That is probably the reason for Ezra's return to the chamber; he cannot stand being confronted by the people in the open, borderless space of the square.

[349] The narrative however is woven in favour of Lot, making therefore the people act and speak in a way that portrays them negatively as homosexuals; the very stuff of alienation. Traditional readings of the text identified the men of Sodom with homosexuality and inhospitality, and sentenced them accordingly. But if we read the narrative with the people in the open, not the one in the house, new insights may come to light. The people are portrayed as being angry with Lot, yet one might ask: Were they really after the visitors or after Lot's egotistic attempt to confine the visitors, in his house, for himself? This could be a plausible view, given that Lot prefers to give up his daughters but not the two men. He prefers to close himself and the two men in the house without giving those in the open a chance. The best Lot could have done is to "come out"

In Judg 19, the story of the Levite and his concubine, the square is identified as the "town square" (ברחוב העיר "in the square of the city"), and that is the place where the Levite, his attendant and concubine intend to spend the night. As strangers into the place (Gibeah) they are invited by a man into his house where he provides for all their needs. Their host, the one with a house, warns them about being in the square in the night. Here again, the guests are being bounded inside. Like the portrayal of the people of Sodom, the men of Gibeah challenge this by demanding that the guests be let out of the house that they may know them. Like Lot, the host negotiates with the men on behalf of his guests by offering them his virgin daughter and the Levite's concubine (v.24). Unlike the Sodom episode, here one of the guests, the concubine (a female), is pushed out by her own man to be raped and abused, to save himself and other men "inside the house."

The square is depicted in other texts as a "red light district," where prostitutes lie in wait for young men (Prov 7:12). Ezekiel refers to the square in his prophecy against Israel's faithlessness (Ezek 16:23–26 [JPS]):

> After all your wickedness (woe, woe to you!)—declares the Lord GOD—you built yourself an eminence and made yourself a mound in every square.
>
> You built your mound at every crossroad; and you sullied your beauty and spread your legs to every passerby, and you multiplied your harlotries. You played the whore with your neighbors, the lustful Egyptians—you multiplied your harlotries to anger Me.

Here the square is the place where Israel adulterates herself with foreign nations. The issue is not the square itself, but what Israel does in the square. Warning against the square is an attempt to prevent Israel from "mingling" with others and exposes the insecurity of the one uttering the warning.

> Isaiah speaks of the square as the place where honesty stumbles:
> And so redress is turned back and vindication stays afar,
> because honesty stumbles in the public square and uprightness cannot enter (Isa 59:14 [JPS]).

---

into the open with his men, rather than "eloping" with them at the cost of his fellowmen and his wife. No wonder that his daughters had to make him drunk in order to preserve his line.

This negative perception is from those in the House, such as Ezra and the officers, whose interests are not served nor taken into account in the square. Any claim of domination is decimated and buried in the square (2 Sam 21:12). In the square, the honour of the displaced is restored (Est 4:6, 6:9, 11). From these references to the square, it is clear that its boundary cannot be marked, simply because it has no boundary. It is an open place where people from all walks of life have the liberty to socialize and express themselves without the interference of those in authority; those in the House.[350]

RELOCATING *TU'A*-WISE

Whereas the text is clearly narrated in favour of the returning exiles and their claims, a *fonua* reading exposes the oppressive forces behind the narration, on the one hand, and reveals transformative alternatives, on the other hand. To read along the grain of the text, the exiles are portrayed as rightful residents returning to reclaim the land granted to their ancestors by Yhwh. In contrast, those who are in the land, "the peoples of the lands," are viewed as foreigners who have polluted the land. Likewise, place is read as a bordered space embodied in the House of God, where only the returnees have access.

To read the text, however, through the category of *fonua*, the returning exiles are perceived as landless subjects (*kumifonua*) who are in search of a place of settlement, whereas "the peoples of the lands" (the alleged impure group) are read as the natives of the land (*kakai-e-fonua*), whose place, the square, is without border and opens to all irrespective of

---

[350]In Ezra 10, the square serves as venue for various meetings between Ezra and "the peoples of the lands." In the square, a response to the prayer of Ezra in 9:5–15 is uttered by another priestly figure, Shecaniah. This response is widely considered by scholars as admission of guilt, a resolution, and a command on behalf of the people (10:2–4). Ezra responds with acts of oath-taking, withdrawal and proclamation (10:5–8). The gathering in Ezra 9 ends as if there was no hope beyond the mixed marriage crisis. This is evident in the sentimentally-driven reactions of Ezra. But the words of Shecaniah express the contrary, reminding the religious leader, יש־מקוה לישראל על־זאת, "there is hope for Israel in spite of this" 10:2e). The truth is, they have married foreign women, and if mixed marriage is an indicator for faithlessness then they are guilty. But what needs to be done is not just to utter a solitary prayer. They need to make a covenant with God to send away their wives and their children according to these authorities: the counsels of Ezra and those who tremble at the commandment and the law of God (10:3). Shecaniah's speech ends with these words: קום כי־עליך הדבר ואנחנו עשה: "Get up! For it is your duty, and we are with you; be strong and do it!" (10:4).

ethnicity, sexual orientation, and social status. A *fonua* reading therefore opens transformative insights from a text that is driven by indifference to others.

CHAPTER 7
REVISIONING EZRA

> When explorers and missionaries crossed the South Pacific Ocean, they viewed the natives as "strangers." This perception was partially accurate, for our ancestors were voyagers who came to our islands—depending on which anthropologist one consults—from different places of origin. . . We natives are not native to the South Pacific Islands! But our ancestors walked the islands before the palefaces arrived. How then did we become the only "strangers" in the islands?
>
> Jione Havea[351]

The second issue raised by the reading of *'ātakai* in Chapter 5 is about social visions that are engraved in, and projected by, the text. This chapter is concerned with that particular aspect, based on the following assumptions:

(i) Every text projects a certain social vision that it invites readers to participate in and accept;

(ii) Every text has a tendency to suppress other social visions that contradict its own;

(iii) Every social vision is an intersection of domination and resistance; and

(iv) Each vision determines to a great extent the way a community is stratified and positioned in relation to power and scarce resources.

---

[351] Havea, "Numbers," 43–51.

My interest in the social vision of the text is also driven by two contextual reasons. First, as a *tu'a* (commoner) reader, I am a part of a Tongan social class that was culturally invented to be at the service, and to live by the visions, of the dominant *'eiki* (chiefly) class.[352] Because some aspects of those visions are oppressive,[353] there is a need to envision new alternatives. Second, community is one of the most vital elements of our (Oceanic) island way of life,[354] and Tongan society in particular. Community defines who we are, and thus shapes the way we live, think and act. Simply put, *one's community is one's home*;[355] it provides some sense of belonging and attachment.[356] As such, there is a need to reread the texts of the Bible for visions that would strengthen that sense of community.

---

[352] For more information on Tongan social classes, consult Gifford, *Tongan Society*, 108–156.

[353] Refer to Chapter 1 for the discussion of the *'eiki* and *tu'a* classes.

[354] See Jovili Meo, "Gems of Pacific Communities: Sharing and Service," *Pacific Journal of Theology* II, no. 16 (1996): 84–101.

[355] The significance of community is captured in this comment with regard to education: "To engage in relational practice, a key consideration is the presence of community." See Mere Kepa and Linita Manu'atu, "Indigenous Maori and Tongan Perspectives on the Role of Tongan Language and Culture in the Community and in the University in Aotearoa-New Zealand," *American Indian Quarterly* 30, no. 1 & 2 (2006): 15. One native Hawaiian scholar views community in terms of survival when she makes this declaration: "There it is. How do we educate our youth for the challenges of the next millennium? We surround them with our community; we give them meaningful experiences that highlight their ability to be responsible, intelligent, and kind. We watch for their gifts, we shape assessment to reflect mastery that is accomplished in real time, not false. We laugh more, plant everything, and harvest the hope of aloha. We help each other, we listen more, we trust in one another again. We find our Hawaiian essence reflected in both process and product of our efforts. *That* is Hawaiian education, and understanding our Hawaiian epistemology is our foundation, our *kumupa'a*. So, let it be said and let it be known: We *have* what we need. We *are* who we need." See Manulani Aluli Meyer, "Our Own Liberation: Reflections on Hawaiian Epistemology," *The Contemporary Pacific* 13, no. 1 (2001): 146.

[356] Tongans who live in diaspora maintain their link with home by establishing groups of different sorts, such as churches and *kava* drinking groups. These groups do become charitable organizations at the same time as they from time to time raise funds to help different projects and families in Tonga. In that sense, diaspora groups do not only serve as cultural networks, but also as economic networks that link Tongans at home with those overseas. Such networks are responsible for the inflow of foreign currencies into Tonga; an economic event that helps to sustain the Tongan economy.

CATEGORY OF ANALYSIS

The assumptions and rationales above call for a rereading of the text through the analytical category of *tākanga*. *Tākanga*, as defined in Chapter 4, is Tongan for a *community*. The hallmarks of *tākanga* are *mateaki* (devotion), *loto tō* (humility), *fetauhi'aki* (reciprocity), and *faka'apa'apa* (unreserved respect). These pre-Christian values are the mechanisms that hold a *tākanga* together. The term *tākanga* however has two variant forms, *tāka'anga* (*tā* [strike or beat]; *ka'anga* [utterly finished or destroyed]) and *taka'anga* (*taka* [to move, drift, wander]; *'anga* [space, place]). These variants signify the dual concern of a reading through *tākanga*: first is to reclaim transformative social visions of biblical texts, and second is to expose claims to power or purity that are proven or potentially oppressive. Through *tākanga*, *tu'a* reading also envisions plurality and difference, and thus resists any biblical vision of society that is purist and exclusivist, because such a vision can tend to predominate in many social arrangements globally. Ezra 9–10 will be read from this perspective.

METHOD OF ANALYSIS

Reading *tākanga* employs the *lau vā* method of *tu'a* reading for analysing Ezra 9–10.[357] This particular method scrutinizes texts based on the categories of *fa'ahinga* (social groups within a community)[358] and *vā* (relation, space). The analysis of *fa'ahinga*, on the one hand, is informed by the notions of *tu'unga* (position, status) and *fa'unga* (constituents, structure), whereas the *vā*, on the other hand, is assessed using the key Tongan social values of *mateaki* (devotion), *loto tō* (humility), *fetauhi'aki* (reciprocity), and *faka'apa'apa* (unreserved respect). The *lau vā* method seeks through these categories to determine whether or not the social visions inscribed in the text foster or impede the goals envisioned through the analytical category of *tākanga*. The primary objective for reading these social aspects is to expose any *tā-kanga* (oppressive) aspects of texts, while at the same time highlighting its *taka-'anga* (liberating) potentials.

---

[357] Chapter 4 offered a detail discussion of this method.
[358] See Gifford, *Tongan Society*, 9.

REVISIONING EZRA 9–10

This chapter is divided into three sections. The first section is concerned with defining the *fa'ahinga*, and reading each one in terms of their *tu'unga* and *fa'unga*. The second section assesses the maintenance and/or transgression of *vā* amongst and within each *fa'ahinga* based on the key social values named above. The third discusses the intersection of transformative (*taka-'anga*) and oppressive (*tā-ka'anga*) visions in the text.

DEFINING *FA'AHINGA*

A *fa'ahinga* encompasses social groups that are constructed in the texts. Each *fa'ahinga* is defined by the way it is located (*tu'unga*) and constituted (*fa'unga*). In Ezra 9–10 there are two main *fa'ahinga*: "the people of Israel" (העם ישראל) and "the peoples of the lands" (עמי הארצות). In the previous chapter, I have defined both groups from a *tu'a* perspective: the former as *kumifonua*; the latter as *kakai-e-fonua*. The term *kumifonua* signifies a routed group of people who are in search of a place of arrival and settlement. In contrast, the *kakai-e-fonua* indicates those who are well-placed and rooted; they are the natives (*fonua*).[359] Each *fa'ahinga* consists of several sub-groups (see Table 1).

Table 1: *Fa'ahinga*

Kumifonua	Kakai-e-fonua
a) העם ישראל (9:1)	a) עמי הארצות (9:1, 11; cf. 3:3)
בני הגולה (10:7, 16; cf. 4:1, 6:19, 20, 8:35,)	עמי הארץ (10:2, 11)
זרע הקדש (9:2)	b) נשים נכריות (10:2, 10, 14, 17, 18, 44)

---

[359] Defining the *fa'ahinga* is significant for several reasons: it brings to light, on the one hand, the reality that every *tākanga* is diversely constituted; it exposes, on the other hand, the illusion of a homogeneous society. The presence of various *fa'ahinga* also highlights that there is always interplay of different roles and often conflicting values in the space of the text; texts also position *fa'ahinga* to protect the interests of those it favours against those it does not. In most cases, the favourites turn out to be those with power and privilege, and texts are often (if not always) written from their perspectives, and to serve their interests.

b) השרים (9:1, 2, 10:8)		c) בנים (10:44)	
c) הכהנים (9:1, cf. 1:5)			
d) הלויים (9:1, cf. 1:5, 2:70, 3:8, 10, 12, 6:20, 7:7, 8:29, 30)			
e) הסגנים (9:2)			
f) אנשים (10:1, 16, 17)			
g) נשים (10:1)			
h) ילדים (10:1)			

The *kumifonua*, on the one hand, is referred to in various terms: "the people of Israel" (העם ישראל), "the holy seed" (זרע הקדש) and "the community of exiles" (בני הגולה). Within this *fa'ahinga*, some are identified by their roles (השרים, הכהנים, הלויים, הסגנים), while others are marked by their genders (אנשים and נשים). The *kakai-e-fonua*, on the other hand, is indistinctly identified as one group, "the peoples of the land(s)," with a particular focus on women, "foreign women" (נשים נכריות).[360]

Tu'unga. Tu'unga refers to "where one stands" (as in *tu'u'anga* [*tu'u* to stand; *'anga* space]) or one's position or location within a community. In Tongan society, each individual has an assigned *tu'unga*: one is either *'eiki* (a chief or of chiefly lineage) or a *tu'a* (a commoner).[361] Each *tu'unga* is defined by various factors (such as worldviews and beliefs expressed in myths and genealogies) that validate the domination of one (*'eiki*) over the other (*tu'a*). In reading texts through *tākanga*, I ask: Are there *'eiki* and *tu'a* subjects in Ezra 9–10? How are they being positioned in relation to power and resources? Are there elements of resistance that resist the positioning of the dominant *fa'ahinga* in the text?

---

[360]From the *kumifonua*, some are accused by their own, particularly the שרים ("chiefs"), for committing an act that they regarded as a serious offence: that is, for not separating themselves (לא־נבדלו, v.1) from the *kakai-e-fonua* or, in other words, marrying foreign women (v.2). The act and prayer that follow the accusation of 9:1–2, namely 9:3–15, rightly admits the guilt of those responsible. Interestingly though, the text tends to shift the blame from the offenders to the *kakai-e-fonua*, and the weight of that blame-shifting falls upon the נשים נכריות ("foreign women") and their בנים ("sons" or "children"). The readings and translations of the texts are dominated by the idea that had there been no peoples in the land, and no "foreign women," Israel would not have sinned. The irony here is that it was Israel's sins that drove them out of the land in the first place (9:6–7). Again, the text constructs both *fa'ahinga* as if the *kumifonua*, on the one hand, has a divine right to dominate, and the *kakai-e-fonua*, on the other hand, should silently accept their ill-treatment by the former.

[361]For the distinctions between the two, see Chapter 1.

The *kumifonua* is first of all identified as העם ישראל ("the people of Israel") in 9:1. This particular reference occurs only fifteen times in the entire Hebrew Bible (MT);[362] otherwise the term בני ישראל is used (cf. Ezra 6:16, 21).[363] Farisani reads העם ישראל, based on Ackroyd's observation,[364] as a reminder that the exile community is to be regarded as "the true successor of all Israel."[365] That would be the case, if the *kumifonua* is to be read as returning residents. But as a routed group, the *kumifonua* does not qualify to be read as such. Mary Douglas argues that the name is a myth that gives Ezra "license to suppose that the people he found in Yehud must be of foreign extraction, although consistently he talks about them as if they were natives."[366] In that sense, the use of the name has a political overtone. Similarly, the use of the phrase, "'peoples of the land,' cheatingly gives him scriptural backing and the basis for the discourse on the uncleanness of idolatry which he uses against them."[367]

The second aspect that defines the *tu'unga* of the *kumifonua* is the term זרע הקדש ("the holy seed," 9:2). What does this phrase entail? What is its significance? The text does not provide a clear explanation of the designation, although it gives the *kumifonua* a very special status. The only other occurrence of the phrase is in Isa 6:13, which predicts the post-destruction situation of Israel as a stump of a tree that has been cut down, but will grow up again as a זרע קדש. In Ezra 9:2, "the holy seed" is expected to be set apart, and not to be mingled with "the peoples of the lands," the *kakai-e-fonua*. To mingle with others, especially in the form of marriage, is to violate the purity of the whole group. Clines reads:

---

[362]Num 21:6; Josh 8:33; 2 Sam 18:7, 19:41, 24:4; 1 Kgs 16:21; Ezra 2:2, 7:13 (in Aramaic), 9:1; Neh 7:7; Ezek 36:8, 38:14, 16; Amos 8:2 and 9:14.

[363]The name ישראל however occurs thirty–one times which is more than Farisani's claim in Elelwani Farisani, "The Use of Ezra-Nehemiah in a Quest for an African Theology of Reconstruction," *Journal of Theology for Southern Africa* 116 (July 2003): 36. He miscounted the occurrence of the name יהודה; the name occurs six times, whereas Farisani only identifies four.

[364]P. R. Ackroyd, "The Theology of the Chronicler," *Lexington Theological Quarterly* 8 (1973): 101–116.

[365]Farisani, "The Use of Ezra-Nehemiah in a Quest for an African Theology of Reconstruction," 36. He also argues that the name "Israel" in Ezra-Nehemiah refers to "the returned exiles who are portrayed as the real representative of the real and pure Israelite community."

[366]Mary Douglas, "Responding to Ezra: The Priests and the Foreign Wives," *Biblical Interpretation* 10, no. 1 (2002): 5.

[367]Ibid.

> [t]he principle of separation (v.1) from other nations of the world, a scheme of the Chronicler's, has been undermined by this mixture (Lev. 19:19) of the holy race with pagans.[368]

This reading clearly takes for granted the view that "the peoples of the lands" are pagans, and therefore are not worthy to interact with "the holy seed." In a similar vein, Fensham offers this observation:

> By mingling with foreign nations and being contaminated with their idol worship, the true religion was in danger of losing its pure character.[369]

While this insight from Fensham sheds some light on the idea of "holy seed," it has its own problem since it assumes that the phrase "the peoples of the lands" means idol worshippers. There is nothing in the text to indicate that the *kakai-e-fonua* have worshipped idols. The comparison in 9:1 to other nations also does not provide any clear evidence as to who is being compared; the *kakai-e-fonua* or those of the *kumifonua* that take "foreign women." Even the nations mentioned in the list (cf. 9:1) are problematic because although they were traditional enemies of Israel, their existence in Ezra's time as ethnic entities is doubtful.[370]

Olyan reads "the holy seed" as an ideological tool for reconfiguring the post-exilic Judaean community.[371] If that was the case, the community is destined to collapse, because the idea of holiness projected by the text is a divisive tool rather than a constitutive one. To define the *kumifonua* as "the holy seed" implicitly portrays their view of the *kakai-e-fonua* on the contrary; that is, they are an unholy group. From

---

[368] Clines, *Ezra, Nehemiah, Esther*, 120.

[369] F. Charles Fensham, *The Books of Ezra and Nehemiah* (Grand Rapids: Eerdmans, 1982), 125.

[370] Allen and Laniak read: "The appeal to holiness is implicitly based on Deut 7:6, where Israel is called "a people holy to the LORD." This holy status is an aspect of the theological particularism that characterizes the OT. In Deut 7 this special relationship with God is stated as the reason why Israel should not intermarry with the traditional seven ethnic groups they found in the promised land . . . They no longer existed as ethnic entities in the postexilic period; the mixed local populations living around the immigrant community are regarded as their virtual equivalents." Leslie C. Allen and Timothy S. Laniak, *Ezra, Nehemiah, Esther* (Peabody: Hendrickson, 2003), 72.

[371] Saul M. Olyan, "Purity Ideology in Ezra-Nehemiah as a Tool to Reconstitute the Community," *Journal for the Study of Judaism* XXXV, no. 1 (2004): 2.

a *tu'a* perspective, the phrase gives the *kumifonua* a *tapu* status, which essentially carries a demand for control and domination.

The third aspect that defines the *tu'unga* of the *kumifonua* is בני הגולה (10:7, 16), which is rendered differently in English versions as "children of the captivity" (KJV), "the exiles" (NIV, NJB), "descendants of the captivity" (NKJV), and "returned exiles" (NRSV) or "all who had returned from exile" (JPS). It is important to note that the phrase בני הגולה literally means "sons of the exile(s)" and thus carries no sense of returning at all. To translate as such (as did the NRSV and NJPS) is to ascribe to the *kumifonua* an event that never happened and a *tu'unga* that they do not deserve. Such a perception would portray the *kumifonua* as former inhabitants of the land—deported and exiled (for example, Ezra 1:11, 2:1, 8:35)—and have now returned as rightful residents. But they are just a group of exiles being allowed by their captors "to build the House of God in Jerusalem which is in Judah" (Ezra 1:2, 3). The decree by Cyrus has no hint that those allowed to return are former inhabitants, nor does it give them any right to take control.[372] The only reason for their re-lease is to act on Cyrus's behalf, rather than to re-claim land or power.

The fourth defining aspect of the *tu'unga* of the *kumifonua* lies in the constructed space of בית אלהים. As discussed in the preceding chapter, בית אלהים, at least in the opinion of the returnees, becomes the centre of power and privilege; it is also projected to be the "command centre" for the community, even in personal matters like who should a man marry or divorce. The House also provides a boundary for Ezra and his שרים, and that is where they make their claims to purity vis-à-vis the impurity of "the peoples of the lands" (9:1–2). The text positions the *kumifonua* within the House, whereas the *kakai-e-fonua* is located outside (*tu'a*). That reflects a desire to position the *kumifonua* as an exclusive group, which thus requires separation from others. Simply put, the House, from a *tu'a* viewpoint, is the emblem of social and religious exclusions.[373] Ironically, while it serves to set apart the *kumifonua*, on the one hand, it ironically alienates them from the whole community, on the other hand.

---

[372]Carroll reads the idea of exile and return as "two sides or faces of the myth that shapes the subtext of the narratives and rhetoric of the Hebrew Bible." Carroll, "Exile! What Exile?" 63. He argues that any journey out of the land or out of a country is equally a journey into a different land or country (it is a zero sum game), so exile and return is an on-going event of going out of and entering into the land.

[373]Exclusion is understood as "those whose quality of life has been reduced and their full participation in society limited by a combination of factors. Socially excluded people experience 'the denial (or non-realisation) of the civil, political and social rights of citizenship.'"

While these four aspects define the *tu'unga* of the *kumifonua*, on the one hand, they reflect, on the other hand, how the text implicitly defines the *tu'unga* of the *kakai-e-fonua*. First, whereas the *kumifonua* is defined as "the people of Israel," the *kakai-e-fonua* is referred to as "the peoples of the land(s)." Second, whereas the *kumifonua* is defined as "the holy seed," the *kakai-e-fonua* is by implication a community of evildoers because they have polluted the land with their abomination and impurity (9:1–2). Third, whereas the *kumifonua* is constructed as returning residents, the *kakai-e-fonua* is viewed as a community of foreigners, hence the phrase נשים נכריות ("foreign women"). In other words, the text locates the *kakai-e-fonua* outside their own *fonua*; they become displaced subjects in the eyes of the narrator and the Ezra faction of the *kumifonua* as well. Fourth, and finally, whereas the *kumifonua* is located inside the House, the *kakai-e-fonua* find themselves in the square, the space *outside* the House (10:1).[374]

Fa'unga. *Fa'unga* indicates the structure or arrangement of something or a group, and thus applies in this work to both texts (as in Chapter 6) and society (as in this chapter). Its longer variant, *fa'u'anga*, points to the components that constitute the whole. To analyse the *fa'unga* of each *fa'ahinga* requires a close look at its constituents, and a salvaging of any members the text may have ignored. Both *fa'ahinga* (*kumifonua* and *kakai-e-fonua*) are constituted by different groups (see Table 1) and defined by several factors.[375]

---

[374] The square is generally regarded by the Hebrew Bible as a place of sinners and is filled with dangers. There the *kakai-e-fonua* is located together with prostitutes, homosexuals, and criminals. See my discussion of the *square* in Chapter 6.

[375] Cataldo has provided an insightful analysis of the social structure of Yehud in Jeremiah Cataldo, "Persian Policy and the Yehud Community During Nehemiah," *Journal for the Study of the Old Testament* 28, no. 2 (2003): 131–143. My concern in this chapter however is not to reconstruct or recover the social world behind the text, but the one that is inscribed in the text in conversation with the social world before the text; the world of the *tu'a* reader. For more insights on the Yehud society the following works are recommended: Carter, *The Emergence of Yehud in the Persian Period: A Social and Demographic Study*, Davies and Halligan, eds. *Second Temple Studies III: Studies in Politics, Class and Material Culture*, Edelman, *The Origins of the 'Second' Temple: Persian Imperial Policy and the Rebuilding of Jerusalem*, Eskenazi and Richards, eds. *Second Temple Studies 2: Temple and Community in the Persian Period*, Michael H. Floyd et al., *Prophets, prophecy, and prophetic texts in Second Temple Judaism* (London: T&T Clark, 2006), Grabbe, *A History of the Jews and Judaism in the Second Temple Period*, David Janzen, *Witch–Hunts, Purity and Social Boundaries* (Sheffield: Sheffield Academic Press, 2002), Lipschitz and Oeming, *Judah and the Judeans in the Persian period*, Ulrich et al., eds. *Priests, Prophets and Scribes: Essays on the Formation and Heritage of Second Temple Judaism in Honour of Joseph Blenkinsopp*, Weinberg, *The Citizen-Temple Community*.

The *kumifonua*, on the one hand, is constituted by three different groups of "returnees" that are distinguished by their roles and restoration agenda The first group—led by a man named Sheshbazzar whose identity is uncertain—brought the vessels for the House of God to Jerusalem (1.8–11). The second group—led by Zerubbabel and Joshua—set their eyes on rebuilding the House of God (3:1–6:22). The third, and last group—directed by Ezra—attempt to re-establish the torah to provide both religious and moral guidelines not only for the מקהל הגולה ("community of exiles," 10:8), but also all inhabitants of the land. In addition to that role is the task of reviving temple worship and rituals (Ezra 7). This Ezra-group sees intermarriage as a problem, hence the tensions in Ezra 9–10; the first two groups seemed to have a problem with "the peoples of the lands"—referred to in 4:1 as "adversaries of Judah and Benjamin" (צרי יהודה ובנימן)[376]—but not with their women since some took their wives from those women (נשים נכריות).

The text predominantly speaks of the male and ranked members of the *kumifonua* group, and rarely about its women and children. As listed in Table 1, the ranked members of the group include the chiefs (השרים), priests (הכהנים), Levites (הלויים), prefects (הסגנים), chiefs of the ancestral house (ראשי האבות לבית אבתם, 10:16), and men in general (אנשים). The only reference to *kumifonua* women and their children is in 10:1, and they are described as weeping subjects. The text allows both groups no voice at all with regard to the issue of intermarriage, nor are the women mentioned as having married foreign men. Even if these women did marry foreign men, the text does not consider it to be an issue for the returnees. It is the men who married "foreign women" that other male returnees are obsessed with (perhaps *they cannot withstand to lose them*[377]). Another devastating aspect of the text is its inconsideration of

---

[376] Those who responded to the initial call to return are identified by the text as ראשי האבות ליהודה ובנימן ("heads of the fathers of Judah and Benjamin") in 1:5. The reference to their foes as צרי יהודה ובנימן allows the possibility to read those enemies as including peoples from other Israelite tribes rather than just foreigners. This view is shared Farisani in Farisani, "The Use of Ezra-Nehemiah in a Quest for an African Theology of Reconstruction," 37.

[377] This opens up another reading possibility; an aspect for a queer reading of the text. While the dominant readings of the text focus on reasons such as inheritance rights and protection of boundaries for the text's anti–exogamy stance, it is also possible that behind that stance lies a homosexual attraction amongst male returnees. This is supported by the fact that they ignored their own women, and hated foreign ones.

children. While they are members of the community, they have no voice, and are vulnerable to expulsion (10:3, 44).[378]

The *kakai-e-fonua*, on the other hand, is regarded by the Ezra-group as foreigners; hence the term נשים נכריות (*nšym nkrywt* "foreign women").[379] Unlike the *kumifonua*, there is no reference in the text to ranked groups within the *kakai-e-fonua*, and there is also no direct reference to male members; "the peoples of the lands" are simply referred to in terms of "foreign women" (10:2, 10, 14, 17, 18, 44) and "their sons" (10:3, 44). Were there no males in the land? Perhaps not, as far as the text is concerned. But the anti-exogamy orientation of the *kumifonua* group singled out this particular feminine group as the epitome of the impurity of "the peoples of the lands," the *kakai-e-fonua*. For a group of men to blame a group of women, especially for something that they are not responsible for is (from a Tongan standpoint) a sign of weakness and insecurity. That is exactly what the men of the Ezra-group in Ezra 9–10 have done.

In terms of ethnicity, the text defined the *kumifonua* group as homogeneous with particular reference to phrases like העם יהודה ובנימן, ישראל, and זרע הקדש. If the *kumifonua* was homogeneous, then objection to intermarriage from some members of the group is perhaps not just to maintain religious purity, but also to preserve ethnic purity as well. The need to protect that purity however is rather ironic, because when the text is read with other texts, purity appears to be an illusion, since some of their ancestors did marry foreign women. Gary N. Knoppers provides six interesting examples of intermarriage from the genealogy of Judah.[380] First, three of Judah's five sons were born by a Canaanite, Bath-shua (1 Chr 2:3). Second, Abigail, the sister of David, gave birth to Amasa, whose father was an Ishmaelite (1 Chr 2:17). Knoppers notes that "if the genealogist found the mixed marriages highly objectionable or reprehensible, he could have criticized them."[381] Instead, the genealogist comments negatively about the first son of Judah, Er, judging him as "evil in the eyes of Yhwh, so Yhwh put him to death" (Gen 38:7). A third case of intermarriage was the one between Sheshan's daughter and

---

[378] Attending to the treatment of children in biblical texts is an obligation of every reader. Not only are they seldom mentioned, but when mentioned they are vulnerable to abuse as in Gen 22 (the binding of Isaac).

[379] This textual orientation stands in contrast to what scholars have found, because the phrase "peoples of the lands" can be read in several ways. See the detail discussion of the phrase in Chapter 7.

[380] Gary N. Knoppers, "Intermarriage, Social Complexity, and Ethnic Diversity in the Genealogy of Judah," *Journal of Biblical Literature* 120, no. 1 (2001): 15–30.

[381] Ibid, 19.

his Egyptian servant, Jarha (1 Chr 2:34–35), from which thirteen generations are listed (2:35–51), unlike most genealogies in the Bible. The fourth case was King David (2 Sam 2:9), the fifth was Mered (1 Chr 4:18). The sixth case involves some of the descendants of Shelah, Judah's son, who married into Moab (4:21–22). These cases clearly expose the fact that purity, ethnic or otherwise, is a mere myth being constructed to serve the interests of the *kumifonua*. In short, the *kumifonua* is far from being ethnically homogeneous.

Unlike the alleged homogeneity of the *kumifonua*, the *kakai-e-fonua* is constructed as a mixed group (cf. the list of ethnic groups in Ezra 9:1–2). Such a mixture is interesting given the fact that they coexist as one *fa'ahinga*, whereas the *kumifonua* group is shown to have some sort of internal struggles (between members of the Ezra-group and those who returned earlier and have taken "foreign wives"). In the light of what I have discussed in Chapter 7, the so-called "peoples of the lands"—despite being perceived negatively by the *kumifonua*—is a community of difference and plurality, where peoples of different ethnicities are able to live together. If exclusion is the measure taken to maintain ethnic purity, I would rather be with the *kakai-e-fonua*, "peoples of the lands" where I can be who I am.

Assessing *Vā*

The analysis of the *fa'ahinga* sets the platform for assessing *vā*. The key for assessing *vā*, as abovementioned, is some of the key fundamental Tongan values such as *mateaki* (devotion), *loto tō* (humility), *fetauhi'aki* (reciprocity), [382] and *faka'apa'apa* (unreserved respect).[383] The several

---

[382] In Tonga, reciprocity is expressed in various occasions, like feasts, weddings, and funerals. When a *katoanga* (feast) is prepared, families, friends, and neighbours contribute to its preparation, because when a *fatongia* (duty) is required of them, others will offer their support in different forms. The same thing happens when it comes to a wedding or funeral. Members of the community work hand in hand to make sure that what is required by culture does not fall heavily on one shoulder. Some Tongan terms express the idea of reciprocity by adding a preformative *fe-* and an afformative -*'aki* to verbs: for examples, *fe'ofa'aki* (to love one another), *fe'uhi'aki* (to care for one another), *fetokoni'aki* (to help one another), *fekau'aki* (to relate to one another), and so on. These positive reciprocal actions are all required to maintain *vā*. For some ideas on reciprocity, see Wood, "Cultural Studies for Oceania," 351–354.

[383] Phyllis Herda et al., eds. *Tongan Culture and History: Papers from the 1st Tongan History Conference 14–17 January 1987* (Canberra: Australian National University, 1990), 231. See also a discussion of some key Tongan values in Kolo, "Historiography: The Myth of Indigenous Authenticity," 1–11.

fa'ahinga in a *tākanga*, though well-defined into groups, have *vā* to maintain and observe. They are not there as exclusive bodies that live only unto themselves without relating to others. This is where *fetauhi'aki* (reciprocity) comes in. *Fetauhi'aki* is about sharing responsibilities and burdens. When it is practiced, the *vā* is properly maintained. Where there is no *fetauhi'aki*, a *vā* is likely to be transgressed; hence, *maumau vā* (breaking *vā*). The *vā* in Ezra 9–10 will be assessed with these insights.

The first *vā* is the one between the *kumifonua* ("people of Israel" or "exiles") and *kakai-e-fonua* ("the peoples of the lands). An ideal way of maintaining *vā* by a routed and landless group like the *kumifonua* is to respect those whose space they have crossed, and to appreciate the fact that they have been well-accepted into the community. Some of the *kumifonua* seem to acknowledge that when they take women from *kakai-e-fonua* as their wives. The *kakai-e-fonua*, as narrated by the text, responds in a similar manner. In Tonga, people do not just allow their daughters to marry foreigners, unless there is a good reason to do so. If the *kakai-e-fonua* prohibits their daughter from marrying the male members of the *kumifonua* group, they are justified in doing that because there may have been economic and political reasons behind the marriage.[384] Yet they generally do not protest; intermarriage to them is just fine. They pay their *faka'apa'apa* to the *kumifonua* by accepting them into their land, and into their households. Contrariwise, the group within the *kumifonua* led by Ezra react in a different manner altogether. Intermarriage to this group is simply abominable (cf. Ezra 9:1–3). To participate in such an act is religiously offensive (to Yhwh) and morally wrong; it will pollute their purity as a holy race. This is the tone that opens Ezra 9–10, and it gives the following impressions. First, the people of Israel are so special and pure and they must always make sure that they maintain that purity. Douglas noted that this is new, because in Leviticus "defilement could not be used to stop the lower classes from intruding on their betters, or commoners from approaching aristocracy, nor for expelling women or foreigners from any assembly."[385]

Second, to maintain their purity they have to separate themselves from other peoples, even those whose places they have trespassed. The reason is that the Ezra group views other peoples as impure irrespective of who they are and what they do. Third, women outside the *kumifonua* group do not deserve *kumifonua* men. This is evident from the language

---

[384]See Danna Nolan Fewell, "Ezra and Nehemiah," in *Global Bible Commentary* (ed. Daniel Patte; Nashville: Abingdon, 2004), 127–134. Also Smith-Christopher, "The Mixed Marriage Crisis in Ezra 9–10 and Nehemiah 13: A Study of the Sociology of Post-Exilic Judaean Community," 243–265.

[385]Douglas, "Responding to Ezra: The Priests and the Foreign Wives," 10.

used in the text to describe "foreign women." They are נכריות (Ezra 10:2; cf. Prov 23:27) and in that sense they are harlots and do not have the protection of the law, as do the גרים (cf. Deut 10:19).

These insights are threatening and disappointing at once, since they do resemble the Tongan attitude of the *'eiki* class to the *tu'a*. Tongan chiefly families would rather allow their sons and daughters to marry amongst themselves than to marry a *tu'a*. There have been cases where marriages were annulled because of that attitude. The driving force behind that is a misconception held by the *'eiki* class that they are an exclusive, sacred and pure group that must be guarded against impurity. Underneath that lies a demand to keep out *tu'a* people from any chance of sharing resources that are reserved exclusively for the *'eiki*. Clearly, there is lack of *faka'apa'apa* for the *tu'a*, and there is no *fetauhi'aki* at all. That is exactly what the *kakai-e-fonua* gets from the Ezra group of the *kumifonua*. They allow their daughters to have landless husbands only to be treated as aliens in their own land and in their own community. Whereas the *kakai-e-fonua* ("peoples of the lands") seeks to maintain their *vā*, the *kumifonua* resorts to *breaking them*.

The second *vā* is one between the *kumifonua* and their deity, Yhwh. Ezra 9–10, and the Ezra narrative in general, is grounded upon a belief that only this *vā* matters, and should be maintained at all costs. The event of "return" is viewed as permitted by Yhwh rather than a liberating act of a foreign ruler (1:2–4). The restoration programme is also perceived as an attempt to re-establish their *vā* with Yhwh in a new way. Upon arrival in the land, they attempt to relive what Yhwh willed for their exodus counterparts (9:12 [JPS]; cf. Deut 7:1–3):

> Now then, do not give your daughters in marriage to their sons or let their daughters marry your sons; do nothing for their well-being or advantage, then you will be strong and enjoy the bounty of the land and bequeath it to your children forever.

To the *kumifonua*, to keep their *vā* with Yhwh means disregarding their *vā* with others. That is well-expressed in their attitude to the *kakai-e-fonua* in Ezra 9–10. The major driving force is the need to possess and inherit land,[386] though masked by a claim to moral impurity. While the *kumifonua*, on the one hand, seeks to pay their *faka'apa'apa* to Yhwh, and to reciprocate what Yhwh supposedly did for them (cf. Ezra 9:8–9), it is certainly an act of utter disrespect, on the other hand, to those whose land they have arrived at. Such a radical religiosity is, from a *tu'a*

---

[386]See Cataldo, "Persian Policy and the Yehud Community During Nehemiah," 248.

standpoint, unacceptable, since it is likely to provoke violence and threaten the kind of community envisioned through *tākanga*. That is parallel to another event of a similar nature in Num 25, where the dislike of foreigners and zeal for Yhwh provided the basis for murdering an innocent woman (vv.7–8), and for waging war against the Midianites (31:1–12). Both these violent incidents received the approval of Yhwh (cf. 25:10–13; 31:1–2).

The third *vā* is the one between the Ezra group and those who had taken wives from the peoples of the lands. As abovementioned, those who have "foreign wives" depart in some ways from the attitude that shapes the narrative. Rather than adhering to the violent demand of their tradition, they negotiate their place in the community through integration rather than segregation.[387] Their *vā* with the *kakai-e-fonua* is elevated above the mere traditionalism of their own *fa'ahinga*. In contrast, those in the Ezra group do not only sever all ties with the *kakai-e-fonua* but also disregard their *vā* with those who married "foreign women," to the extent that their possessions would be confiscated if they did not comply (10:8). This tension is expressed in the beginning of Ezra 9 when some chiefs (שרים) reported other chiefs, accusing them of the problem of intermarriage. Their attitude to intermarriage tends to cause more problems for themselves, rather than the *kakai-e-fonua*. While, on the one hand, they seek to reconstruct a community based on the Law of Moses, they build, on the other hand, a community that is divided against itself. The rebuilding programme in that sense is no more than a deception. They violate all the *vā* they need to maintain, because there is lack of *faka'apa'apa* (respect) and *fetauhi'aki* (reciprocity) with the *kakai-e-fonua*.

The fourth *vā* is the one between two community leaders, Ezra ben Seraiah (7:1) and Shecaniah ben Jehiel (10:2). The former is a leader of the *kumifonua* group, particularly those who oppose intermarriage; the latter is a leader from the *kakai-e-fonua* group, and is speaking on behalf of the exogamists. Ezra, as portrayed by the text, is clearly judgmental, upset, and outraged when he learns of the intermarriage saga. His reaction to the issue of intermarriage is described in the following words (9:3):

---

[387]There may have been political and economic reasons, but the fact that they move beyond the confinement of their own kind is more inviting than the exclusionary tendency of other *kumifonua* men, like the chiefs (שרים).

> *And as I heard this word, I rent my garment and my robe, and pulled the hair from my head and beard, and I sat appalled.*

Such an act from a Tongan viewpoint can only be found on two occasions: death of a loved one and marriage of one's son or daughter with somebody undesirable. In the case of Ezra, no one has died and certainly none of those who married foreign women was his own. In other words, his reaction is utterly unfounded.

In contrast, Shecaniah does not make a fool out of himself by responding to Ezra in the same manner. He instead offers advice and options, while at the same time gives Ezra the decision making task (10:2–4). In a very clever way, he admits wrong-doing on behalf of the people, and then recommends what should be done. Whereas Ezra resorts to prayer and strange acts, Shecaniah proposes covenant-making and calls for actions. In other words, if intermarriage is a problem for the community, then Ezra should address the problem with the community rather than by way of accusation, confession and mourning.[388]

RE-VIS[ION]ING *TĀKANGA*

The above analysis of *fa'ahinga* and *vā* aims to shed light on visions of society inscribed in the text, and to assess whether or not they hinder or promote the goals of *tākanga*. A *tākanga* requires a relationship that is characterized by trust, respect, equal participation, solidarity and responsibility. The key assumption for *tākanga* is that a society or community cannot function well if there is lack of respect, trust, participation, solidarity and responsibility amongst its members. *Tākanga* also presupposes plurality, because community is not about individuals; it presupposes hybridity because everything, human and non-human, is a mixture of different elements; it presupposes solidarity because "no man is an island"; it requires reciprocity because no one has the ability and resources to do everything; we always need the assistance of others. Individualism and ethnocentrism are heresies in *tākanga*. *Tākanga*, however, always expects contradictory visions of society based on its two variants: *tā-a'anga* and *taka-'anga*. The former occurs when the goals of *tākanga* are ignored; the latter happens when they are upheld.

---

[388] I will further discuss the differences between the Ezra and Shecaniah below in Chapter 8.

Tā-ka'anga. *Tā-ka'anga*, the second variant of *tākanga*, means "to be utterly beaten" or "to brutalize." The term indicates an act of violence against something or someone that is often fuelled by hatred. A *tākanga* that is overruled by hatred breeds violence. Ezra 9–10 is woven with a vision to control and dominate; a *tā-ka'ang*a vision. The *tā-ka'anga* vision is dictated by a single belief and value systems that does not tolerate alternatives. It is characterized by a strict imposition of values, interests, beliefs and norms. It demands conformity and total obedience; resistance invites harsh judgments. In other words, there is only one true guide for life and faith; the rest are wrong and abominable. Such a vision is held and controlled by an elite minority, and it promotes an I-I/I-It relation that is ruled by self-interests and egotistic values. In Ezra 9–10, this is the social tendency of Ezra and his group of returnees. To them, the community in which they settled should be homogenized into a single belief and value system. A system that is socially purist, racist, and elitist; religiously fanaticist (Yahwist), temple-centred, torah-led. This is the kind of vision that dominates the text, and it is the kind of vision the text promotes and would like the readers to believe. Such an aggressive vision of society, from a *tu'a* perspective, evokes both the colonial and the *'eiki* visions of society as experienced by colonial and *tu'a* subjects respectively. The difference however lies in the fact that the colonial vision came from outside; the *'eiki* vision was an internal issue. That my own people are discriminating against me makes it worse than the experience of the colonised.

Taka-'anga. *Taka-'anga*, the second variant of *tākanga*, designates a place or community where people preferred to visit or to be a part of. It is a space of choice that offers a sense of *faka-lata* (belonging; at home). Such a space creates an ideal environment that promotes the kind of community envisioned by *tākanga*. It offers a liberating alternative to the violent tendency of *tā-ka'anga*. *Taka-'anga* promotes freedom of individuals to move and drift without restriction; it allows peoples to be different. In the Ezra narrative, those who held such a vision of society are the *kakai-e-fonua* and those men who married "foreign women." The reading through *tākanga* allows the *kakai-e-fonua* to be read and imagined in this way from the briefest hints in the text that I have exposed above. This alternative vision of society offers *tu'a* and displaced subjects a glimpse of hope amidst the stark reality of social exclusion and religious fanaticism that confront the readers, and where readers are invited to by the text.

REVISIONING *TU'A*-WISE

This reading of Ezra 9–10 through *tākanga* offers some significant implications for interpretation. First, focusing on *fa'ahinga* and redefining them opens up the fact that there are diverse constituents in every community; there is the presence of multiple positions, structures, ways of being and ways of thinking. Second, analysing the *vā* exposes internal and external tensions amongst groups which the text portrays. It also reveals the way texts promote one *vā* at the costs of others, a tendency that has the potential to affect readers and reading communities if adhered to. Third, reading *tākanga* witnesses to the fact that to situate one's interpretation of biblical texts from an alternative standpoint unpacks some important insights that are ignored by other readings.

CHAPTER 8
RE-STOR[Y]ING EZRA

> For events in island-storytelling to happen, I ask you, our readers, two things: reread the passages until you have an intuitive awareness of the stories, and be free to redirect the stories where and when you can. Our purpose is not to recover these stories but to let them loose, by leisurely telling them in conversation.
>
> Jione Havea[389]

This final reading of Ezra is based on the last issue I have raised in Chapter 5, which revolves around the belittling rhetoric woven into the text to characterize and condemn peoples: "the peoples of the lands." I, as a *tu'a* reader, am sensitive to such characterization since a *tu'a* is a victim of cultural and colonial misrepresentation. In that sense, I will reread the text through the lens of *tālanga*.

CATEGORY OF ANALYSIS

This reading is not an attempt to recover what happened; rather it seeks to *re-story* the text from an-other perspective. The term *tālanga* entails orality, and it means to engage in a conversation, where two or more parties offer their views on a subject of concern. *Tālanga* involves the acts of *speaking* and *listening*; it does not seek consensus, nor does it expect a final word. It is always an open-ended forum that invites multiple perspectives, options, solutions, and/or meanings. Like *tākanga*, it has two possible variants: (i) *tala'anga* (*tala* [to tell, inform, expose];

---

[389]Havea, "Numbers," 46.

'*anga* [space/place for conversation]); (ii) *tā-langa* (*tā* [cut, beat, strike]; *langa* [to be in pain, to build]). These variant forms give *tālanga* a dual tendency; that is, language and orality can serve as a means of obtaining information or communication, and a powerful tool for strengthening community, on the one hand; when used negatively, on other hand, it becomes a violent means of repression and displacement. To avoid the violent tendency of *tālanga*, *tu'a* reading seeks, through the process of *faka-'uhinga* (interpretation), to scrutinize the dominant voices, but also to recover repressed and unheard voices, in biblical texts. Moreover, *tu'a* reading examines the function of language (what language *does*) to expose the rhetoric of domination.

METHOD OF ANALYSIS

Tālanga reading employs the *lau lea* method of *tu'a* reading for analysing Ezra 9–10. The word *lea* is Tongan for "speech, language, word" or simply the "act of speaking." To analyse the *lea* in texts, *lau lea* focuses on the ways language and speeches are woven into the narrative (Tongan: *tufunga lea*), as well as *ways of speaking* (Tongan: *tō'onga lea*). *Lea* is understood herein as a tool of representation and construction. It embodies certain viewpoints, ideas, and attitudes; it is the vehicle for constructing voices, characters, and space.

RE-STOR[Y]ING EZRA 9–10

Ezra 9–10 is interlaced with various ways of speaking: some aim to dominate; others tend to subvert. This analysis will focus on the categories of *tufunga lea* and *tō'onga lea*. Each category provides the tools for analysis, and will be defined as the discussion proceeds.

ANALYSING *TUFUNGA LEA*

The word *tufunga lea* (*tufunga* [to build, make; builder, artist]; *lea* [language, speech, language]) can be used both as a verb and a noun; it designates an act and signifies a person at once. As a verb, it indicates the act of composing a speech or weaving speeches together. As a noun, it designates an artist; the *tufunga* of *lea*. The act of *tufunga lea* is a selective event. It includes as much *lea* as it excludes, depending on what serves the interest of the *tufunga*. The way *lea* is woven is also determined likewise.

Lau lea views texts in a similar manner. It is a work of a *tufunga* who weaves together different strands that fit his or her purpose, and excludes those which do not. *Lau lea* is a type of analysis that not only reads what is written, but it also allows a reading of the unwritten—viz. those voices that are not heard.

In the preceding chapter, a reading of *tākanga* sheds light on the various *fa'ahinga* and *vā* that are mentioned in Ezra 9–10. When viewed through the analytical category of *tālanga* and analysed with the method of *lau lea*, some characters are clearly given the chance to speak, whereas others remain silent. The discussion of the *'ā-ki-loto* and its *fa'unga* in Chapter 6 laid the groundwork for this part.

Ezra 9 is narrated in the first person where the narrator's voice colludes with the voice of the narrative's protagonist, Ezra, thus making the voice of the latter so predominant. The only other voice in Ezra 9 is that of those who bring the issue of intermarriage to Ezra's attention: the chiefs (שרים) (9:1b–2). What is most striking about these two voices is that despite the domination of Ezra's voice, it is the chiefs' voice that has proven so effective. Their short report sets the events in Ezra 9–10 in motion. If that voice is to be omitted, the rest of the narrative would make no sense (see the pattern below; N = narration; D = direct speech).

```
9:1a            N (Ezra)

        1b–2            D (Officers)

3–6a            N¹ (Ezra)

        6b–15           D¹ (Ezra)
```

In Ezra 10, the voice of the narrator continues to dominate the narrative, but in the third person. Here the narrator distanced itself from Ezra, as the latter is locked in a conversation with Shecaniah (10:2b–4) and the people (10:12b–14). Taking a central position in the narrative is Ezra's voice, while Shecaniah's and the people's voices provide a frame.

10:1–2a   N

  2b–4   **D** (Shecaniah)

    5–10a   N

      10b–11   **D** (Ezra)

        12a N^1

     12b–14 D^1 (People)

  15–17 N^2

The centrality of Ezra's voice however comes to an end when both chapters are read as one narrative. The emphasis shifts from Ezra's voice to Shecaniah's; the voice of the accused (10:2b–4) becomes the centre, whereas the accuser's (9:6b–15; 10:10b–11) provides the frame. Similarly, whereas in Ezra 9 the voice of the chiefs stands in parallel to Ezra's voice, it is positioned in parallel to those they accused (the people [10:12b–14]).

 9:1a   **N** (Ezra)

  1b–2   **D** (Officers)

   3–6a   **N** (Ezra)

    6b–15   **D** (Ezra)

     10:1–2a   N

      2b–4   **D** (Shecaniah)

     5–10a N^1

    10b–11 D^1 (Ezra)

   12a N^2

  12b–14 D^2 (People)

 15–17 N^3

The above analysis indicates that although *lea* is being constructed to amplify Ezra's voice and the concern of those who returned with him from exile, it is not as persistent and unwavering as the text would like it to be. What is being woven to make an impact on those who married foreign women is equally met by yet another voice that is uttered with force (10:2b–4):

> *We have acted faithlessly against our God when we brought (literally, "caused to dwell") foreign women from the peoples of the land, but now there is hope for Israel beside this.*
>
> *Now let us make a covenant to our God to release all women and those born from them, with the advice of my lord and those who trembled at the commandment of our God, and let it be done according to the law.*
>
> *Get up! For upon you is this matter and we are with you; be strong and do it.*

This speech by Shecaniah shows how resourceful and thoughtful he is with regard to the issue at hand. Instead of weeping and falling on his knees like Ezra, he proposes a clear plan of what they should do, and demands that action should follow. Ezra's action in v. 5 is a direct response to that advice rather than of his own idea:

> *Then Ezra rose and made the chiefs of the priests, the Levites, and all Israel swear according to this word, and they swore.*

The passiveness of Ezra here is parallel to 9:3 where he responds to the report that the chiefs bring in 9:1–2. There is also a significant difference between the two incidents. The chiefs in 9:1–2 offer only an issue and Ezra reacts to it in his own way. In 10:2b–4 Shecaniah gives Ezra a solution to which Ezra responds accordingly. The one constructed by the text to be at the helm of the community is here guided by another. The leader is now being led.

There are interesting aspects of Shecaniah's speech that need more emphasis. First, the use of the phrase "our God" (אלהינו) (10:2) implies that the God being claimed by the chiefs and Ezra to have forbidden intermarriage (cf. 9:6–15) is not just of the *kumifonua* (the exiles); that God is also worshipped by the *kakai-e-fonua* ("the peoples of the lands"). The use of the divine name אלהים seems to be an intentional attempt to shift the attention from the exclusiveness of Yhwh to the inclusiveness of אלהים. The *kumifonua* cannot just claimed that God for themselves; אלהים is for all.

Second, the term להוציא in verse 2 is generally rendered as "to put away" (NKJV), "to send away" (NIV, NJB, NRSV), and "to expel" (JPS).[390] I opted to translate the term להוציא as "to release" based on how the term is being used in other texts, where it carries some sense of emancipation, rather than the negative sense of divorce and expulsion. In Exod 6:13 and 27, the word is used with reference to the need to bring out Israel from Egypt. Verse 13 reads:

וידבר יהוה אל־משה ואל־אהרן ויצום אל־בני ישראל ואל־פרעה מלך
מצרים להוציא את־בני־ישראל מארץ מצרים

And Yhwh spoke to Moses and Aaron, and commanded them regarding the people of Israel and Pharaoh king of Egypt, to free the people of Israel from the land of Egypt.

That is also the case when it is used in Isa 42:7, which refers to the *release* of those who are held captive.

לפקח עינים עורות להוציא ממסגר אסיר מבית כלא ישבי חשך

To open eyes that are blind, to release prisoners out of the dungeon, from the house of confinement those who dwell in darkness.

From the perspective of a *tu'a* reader, the latter is the sense of להוציא in Shecaniah's speech. He acknowledges that some of the men have acted against the law, and they should be held accountable. But for their wives and children, they should be released and be freed because they have nothing to do with the issue at stake. Clines notes that "a Jehiel of the family of Elam was amongst those who had married foreign wives (10:26)."[391] He then reads: "Shecaniah himself in this case would have been advocating his own excommunication, so we can only suppose that

---

[390]Most, if not all, readings of that verse agree that the solution is to expel or divorce foreign women with their children. See at least Fensham, *The Books of Ezra and Nehemiah*, 132. Clines, *Ezra, Nehemiah, Esther*, 124. Blenkinsopp, *Ezra-Nehemiah*, 188. Allen and Laniak, *Ezra, Nehemiah, Esther*, 79. Brown II, "The Problem of Mixed Marriages in Ezra 9–10," 454.

[391]Clines, *Ezra, Nehemiah, Esther*, 126.

his father was another Jehiel of that family."[392] No man in his right mind would want to be divorced from his own wife and children, nor would he want his own mother (if regarded as a foreigner) to be expelled. I doubt that Shecaniah would want that to happen to his own family, and a covenant with God would be the only way to ensure their well-being, as he proposes in Ezra 10:3.

Third, the way Shecaniah speaks to Ezra is in a very authoritative tone. The imperative קום is most frequently used in divine commands to kings, prophets, and judges.[393] The most interesting use of the term outside divine commands is in v.4 by Shecaniah and by Jezebel in 1 Kgs 21:7, 15. The narrative in 1 Kgs 21:1–21, the event concerning Naboth's vineyard, is woven together to justify the Deuteronomist's hatred of Jezebel, a Sidonian princess. The story however is largely driven by Jezebel's voice, which stands in parallel to Yhwh's voice. Whereas Elijah the prophet acts on Yhwh's command, Ahab and all the people of Jezreel behaved in accordance with Jezebel's advice. In vv. 4–10, Ahab was disappointed that his request was resisted by one of his subjects, Naboth. In response, Jezebel advised the king on how a king was supposed to act. She then wrote a letter outlining what the people of the town should do, and they did accordingly. Phyllis Trible comments that Jezebel's "view of kingship enjoys a precedent in Israel."[394] The point being made here is that despite what the text constructs and what interests it seeks to serve, it tends to weave in (somehow unconsciously) alternative voices that resist those that are dominant, thereby deconstructing the text itself.

The voices a text includes are as significant as those it ignores, because in some cases it tends to ignore the very voice that it should have included together with those it ignores deliberately. That is the case with Ezra 9–10, and the rest of the Ezra narrative. The text appears to have ignored the voices of the following: "peoples of the lands" (*kakai-e-fonua*, עמי הארצות), "foreign women" (נשים נכריות), their husbands, as well as their children. That is sensible enough not to allow any voices of resistance from the accused while it seeks to build its case against them. The voiceless are positioned not to have a chance to defend themselves against the verbal onslaught of the *kumifonua* group. The irony of the

---

[392]Ibid.

[393]See Gen 13:17, 19:15, 28:2, 31:13, 35:1, 44:4; Num 22:20, 23:18; Deut 9:12, 10:11; Josh 1:1; Judg 4:14, 5:12, 7:9, 8:20, 21, 9:32; 1 Sam 16:12, 23:4; 2 Sam 19:7, 1 Kgs 17:9, 19:5, 7, 21:7, 15, 18; 2 Kgs 1:3, 1 Chr 22:16; Jer 13:6, 18:2; Ezek 3:22; Jonah 1:2, 6, 3:2; Mic 6:1.

[394]Phyllis Trible, "Exegesis for Storytellers and Other Strangers," *Journal of Biblical Literature* 114, no. 1 (1995): 10.

matter, however, is that the one (Yhwh) claimed by the text to have set the rules for their social engagements seems to have no voice or is given no chance to speak at all. His words are referred to indirectly as a past event (9:6–15) rather than a present reality. In a sense, words ascribed to Yhwh are no more than words being forced into Yhwh's "mouth." In a situation where Yhwh is expected to intervene as in 1 Kgs 21:1–21, Yhwh is being pushed into the remote past only to be heard "whispering" through the mouths of priests and others who perhaps view themselves as spokespeople for the divine. This is a case where the selectivity of the *tufunga lea* has gone wrong. The silence of Yhwh seems to indicate that the *kumifonua* has only used the divine for their own political agenda and to validate their indifference to the peoples of the lands.

The analysis of the *tufunga lea* can be summed up as follows. First, Ezra 9–10 is obviously designed to give Ezra and his group an advantage in terms of speaking. That is significantly challenged, however, by the voice of somebody whom the author of the text perhaps did not think would make an impact: Shecaniah. The implication here is that despite the frequency and intensity of voices that are woven to dominate, there is always an alternative voice that, though ignored by both texts and readers, offers transformative insights. Second, Ezra 9–10 completely suppresses voices of those who had been accused of polluting both the land and the holy race. Ironically, it also silenced the voice of the one they intend to serve: Yhwh. In sum, voice and silence alike signify that *tufunga lea* (use and arrangement of language and speeches) is a political process that is driven by certain interests; it is biased and perspectival.

ANALYSING *TŌ'ONGA LEA*

Having analysed the aspects of *tufunga lea*, I will now focus on *tō'onga lea* or ways of speaking. Each *lea*, on the one hand, is uttered to have an effect on the hearers, and to drive home a message. When ways of speaking are analysed, they tend, on the other hand, to say something about the speakers, revealing in most cases the kinds of intention that shape the utterances. Reading *tālanga* will analyse ways of speaking that are woven together in the text, the way they portray speaking subjects, and the significant contribution they make to the meaning of the text as a whole. I will deal particularly with three Tongan ways of speaking: *lea hualela, lea akonaki*, and *lea faka-punake*. Analysis of these *tō'onga lea* will focus on the flow of direct speeches in Ezra 9–10, and they are progressed as follows:

A   9:1b–2 (Chiefs)

B   9:6b–15 (Ezra)

C   10:2b–4 (Shecaniah)

B¹   10:10b–11 (Ezra)

A¹   10:12b–14 (People)

Direct speeches are knitted together, and form a chiastic structure where the speech uttered by the chiefs in 9:1b–2 (A) is parallel to the speech spoken by the people in 10:12b–14 (A¹). Similarly, Ezra's prayer in 9:6b–15 (B) is parallel to his speech in 10:10b–11 (B¹). At the centre lies Shecaniah's speech in 10:2b–4 (C). I will analyze the speeches in the order shown above.

A   9:1b–2

The first speech in 9:1b–2 contains a report of what is supposedly regarded as a problem: the people of Israel have not separated themselves from the peoples of the lands. Mingling with others is here seen as a transgression, and it is based on a belief that "the peoples of the lands" have committed abhorrent practices that are compared to peoples whom Israel views as having similar moral tendencies (vv.1b–2):

> *The people of Israel, the priests, and the Levites have not separated themselves from the peoples of the lands— their abominations are likened to the Canaanites, the Hittites, the Jebusites, the Ammonites, the Moabites, the Egyptians, and the Amorites—for they have taken from their daughters for them and for their sons, and the holy race have exchanged pledges with the peoples of the lands, and the hand of the chiefs and the prefects was first in this treacherous act.*

The actual problem is specifically identified as intermarriage: Israelite men and their sons have taken wives from women of the lands, whom the text regards as "foreign." Such a practice is considered a threat because the "holy seed" is at risk of being polluted by the peoples of the lands. The offenders include members of the community of exiles, led by high ranking officials: chiefs (שרים) and prefects (סגנים). This is all expressed from the point of view of some "chiefs" and not the whole community, and the one who receives the report, Ezra, reacted with guilt and fear as if the whole world has collapsed. The reference to traditional enemies of Israel in terms of their ethnicities (despite not existing at the time[395]) is probably an attempt to intensify the emotion of the leader, Ezra, that their own have been dwelling with the enemies.[396]

Through the lens of *tālanga* the report is a *lea hualela* on the part of the chiefs. It is uttered in a way to provoke judgment upon the so-called offenders, on the one hand, and to belittle the practices of "the peoples of the lands," on the other hand. In that sense, the speakers themselves give the impression that they are innocent of this practice, while their fellows are guilty. In addition, the speakers clearly draw a distinction between themselves and others—between the "holy self" and "the unholy other." The two therefore must not be allowed to mingle; they have to remain separate.[397] As a *hualela* expresses a false impression of oneself, so is this report by the chiefs—viewing themselves as "holy" (*tapu*) is a false impression on the returnees'

---

[395] See Fensham, *The Books of Ezra and Nehemiah*, 124–125. Clines, *Ezra, Nehemiah, Esther*, 119. Allen and Laniak, *Ezra, Nehemiah, Esther*, 72.

[396] Allen and Laniak read: "Outsiders belonging to "the peoples of the lands" had no place in the new Israel, as the narratives of 4:1–4 and 6:21 had made clear, using similar language. The latter verse mentioned proselytes who had renounced such a tainted practices. Here, however, conversion was not envisioned as an option, and racial purity was pursued on religious grounds . . . They felt overwhelmed by an established, culturally heterogeneous population, in a setting where religion played a large role in culture. Consequently only marriage inside the community was expedient and indeed necessary—so strong was the scent of spiritual danger." *Ezra, Nehemiah, Esther*, 73. This reading clearly attempts to do justice to the text and its meaning, but when it is viewed *tu'a*-wise, the text stands in contrast to what *tu'a* reading is looking for: heterogeneity, racial and religious tolerance. A text that discounts those visions is indeed a text of terror.

[397] Walter Brueggemann offers this comment with regard to the issue, "It was an act of immense authority that readily terminated marriages and disrupted families for the sake of a particular religious passion rooted in a particular notion of Israel as "holy seed." This exclusionary propensity is a hallmark of the returnees from Babylon. This intense religious passion may be understood as a response to the felt jeopardy of the community . . . Two suspicions about this religious propensity, however, may be registered. First, it is clear, as Fernando Belo has shown, that *purity* is not the only issue in Torah [sic] that might taken as *Leitmotiv* for reform, for *debt* is an alternative agenda of comparable importance." Walter Brueggemann, *An Introduction to the Old Testament: The Canon and Christian Imagination* (Louisville: Westminster John Knox, 2003), 365–366.

behalf, and thus disguises a demand to assert their control over the inhabitants of the land.[398]

B   9:6b–15

The second speech is a response to the report uttered in the first one. The speaker here is Ezra, and his speech is directed to Yhwh their God in the form of a prayer. Different subjects and issues are knitted together in this prayer.

- A   Confession of Sin (9:6–7)
  - Expression of Shame (9:6a)
  - Admission of Guilt (9:6b)
  - Consequences of Sin (9:7)
- B   Praise of Divine Mercy (9:8–9)
  - Preservation of Remnant (9:8a)
  - A Stake in the Holy Place (9:8b)
  - Slaves Yet Not Forsaken (9:9a)
  - New Life and Restoration (9:9b)
- A^1 Confession of Sin (9:10–12)
  - Rhetorical Question (9:10a)
  - Admission of Guilt (9:10b)
  - Appeal to Tradition (9:11–12)
    - Pollution of Land by Peoples of the Lands (9:11)
    - Prohibition of Mixed Marriages (9:12a)
    - Issue of Inheritance Raised (9:12b)
- B^1 Question of Divine Mercy (9:13–14)
  - Divine Mercy Undeserved (9:13)
  - Rhetorical Question (9:14)
    - Concerning Mixed Marriage (9:14a)

---

[398] Ron L. Stanley, reading from a queer perspective, exposes the fact that the issue here is in direct contrast to what Ezra and the returnees were commissioned to do: "The actions taken by Ezra once he arrived, however, do not stack up to what he was commissioned to do by the king." Ron L. Stanley, "Ezra-Nehemiah," in *The Queer Bible Commentary* (ed. Deryn Guest, et al.; London: SCM, 2006), 269. He also comments on Ezra's lack of leadership quality which also supports the point I made above between Ezra and Shecaniah: "Ezra was not the leader of the people that he could have been. First, Ezra had to be told about the intermarriage of Judaeans with foreigners around them, and it was a leader in the community, Shecaniah, not Ezra, who offered a solution to the problem. Shecaniah even had to encourage Ezra to take action on the matter . . . Second, there is no record that Ezra fulfilled his role as a teacher of the law until much later . . . Ezra was reluctant to take a leading role with his people and did not accomplish all that the king sent him to do" (Ibid, 269–270).

		○ Concerning Remnant (9:14b)
A²		Confession of Sin (9:15)
		• Acknowledge Divine Mercy (9:15a)
		• Admission of Guilt (9:15b)

Confessions (9:6–7, 10–12, 15) dominate the prayer though interspersed with recollections of God's merciful acts toward Israel (9:8–9, 13–14). With regard to the faithfulness of God, the prayer recalls how God has been graciously and actively involved in Israel's history, particularly in allowing a remnant to return to the land given to their ancestors to rebuild and restore. In contrast, the prayer admits the sins of Israel, heightened with hyperboles, ironies and rhetorical questions. Moreover, sins are seen as results not of the returnees own doing, but of mingling with the "peoples of the lands" and marrying with "foreign women." The prayer is more political than religious; it tends to solidify the positions of the accusers and condemns the accused and their foreign wives at once. Through prayer, Ezra appeals to divine authority and invokes traditional texts, staging the platform for the returnees' restoration claims.

The prayer combines two *tō'onga lea* which come under *lea faka-punake*: *fakalangilangi* and *fakahekeheke*. *Fakalangilangi* is an attempt to speak in a way to exalt or glorify somebody higher than oneself. Such a way of speaking mostly employs positive languages and imageries, and that is featured particularly in those parts of the prayer that recount the gracious intervention of divine mercy in Israel's history (9:8–9, 13–14). Vv. 8 and 9 read:

> *And now, for a little moment, a favour has come from Yhwh our God who granted to us an escape, and gave us a peg in his holy place, and our God has enlightened our eyes and given a little sustenance in our servitude.*
>
> *For slaves we are, and in our servitude our God has not forsaken us, but has stretched out kindness before the kings of Persia who gave us sustenance to raise the house of our God, erecting its ruins and giving us a wall in Judah and in Jerusalem.*

From these two verses, there are two significant claims uttered by Ezra. First, those who returned from exile are a surviving remnant. Second, this remnant is destined by God to rebuild the House of God and to have a hold in Judah and Jerusalem. Both claims are woven to justify their presence in Judah, and their attempt to reconstruct the House of God.

Both claims portray the returnees as having a God-given right to do what they are doing, despite its impact on the wider community. When *fakalangilangi* is uttered in this way, it becomes a *fakahekeheke*; it utters more lies than truths, and it tends to exaggerate. An example of *fakahekeheke* is verse 6:

> and I said, "My God, I am ashamed and humiliated to lift my face to you, my God, because our iniquities have become higher than our head, and our wrong-doings have grown up to the heavens."

Here the speaker overstresses their iniquities by comparing it to the height of the heavens. It may have been an attempt to point to the enormity of the sin they have committed, but given that the problem is only intermarriage, such a comparison seems laughable. The prayer ends Ezra 9.

C   10:2b–4

Whereas Ezra 9 ends with Ezra's prayer, Ezra 10 opens with a different speaker: Shecaniah. I have discussed this speech above, but I will focus here on the way the speech is being uttered. The structure of the speech is as follows:

2b	Admission of guilt
2c	Fostering hope
3	Recommendation
4	Call for action

As Ezra's prayer is a response to the report of the chiefs, this speech is uttered as a response to Ezra's prayer. Verse 2b resembles the opening of Ezra's prayer in 9:6–15 in the sense that it begins by admitting that they have done wrong by marrying נשים נכריות ("foreign women"). But instead of being sentimentally driven and distressed like Ezra, Shecaniah in verse 2c offers a sound reminder:

ועתה יש־מקום לישראל על־זאת

[b]ut now there is hope for Israel beside this.

The truth is that some have married foreign women. If mixed marriage is the indicator for faithlessness then they are guilty. But what needs to be done is not just to utter a solitary prayer. They need to make a covenant with God *to release* their wives and their children according to these authorities: the counsels of Ezra and those who tremble at the commandment and the law of God (10:3). Shecaniah's speech ends with a call for action: Get up! For upon you is this matter and we are with you; be strong and do it (10:4). In Ezra 9, Ezra is the dominant subject in terms of both actions and words. Now in Ezra 10 he becomes silent (for once), which signals a twist in the story. From this point onward, Ezra slowly fades away from the scene, while the voiceless subjects of Ezra 9 become audible and visible.

If Shecaniah's words are to be read from the narrator's point of view, we sense affirmation and submission on the people's part. But if one reads *tu'a*-wise, features of *akonaki*, *fetau* and *heliaki* are traceable. A *akonaki* is a *tō'onga lea* that imparts advice and instruction, and is usually uttered by a person who has experience, authority and wisdom. That is what Shecaniah's speech has offered Ezra. *Fetau* offers a counterproposal or counterargument, and that is also a feature of Shecaniah's speech. Shecaniah did hear Ezra's prayer, and understands well where the prayer is directed. His immediate reaction and proposal may have gotten Ezra off balance. In Ezra's prayer, he was speaking of men being separated from their wives. Here, Shecaniah suggests otherwise: to send away their wives and children. The mentioning of the children alongside their mothers adds some personal and emotional tones to the speech. That there are innocent children involved in this crisis had probably never crossed Ezra's mind. Finally, a *heliaki* tends to disguise the real intentions behind a speech; at times, it seeks to misguide the hearer, while the speaker acts otherwise. Following Shecaniah's speech, Ezra reacts according to the advice provided. The end of the narrative in 10:17 duly focuses on the men who married "foreign women," and thus implies that the latter have been released, as Shecaniah had proposed.

B¹   *10:10b–11*

This fourth speech is Ezra's response to Shecaniah's advice, and stands in parallel to his prayer in 9:6–15. For the first time in the narrative, Ezra has the courage to speak directly to those accused of marrying "foreign wives." In his prayer (9:6–15), he directs his speech to God; here he talks to the accused face to face. The way he uttered his speech however still resembles both the *hualela* orientation of the chiefs' report (9:1b–2) and his prayer (9:6–15). Verses 10b–11 read:

> *You have acted unfaithfully and have brought foreign women, thus increasing the guilt of Israel. So now make a confession to Yhwh, God of your fathers, and do his will, and separate yourselves from the peoples of the land and from the foreign women.*

This speech reveals the stereotypic association of the root מעל (*m'l*, "faithless acts") and נשים נכריות ("foreign women") (10:10), as well as the roots ידה (*ydh*, "to confess" 10:1, 11) and בדל (*bdl* "to separate" 9:1, 10:11). These associations somehow give some indications of the worldview that shape the text: foreigners are faithless, and confession of faithlessness requires separation from foreigners. This is the view that generates the tensions between the בני הגולה (literally, "sons of the exiles") and the עמי הארצות ("peoples of the lands"), as well as between the זרע הקדש ("the holy race/seed") and the נשים נכריות ("foreign women"). It also draws a boundary between two factions of the returnees: the separatists (represented by those, like the "chiefs" of 9:1, who conspire to expel "foreign women") and the assimilationists (represented by those who married foreign women and peoples of the lands).

Here Ezra points out the problem, and demands a public confession which is to go hand in hand with separating the returnees from the "peoples of the lands" and their "foreign women." In 9:1–2 the reason for the call to separate is to safeguard the "holy seed" from being polluted by the impurity of the "peoples of the lands." In this speech, the reason for separation is that it is the will of Yhwh. Like any *hualela*, this speech gives the false impression that returnees are morally superior to the peoples of the lands, while the fact points otherwise (cf. 9:6).

A^1 *10:12b–14*

The last speech in Ezra 9–10 is a direct response of the people to Ezra's speech in 10:10b–11. This speech reads:

> *So as you said, we must do.*
>
> *But the people are many and the time is rain, and we have no strength to stand in the outside, nor is this the work of a day or two, for we have transgressed greatly in this matter*

> *Let our chiefs be standing for the entire congregation, and all in our town who dwelled with foreign women shall come in appointed times, and with them the elders and judges of each town, until the anger of our God is averted from us in regard to this matter.*

The reaction of the people to Ezra's speech features antithetical *rhetoric of avowal* and *disavowal* (10:12–15), carrying further the *heliaki* tone of Shecaniah's speech. In 10:12 an intense rhetoric of avowal is pronounced: כן (כדבריך) [כדברך] עלינו לעשות (*"So as you said, we must do"*). This expression of earnestness[399] is deconstructed in the following verses with the people's counter-proposal introduced by the adversative אבל (*'bl*, "but" or "on the contrary" 10:13), the withdrawal of the people from the gathering (10:14), and the actual opposition (עמד *'md*, "to stop" or "to take one's stand" 10:15a) from Jonathan and Jahzeiah, supported by Meshullam and Shabbethai (10:15b).

The *rhetoric of disavowal* offers a *fetau* to the *rhetoric of avowal* set forth in verse 12b. The intensity of the response indicates that the suppressed voices in the previous gatherings are now very much audible. The people's withdrawal from the gathering is parallel to Ezra's withdrawal in 10:6, showing the rise of the displaced subjects. The opposition of the people shatters the rather imposing authority of Ezra and his cohorts. The people seem to drive home the message that they can neither be controlled nor silenced. The next section is an attempt to re-story the text from the perspective of *kakai-e-fonua* ("the peoples of the lands").

RE-STOR[Y]ING *TU'A*-WISE

Those without voice always carry the hope that they will eventually have the chance to speak. Here the voiceless subjects of Ezra are given that chance:

> Aliens we are, you say
> > but we are the *kakai-e-fonua*
> > out of the *fonua* we grew
> > upon it we shall remain

---

[399] Loring W. Batten, *The Books of Ezra and Nehemiah: A Critical and Exegetical Commentary* (Edinburgh: T&T Clark, 1913), 344.

Abhorrent are our ways, you cry
> but that is our *tala-e-fonua*
> you have the choice
> to live it or leave out

We are impure, you claim
> but who on earth is pure?
> wake up, holy ones!
> oh, self-righteous ones, wake up!

Our women are harlots, you gaze
> whose seeds are you, anyway?
> despite your vilifying words
> they are our mothers, sisters, and wives.

Like your forebears, you are
> Naming game, you played
> Blaming names, your game
> Your attitudes never changed

We are of the *fonua*,
> and the *fonua* is us
> here is our place
> here is our people

We are a *tākanga*,
> together we imagine
> a community that nurtures
> a world of freedom and justice

From the above analysis, there are significant insights a *tālanga* reading has opened up from the text. First, the analysis of *tufunga lea* stresses the fact that in every text, voices are constructed, arranged, and suppressed to serve certain interests; in this case, it is the interest of those who returned from exile (the *kumifonua*). In Ezra 9 the peoples of the lands have no voice at all, and there is no opportunity for dialogue and engagements. In contrast, Ezra 10 allows dialogue between parties, and only here we find alternative views to the one that dominates Ezra 9. Second, the analysis of *tō'onga lea* offers the following insights: different ways of speaking do shed light on the relationship between the speaker and the hearer. *Hualela* speeches expose a tendency to dominate on the part of the speaker. *Heliaki* speeches tend to resist dominant views by providing alternatives. Here plurality of voices and multiple viewpoints are promoted.

CONCLUSION

This work has reconsidered the task of biblical interpretation from Oceania by asserting that constructing an alternative way of reading the Bible, using Tongan imaginations, makes a difference. This was prompted by an awareness of the situated, contextual and perspectival nature of the interpretive task, on the one hand, and the illusion of an objective, neutral and/or universal reading of the Bible, on the other hand. The task undertaken, therefore, focused on developing an alternative approach (that is, *lau faka-tu'a* [*tu'a* reading]), which was then put to the test by reading Ezra 9–10.

The development of *tu'a* reading began, first of all, by situating it in the social location of Tongan commoners (*tu'a*), and within the terrain of contextual biblical interpretation. Situating my approach in the social location of Tongan *tu'a* indicated that I, as a reader, am from a particular social class, and that reading from that location reflects not only my position as a Tongan, but also represents the positions of Oceanic readers in the field of biblical studies. There is lack of respect for that location, and, in most cases, no worthwhile contribution is expected. Locating *tu'a* reading in the terrain of contextual biblical interpretation indicates that it takes the interests and values of real readers very seriously in the process of interpretation; a *tu'a* reader is a real reader. It also opens up some gaps that invite alternatives. This work has offered one alternative from Oceania.

Tu'a reading has been developed as a multi-dimensional approach, both in terms of theory and methodology. Theoretically, it has three categories of analysis: namely, *fonua* (place, people), *tākanga* (community), and *tālanga* (orality). Each category offers a unique perspective for interpretation. Methodologically, it is constituted of four methods: *lau fe'unu* (text analysis), *lau lea* (speech/language analysis), *lau vā* (space/relation analysis) and *lau tu'unga* (rationale/ideological analysis). These methods, like the categories, have been constructed from several aspects of Tongan ways of being and ways of knowing. Each method scrutinizes different aspects of the text based on the perspectives provided by the analytical categories. All these categories and methods have been employed in the readings of Ezra 9–10.

Whereas the text is clearly narrated in favour of the returning exiles and their claims, a *fonua* reading exposes the oppressive forces behind the narration, on the one hand, and reveals transformative alternatives, on the other hand. To read along the grain of the text, the exiles are portrayed as rightful residents returning to reclaim the land granted to their ancestors by Yhwh. In contrast, those who are in the land, "the peoples of the lands," are viewed as foreigners who have polluted the land. Likewise, place is read as a bordered space embodied in the House of God, where only the returnees have access. To read the text, however, through the analytical category of *fonua*, the returning exiles are perceived as landless subjects (*kumifonua*) who are in search of a place of settlement, whereas "the peoples of the lands" (the alleged impure group) are read as the natives of the land (*kakai-e-fonua*), whose place, the square, is without border and opens to all irrespective of ethnicity, sexual orientation, and social status. A *fonua* reading therefore opens transformative insights from a text that is driven by indifference to others.

The reading of Ezra 9–10 through the analytical category of *tākanga* foregrounded an approach that perceived every text to have projected a certain social vision that it invites readers to participate in and accept; every text tended to suppress other social visions that contradict its own; every social vision is an intersection of domination and resistance; and each vision determined to a great extent the way a community is stratified and positioned in relation to power and scarce resources. The interest in the social vision of the text is also driven by the oppressive nature of the visions behind the construction of the Tongan social hierarchy, and the vitality of community life to Tongans and Oceanic islanders. The reading through *tākanga* revealed, first of all, that there are diverse constituents in every community; there is the presence of multiple positions, structures, ways of being and ways of thinking. Second, analysing the *vā* exposed the internal and external tensions amongst groups which the text portrays. It also reveals the way texts promote one *vā* at the costs of others, a tendency that has the potential to affect readers and reading communities if adhered to. Third, reading *tākanga* witnesses to the fact that to situate one's interpretation of biblical texts from an alternative standpoint unpacks some important insights that are ignored by other readings.

The final reading of Ezra 9–10 through the analytical category of *tālanga* directed the attention of *tu'a* reading to the demeaning rhetoric employed by the text to characterize peoples it hates and/or condemns, and thus focused on the two aspects of *tufunga lea* (employment and arrangement of language and speeches) and *tō'onga lea* (ways of speaking). The analysis of *tufunga lea* stresses the fact that in every text, voices are constructed, arranged and suppressed to serve certain interests; in this case, it is the interest of those who returned from exile (the *kumifonua*). In Ezra 9 the peoples of the lands have no voice at all, and there is no opportunity for dialogue and engagements. In contrast, Ezra 10 allows dialogue between parties, and only here we find alternative views to the one that dominates Ezra 9. The analysis of *tō'onga lea* offered the following insights: different ways of speaking did shed light on the relationship between the speaker and the hearer. *Hualela* speeches expose a tendency to dominate on the part of the speaker. *Heliaki* speeches tend to resist dominant views by providing alternatives. Both the *tufunga lea* and *tō'onga lea* aspects of the text exposed on the one hand the politics of orality, where voices are suppressed, and revealed on the other hand through the notion of *heliaki* and *fetau* the transformative aspects of the text, which have never been considered in the interpretation of Ezra 9–10.

These readings have proven that a Tongan reading of biblical texts does make a difference to biblical interpretation. The work however is not an end in itself. What I have done thus far is only the beginning. There are still uncharted waters that require further exploration. Given the diversity of Oceanic cultures, other readers (academic and non-academic) can utilize other areas such as Oceanic belief systems and world-views, indigenous epistemologies, the many contextual issues that the region faced, particularly those social violence against women and children and environmental degradation. Likewise, Tongan readers can also formulate new ways of readings based on their own social locations, and on other aspects of culture that are not dealt with in this work.

This work extends an invitation to biblical scholars in the region to develop approaches to biblical interpretation that are shaped by their own ways of being and ways of knowing, rather than continuing to rely solely on borrowed insights. It is also a challenge to biblical studies as a discipline to open its doors to insights, not only from Western and continental scholars, but also from those in island contexts. Only in so doing, can voices from the region be heard, the dehumanizing aspects of the Bible be avoided, and the transformation of displaced subjects like Tongan *tu'a* can be realised. Such a task has its own risks, but they are indeed worth taking. I conclude with two questions: Are Oceanic biblical scholars courageous enough to take the risks? Can the field of biblical interpretation take into account indigenous approaches from Oceanic readers, like the *tu'a*?

BIBLIOGRAPHY

Ackroyd, Peter R. "The Theology of the Chronicler." *Lexington Theological Quarterly* 8 (1973): 101–116.
———. *I & II Chronicles, Ezra, Nehemiah*, Torch Bible Commentaries. London: SCM, 1973.
Adam, A. K. M. *Faithful Interpretation: Reading the Bible in a Postmodern World*. Minneapolis: Fortress, 2006.
———. *Handbook of Postmodern Biblical Interpretation*. St. Louis: Chalice, 2000.
———. *What Is Postmodern Biblical Criticism?* Edited by Dan O. Via, Jr., Guides to Biblical Scholarship. Minneapolis: Fortress, 1995.
Adamo, David Tuesday. "African Cultural Hermeneutics." Pages 66–90 in *Vernacular Hermeneutics*. Edited by Sugirtharajah, R. S. Sheffield: Sheffield Academic Press, 1999.
Adeney, Walter F. *Ezra, Nehemiah, and Esther*, The Expositor's Bible. New York: A. C. Armstrong, 1893.
Allen, Leslie C., and Timothy S. Laniak. *Ezra, Nehemiah, Esther*, New International Biblical Commentary. Old Testament Series 9. Peabody: Hendrickson, 2003.
An, Choi Hee, and Katheryn Pfisterer Darr, eds. *Engaging the Bible: Critical Readings from Contemporary Women*. Minneapolis: Fortress, 2006.
Ariarajah, Wesley. "Intercultural Hermeneutics—A Promise for the Future?" *Exchange* 34, no. 2 (2005): 89–101.
Ashcroft, B., and P. Ahluwalia. *Edward Said*. London: Routledge, 2001.
Ateek, Naim. "Pentecost and Intifada." Pages 69–81 in *Reading from this Place: Social Location and Biblical Interpretation in Global Perspective*. Edited by Segovia, Fernando F., and Mary Ann Tolbert. Vol. 2. Minneapolis: Fortress, 1995.
Austin, Jon. "Space, Place & Home." Pages 107–115 in *Culture and Identity*. Edited by Austin, Jon. Frenchs Forest, NSW: Pearson, 2005.
Bailey, Randall C. "The Danger of Ignoring One's Own Cultural Bias in Interpreting the Text." Pages 66–90 in *The Postcolonial Bible*. Edited by Sugirtharajah, R. S. Sheffield: Sheffield Academic Press, 1998.

———, ed. *Yet With A Steady Beat: Contemporary U. S. Afrocentric Biblical Interpretation*, Vol. 42. Atlanta: SBL, 2003.
Bal, Mieke. *Anti-Covenant: Counter-Reading Women's Lives in the Hebrew Bible*. Sheffield: Almond, 1989.
Barthes, Roland. "The Death of the Author." Pages 259–263 in *Literature in the Modern World: Critical Essays and Documents*. Edited by Walder, Dennis. Oxford: Oxford University Press, 2004.
———. *The Death of the Author* 1977 [cited 29 March 2007]. Available from http://social.chass.ncsu.edu/wyrick/debcllass/whais.htm.
———. *The Pleasure of the Text*. Translated by Miller, Richard. New York: Hill and Wang, 1975.
———. *Structural Analysis and Biblical Exegesis: Interpretational Essays*, PTMS 3. Pittsburgh: Pickwick, 1974.
Batten, Loring W. *The Books of Ezra and Nehemiah: A Critical and Exegetical Commentary*. Edited by Briggs, Charles A., ICC. Edinburgh: T&T Clark, 1913.
Becking, Bob. "Ezra's Re-enactment of the Exile." Pages 40–61 in *Leading Captivity Captive: 'The Exile' as History and Ideology*. Edited by Grabbe, Lester L. Sheffield: Sheffield Academic Press, 1998.
Bennett, Harold V. *Injustice Made Legal: Deuteronomic Law and the Plight of Widows, Strangers and Orphans in Ancient Israel*. Grand Rapids: Eerdmans, 2002.
Beuken, Wim, and Seán Freyne, eds. *The Bible as Cultural Heritage*. London: SCM, 1995.
Bhabha, Homi K. *The Location of Culture*. London: Routledge, 1994.
Biblia Hebraica Stuttgartensia. Stuttgart: Deutsche Bibelgesellschaft, 1977.
Blenkinsopp, Joseph. *Ezra-Nehemiah*. Edited by Ackroyd, Peter, et al. Old Testament Library. Philadelphia: Westminster, 1988.
Block, Daniel I. "The Role of Language in Ancient Israelite Perceptions of National Identity." *Journal of Biblical Literature* 103, no. 3 (1984): 321–340.
Blumenthal, David R. *Facing the Abusing God: A Theology of Protest*. Louisville: Westminster John Knox, 1993.
Boda, Mark J., and Paul L. Redditt, eds. *Unity and Diversity in Ezra-Nehemiah: Redaction, Rhetoric, and Reader*. Sheffield: Sheffield Phoenix Press, 2008.

Boer, Roland C. "No Road: On the Absence of Feminist Criticism of Ezra-Nehemiah." Pages 233–252 in *Her Master's Tools? Feminist and Postcolonial Engagements of Historical-Critical Discourse*. Edited by Stichele, Caroline Vander, and Todd C. Penner. Atlanta: SBL, 2005.

Bott, Elizabeth. *Tongan Society at the Time of Captain Cook's Visits: Discussions with Her Majesty Queen Salote Tupou*. Wellington: The Polynesian Society, 1982.

Brah, A. *Cartographies of Diaspora: Contesting Identities*. London: Routledge, 1996.

Braxton, Brad Ronnell. "The Role of Ethnicity in the Social Location of 1 Corinthians 7:17–24." Pages 19–32 in *Yet With A Steady Beat: Contemporary U. S. Afrocentric Biblical Interpretation*. Edited by Bailey, Randall C. Atlanta: SBL, 2003.

Breneman, Mervin. *Ezra, Nehemiah, Esther*. Vol. 10, New American Commentary. Nashville: Broadman & Holman, 1993.

Brenner, Athalya, and Carole Fontaine, eds. *A Feminist Companion to Reading the Bible: Approaches, Methods, and Strategies*. Sheffield: Sheffield Academic Press, 1997.

Brett, Mark G. *Ethnicity and the Bible*. Leiden: Brill, 1996.

Brown, Francis, S. R. Driver, and Charles A. Briggs. *The Brown-Driver-Briggs Hebrew and English Lexicon*. Peabody: Hendrickson, 2003.

Brown II, A. Philip. "The Problem of Mixed Marriages in Ezra 9–10." *Bibliotheca Sacra* 162 (October–December 2005): 437–458.

Brueggemann, Walter. *An Introduction to the Old Testament: The Canon and Christian Imagination*. Louisville: Westminster John Knox, 2003.

———. *The Land: Place as Gift, Promise, and Challenge in Biblical Faith*. 2nd ed. Overtures to Biblical Theology. Minneapolis: Fortress, 2002.

Buber, Martin. *I and Thou*. New York: Scribner's, 1970.

Caldwell, Larry W. "Towards the New Discipline of Ethnohermeneutics: Questioning the Relevancy of Western Hermeneutical Methods in the Asian Context." *Journal of Asian Missions* 1, no. 1 (1999): 23–43.

Callaway, Mary C. "Canonical Criticism." Pages 121–134 in *To Each Its Own Meaning: An Introduction to Biblical Criticism and Their Applications*. Edited by McKenzie, Steven L., and Stephen R. Haynes. Louisville: Westminster John Knox, 1993.

Carroll R., M. Daniel. "Introduction: Issues of 'Context' Within Social Science Approaches to Biblical Studies." Pages 13–21 in *Rethinking Contexts, Rereading Texts: Contributions from the Social Sciences to Biblical Interpretation*. Edited by Carroll R, M. Daniel. Sheffield: Sheffield Academic Press, 2000.

Carroll, Robert P. "Exile! What Exile?" Pages 62–79 in *Leading Captivity Captive: 'The Exile' as History and Ideology*. Edited by Grabbe, Lester L. Sheffield: Sheffield Academic Press, 1998.

———. "The Myth of the Empty Land." *Semeia* 59 (1992): 79–93.

Carter, Charles E. *The Emergence of Yehud in the Persian Period: A Social and Demographic Study*, JSOT Supplement Series 294. Sheffield: Sheffield Academic Press, 1999.

———. "Opening Windows onto Biblical Worlds: Applying the Social Sciences to Hebrew Scripture." Pages 421–451 in *The Face of Old Testament Studies: A Survey of Contemporary Approaches*. Edited by Baker, David W., and Bill T. Arnold. Grand Rapids: Baker Books, 1999.

———. "The Province of Yehud in the Post-exilic Period: Soundings in Site Distribution and Demography." Pages 106–145 in *Second Temple Studies: 2. Temple and Community in the Persian Period*. Edited by Eskenazi, Tamara Cohn, and Kent H. Richards. Sheffield: Sheffield Academic Press, 1994.

Cataldo, Jeremiah. "Persian Policy and the Yehud Community During Nehemiah." *Journal for the Study of the Old Testament* 28, no. 2 (2003): 131–143.

Chalcraft, David J., ed. *Social-scientific Old Testament Criticism*. Sheffield: Sheffield Academic Press, 1997.

Classen, Carl Joachim. *Rhetorical criticism of the New Testament*. Tübingen: Mohr Siebeck, 2000.

Clifford, James. "Indigenous Articulations." *The Contemporary Pacific* 13, no. 2 (2001): 468–490.

Clines, David J. A., ed. *The Dictionary of Classical Hebrew*, Vol. V. Sheffield: Sheffield Academic Press, 2001.

———. *Ezra, Nehemiah, Esther*. New Century Bible Commentary. Grand Rapids: Eerdmans, 1984.

Collins, John J. "The Zeal of Phinehas: The Bible and the Legitimation of Violence." *Journal of Biblical Literature* 122, no. 1 (2003): 3–21.

Collocott, E. E. "Notes on Tongan Religion I." *The Journal of the Polynesian Society* 30, no. 119 (1921): 152–163.

———. "Notes on Tongan Religion II." *The Journal of the Polynesian Society* 30, no. 120 (1921): 227–240.
———. "Tongan Myths and Legends, III." *Folklore* 35, no. 3 (1924): 275–283.
Cook, Stephen L. *The Social Roots of Yahwism*. Studies in Biblical Literature 8. Atlanta: SBL, 2004.
Corwin, Rebecca. *The verb and the sentence in Chronicles, Ezra and Nehemiah*. Borna: Noske, 1909.
Cosgrove, Charles H. "Introduction." Pages 1–22 in *The Meanings We Choose: Hermeneutical Ethics, Indeterminacy and the Conflict of Interpretations*. Edited by Cosgrove, Charles H. London: T&T Clark, 2004.
———, ed. *The Meanings We Choose: Hermeneutical Ethics, Indeterminacy and the Conflict of Interpretations*. Edited by Brenner, Athalya. London: T&T Clark, 2004.
———, Herold Weiss, and K. K. (Khiok-Khng) Yeo. *Cross–Cultural Paul: Journeys to Others, Journeys to Ourselves*. Grand Rapids: Eerdmans, 2005.
Court, John M. *Biblical Interpretation: The Meanings of Scripture – Past and Present*. London ; New York: T&T Clark, 2003.
Davies, Philip R., and John M. Halligan, eds. *Second Temple Studies III: Studies in Politics, Class and Material Culture*. Edited by Clines, David J. A., and Philip R. Davies. Sheffield: Sheffield Academic Press, 2002.
Davis, Jeffrey Sasha. "Representing Place: 'Deserted Isles' and the Reproduction of Bikini Atoll." *Annals of the Association of American Geographers* 95, no. 3 (2005): 607–625.
Derrida, Jacques. *Structure, Sign, and Play in the Discourse of the Human Sciences* 2007 [cited 19 April 2007]. Available from http://www.hydra.umn.edu/derrida/sign-play.html.
———. *Writing and Difference*. Chicago: University of Chicago Press, 1978.
Detweiler, Robert. *Reader response approaches to Biblical and secular texts*. Atlanta: Scholars Press, 1985.
Diaz, Vicente M., and J. Kehaulani Kauanui. "Native Pacific Cultural Studies on the Edge." *The Contemporary Pacific* 13, no. 2 (2001): 315–342.
Dietrich, Walter, and Ulrich Luz, eds. *The Bible in a World Context: An Experiment in Contextual Hermeneutics*. Grand Rapids: Eerdmans, 2002.

Dilthey, Wilhelm. "The Development of Hermeneutics." Pages 93–105 in *Hermeneutical Inquiry*. Edited by Klemm, David E. Atlanta: Scholars Press, 1986.

Donaldson, Laura. "The Sign of Orpah: Reading Ruth Through Native Eyes." Pages 20–36 in *Vernacular Hermeneutics*. Edited by Sugirtharajah, R. S. Sheffield: Sheffield Academic Press, 1999.

———, and R. S. Sugirtharajah. *Postcolonialism and Scriptural Reading*. Atlanta: Scholars Press, 1996.

Douglas, Mary. "Responding to Ezra: The Priests and the Foreign Wives." *Biblical Interpretation* 10, no. 1 (2002): 1–23.

Drewes, Barend F. "Reading the Bible in Context: An Indonesian and a Mexican Commentary on Ecclesiastes: Contextual Interpretations." *Exchange* 34, no. 2 (2005): 120–133.

Dube, Musa W. *Postcolonial Feminist Interpretation of the Bible*. St. Louis: Chalice, 2000.

———. "Readings of *Semoya*: Batswana Women's Interpretation of Matthew 15:21–28." *Semeia* 78 (1996): 111–129.

———. "Towards a Postcolonial Feminist Interpretation of the Bible." *Semeia*, no. 78 (1997): 11–26.

Duggan, Michael W. *The Covenant Renewal in Ezra-Nehemiah (Neh 7:72b–10:40): An Exegetical, Literary, and Theological Study*. Vol. 164, SBL Dissertation Series. Atlanta: SBL, 2001.

Duncan, Christopher R. "Savage Imagery: (Mis)representations of the Forest Tobelo of Indonesia." *The Asia Pacific Journal of Anthropology* 2, no. 1 (2001): 45–62.

Dyck, Elmer. "Canon as Context for Interpretation." Pages 33–64 in *The Act of Bible Reading*. Edited by Dyck, Elmer. Downers Grove: InterVarsity, 1996.

Edelman, Diana Vikander. *The Origins of the 'Second' Temple: Persian Imperial Policy and the Rebuilding of Jerusalem*. London: Equinox, 2005.

Ekblad, Bob. *Reading the Bible with the Damned*. Louisville: Westminster John Knox, 2005.

Elliott, John H. *What is Social-Scientific Criticism?*, Guides to Biblical Scholarship, New Testament Series. Minneapolis: Augsburg Fortress, 1993.

Ernesti, Johann August, and Moses Stuart. *Elements of Interpretation*. 2nd ed. Andover: Flagg and Gould, 1824.

Eskenazi, Tamara Cohn. "Ezra-Nehemiah." Pages 123–130 in *Women's Bible Commentary*. Edited by Newsom, Carol A., and Sharon H. Ringe. Louisville: Westminster John Knox, 1998.

———. *In An Age of Prose: A Literary Approach to Ezra-Nehemiah*. SBL Monograph Series 36. Atlanta: Scholars Press, 1988.

———, and Eleanore P. Judd. "Married to a Stranger in Ezra 9–10." Pages 266–285 in *Second Temple Studies: 2. Temple and Community in the Persian Period*. Edited by Clines, David J. A., and Philip R. Davies. Sheffield: JSOT, 1994.

———, and Kent H. Richards, eds. *Second Temple Studies 2: Temple and Community in the Persian Period*. Sheffield: JSOT, 1994.

Estermann, Josef. "Like a Rainbow or a Bunch of Flowers: Contextual Theologies in a Globalized World." *Pacific Journal of Theology* II, no. 30 (2003): 4–33.

Fanon, Frantz. *The wretched of the earth*. New York: Grove, 1968.

Farisani, Elelwani. "The Use of Ezra-Nehemiah in a Quest for an African Theology of Reconstruction." *Journal of Theology for Southern Africa* 116 (July 2003): 27–50.

Fee, Gordon D. "History as Context for Interpretation." Pages 10–32 in *The Act of Bible Reading: A Multi-disciplinary Approach to Biblical Interpretation*. Edited by Dyck, Elmer. Downers Grove: InterVarsity, 1996.

Felder, Cain Hope. "Racial Motifs in the Biblical Narratives." Pages 172–188 in *Voices from the Margin*. Edited by Sugirtharajah, R. S. London: SPCK, 1991.

Fensham, F. Charles. *The Books of Ezra and Nehemiah*, New International Commentary on the Old Testament. Grand Rapids: Eerdmans, 1982.

Fewell, Danna Nolan. "Ezra and Nehemiah." Pages 127–134 in *Global Bible Commentary*. Edited by Patte, Daniel. Nashville: Abingdon, 2004.

———, and David M. Gunn. *Reading Between Texts: Intertextuality and the Hebrew Bible*. Louisville: Westminster John Knox, 1992.

Finlayson, James Gordon. *Habermas: A Very Short Introduction*. Oxford: Oxford University Press, 2005.

Firth, Stewart. "Colonial Administration and the Invention of the Native." Pages 253–288 in *The Cambridge History of the Pacific Islanders*. Edited by Denoon, Donald, et al. Cambridge: Cambridge University Press, 1997.

Fish, Stanley. *Is There a Text in this Class?: The Authority of Interpretive Communities*. Cambridge: Harvard University Press, 1980.

Floyd, Michael H. et al., *Prophets, prophecy, and prophetic texts in Second Temple Judaism*, Library of Hebrew Bible/Old Testament studies 427. London: T&T Clark, 2006.

Foskett, Mary F., and Jeffrey Kah-Jin Kuan, eds. *Ways of Being, Ways of Reading: Asian American Biblical Interpretation*. St. Louis: Chalice, 2006.

Foucault, Michel. "What Is an Author?" Pages 9–22 in *The Death and Resurrection of the Author?* Edited by Irwin, William. Westport/London: Greenwood, 2002.

Gadamer, Hans-Georg. *Truth and Method*. 2nd ed. New York: Continuum, 1994.

Gegeo, David W., and Karen Ann-Watson Gegeo. "How We Know: Kwara'ae Rural Villagers Doing Indigenous Epistemology." *The Contemporary Pacific* 13, no. 1 (2001): 55–88.

Genette, Gerard. *Palimpsests: Literature in the Second Degree*. Translated by Channa Newman and Claude Doubinsky. Nebraska: University of Nebraska Press, 1997.

———. *Paratexts: Thresholds of Interpretation*. Translated by Lewin, Jane E. Cambridge: Cambridge University Press, 1997.

Gifford, Edward Winslow. *Tongan Myths and Tales*. Honolulu: Bernice P. Bishop Museum, 1924.

———. *Tongan Society*. Honolulu: Bernice P. Bishop Museum, 1921.

Goldsworthy, Graeme. *Gospel-Centered Hermeneutics: Foundations And Principles Of Evangelical Biblical Interpretation*. Downers Grove: IVP, 2006.

González, Justo L. "*Revelation*: Clarity and Ambivalence: A Hispanic/Cuban American Perspective." Pages 47–61 in *From Every People and Nation: The Book of Revelation in Intercultural Perspective*. Edited by Rhoads, David. Minneapolis: Fortress, 2005.

Goss, Robert E., and Mona West, eds. *Take Back The Word: A Queer Reading of the Bible*. Cleveland: Pilgrim, 2000.

Gottwald, Norman K., and Richard A. Horsley, eds. *The Bible and Liberation: Political and Social Hermeneutics*. Rev. ed. Maryknoll: Orbis, 1993.

Gowler, David B., et al., eds, *Fabrics of Discourse: Essays in Honor of Vernon K. Robbins*. Harrisburg: Trinity, 2003.

Grabbe, Lester L. *A History of the Jews and Judaism in the Second Temple Period*, Library of Second Temple Studies 47. London: T&T Clark, 2004.

Graham, Matt Patrick. *The Chronicler as Historian*. Sheffield: Sheffield Academic Press, 1997.

———. et al., eds. *The Chronicler as Theologian: Essays in Honor of Ralph W. Klein*, JSOT Supplement Series 371. London: T&T Clark, 2003.

Gutierrez, Gustavo. "Song and Deliverance." Pages 129–146 in *Voices from the Margin*. Edited by Sugirtharajah, R. S. London: SPCK, 1991.

Habel, Norman C. *The Land Is Mine: Six Biblical Land Ideologies*. Minneapolis: Fortress, 1995.

———. *Literary Criticism of the Old Testament*. Philadelphia: Fortress, 1971.

———, ed. *Readings from the Perspective of Earth*, Vol. 1. Sheffield: Sheffield Academic Press, 2000.

Hall, Stuart. "Culture, Community, Nation." *Cultural Studies* 7, no. 3 (1993): 349–363.

Hau'ofa, 'Epeli, Vijay Naidu, and E. Waddell, eds. *A New Oceania: Rediscovering Our Sea of Islands*. Suva: Institute of Pacific Studies, USP, 1993.

Havea, Jione. *Elusions of Control: Biblical Laws on the Words of Women*. SBL Semeia Studies 41. Atlanta: SBL, 2003.

———. "The Future Stands Between Here and There: Towards an Island(ic) Hermeneutics." *Pacific Journal of Theology* II, no. 13 (1995): 61–68.

———. "Numbers." Pages 43–51 in *Global Bible Commentary*. Edited by Patte, Daniel. Nashville: Abingdon, 2004.

———. "A resting king David: 2 Samuel 7 and [dis]placements." Paper presented at the AAR/SBL (Post-Structuralist Research on the Hebrew Bible section). San Francisco, November 22–24, 1997.

———. "Shifting the Boundaries: house of God and politics of reading." *Pacific Journal of Theology* II, no. 16 (1996): 55–71.

Hayes, John. *Methods of biblical interpretation: excerpted from the Dictionary of biblical interpretation*. Nashville: Abingdon, 2004.

Heidegger, Martin. *Being and Time: A Translation of Sein und Zeit*. Translated by Stambaugh, Joan. Albany: SUNY Press, 1996.

Helu-Thaman, Konai. "Decolonizing Pacific Studies: Indigenous Perspectives, Knowledge, and Wisdom in Higher Education." *The Contemporary Pacific* 15, no. 1 (2003): 1–17.

Helu, 'I. Futa. *Critical Essays: Cultural Perspectives from the South Seas*. Canberra: Journal of Pacific History, 1999.

———. "Aesthetics of Tongan Dance: A Comparative Approach." Pages 261–269 in *Critical Essays: Cultural Perspectives from the South Seas*. Canberra: The Journal of Pacific History, 1999.

———. "Tongan Dress." Pages 288–292 in *Critical Essays: Cultural Perspectives from the South Seas*. Canberra: The Journal of Pacific History, 1999.

Herda, Phyllis. "Genealogy in the Tongan construction of the past." Pages 21–29 in *Tongan culture and History*. Edited by Herda, Phyllis, Jennifer Terrell, and Niel Gunson. Canberra: Department of Pacific and Southeast Asian History, Research School of Pacific Studies, ANU, 1990.

———, Jennifer Terrel, and Niel Gunson, eds. *Tongan Culture and History: Papers from the 1st Tongan History Conference 14–17 January 1987*. Canberra: Australian National University, 1990.

Hirsch Jr., E. D. *The Aims of Interpretation*. Chicago: University of Chicago Press, 1976.

———. *Validity in Interpretation*. New Haven: Yale Divinity Press, 1967.

Howitt, William. *Colonization and Christianity: A Popular History of the Treatment of the Natives by the Europeans in all their Colonies*. London: Longman, Orme, Brown, Green, & Longmans, 1838.

Hull, Michael. "Knowing One's Place: On Venues in Biblical Interpretation." *Dunwoodie Review* 26 (2003): 82–97.

Iser, Wolfgang. *The Act of Reading: A Theory of Aesthetic Response*. Baltimore: John Hopkins University Press, 1978.

James, K. E. "The Female Presence in Heavenly Places: Myth and Sovereignty in Tonga." *Oceania* 61, no. 4 (1991): 287–308.

———. "Is There a Tongan Middle Class? Hierarchy and Protest in Contemporary Tonga." *The Contemporary Pacific* 15, no. 2 (2003): 309–336.

Janzen, David. *Witch-Hunts, Purity and Social Boundaries*. JSOTSup 350. Sheffield: Sheffield Academic Press, 2002.

Jasper, David. *A Short Introduction to Hermeneutics*. Louisville: Westminster John Knox, 2004.

Johnson, Willa Mathis. "The Holy Seed Has Been Defiled: The Interethnic Marriage Dilemma in Ezra 9–10." Ph.D., Vanderbilt University, 1999.
Ka'ili, Tevita 'O. "*Tauhi vā*: Nurturing Tongan Sociospatial Ties in Maui and Beyond." *The Contemporary Pacific* 17, no. 1 (2005): 83–114.
Kaeppler, Adrienne L. "Rank in Tonga." *Ethnology: An International Journal of Cultural and Social Anthropology* 10, no. 2 (1971): 174–193.
Kanyoro, Musimbi. "Reading the Bible from an African Perspective." *Ecumenical Review* 51, no. 1 (1999): 18–24.
Keil, Karl Friedrich, and Sophia Taylor. *The Books of Ezra, Nehemiah, and Esther*. Clark's Foreign Theological Library 38. Edinburgh: T&T Clark, 1873.
Kelly, William. "Postcolonial Perspective on Intercultural Relations: A Japan-U.S. Example." *The Edge: The E-Journal of Cultural Relations* 2, no. 1 (2001).
Kepa, Mere, and Linita Manu'atu. "Indigenous Maori and Tongan Perspectives on the Role of Tongan Language and Culture in the Community and in the University in Aotearoa-New Zealand." *American Indian Quarterly* 30, no. 1 & 2 (2006): 11–27.
Kidner, Derek. *Ezra and Nehemiah: An Introduction and Commentary*, The Tyndale Old Testament Commentaries. Downers Grove: Inter-Varsity, 1979.
Klemm, David E. "Hermeneutics." Pages 497–502 in *Dictionary of Biblical Interpretation*. Edited by Hayes, John H. et al. Nashville: Abingdon, 1999.
Knoppers, Gary N. "Intermarriage, Social Complexity, and Ethnic Diversity in the Genealogy of Judah." *Journal of Biblical Literature* 120, no. 1 (2001): 15–30.
Koch, Klaus. *The Growth of the Biblical Tradition: The Form-Critical Method*. Translated by Cupitt, S. M. New York: Scribner's, 1969.
Koehler, Ludwig, and Walter Baumgartner. *Hebrew and Aramaic Lexicon of the Old Testament*. Translated by Richardson, M. E. J. English ed. 5 vols. Vol. 2. Leiden: Brill, 1995.
Kolo, Finau 'O. "Historiography: The Myth of Indigenous Authenticity." Pages 1–11 in *Tongan Culture and History*. Edited by Herda, Phyllis, Jennifer Terrel, and Niel Gunson. Canberra: Australian National University, 1990.

Kristeva, Julia. *Powers of Horror: An Essay on Abjection*. Translated by Roudiez, Leon S. New York: Columbia University Press, 1982.

Kwok, Pui-Lan. *Discovering the Bible in the Non-Biblical World*. New York: Orbis, 1995.

———. "Discovering the Bible in the Non-Biblical World." Pages 299–315 in *Voices from the Margin: Interpreting the Bible from the Third World*. Edited by Sugirtharajah, R. S. London: SPCK, 1991.

———. "Overlapping Communities and Multicultural Hermeneutics." Pages 203–215 in *A Feminine Companion to Reading the Bible*. Edited by Brenner, Athalya, and Carole Fontaine. Sheffield: Academic, 1997.

———. "Sexual Morality and National Politics." Pages 21–46 in *Engaging the Bible*. Edited by An, Choi Hee, and Katheryn Pfisterer Darr. Minneapolis: Fortress, 2006.

Lātūkefu, S. *Church and State in Tonga, 1822–1875*. Canberra: ANU Press, 1974.

Lee, Archie C. C. "The Bible in Asia: Contextualizing and Contesting." Paper presented at the Society of Asian Biblical Studies. Seoul, South Korea, 14–16 July 2008.

———. "Exile and Return in the Perspective of 1997." Pages 97–108 in *Reading from this Place: Social Location and Biblical Interpretation in Global Perspective*. Edited by Segovia, Fernando F., and Mary Ann Tolbert. Vol. 2. Minneapolis: Fortress, 1995.

Lipschitz, Oded, and Manfred Oeming. *Judah and the Judeans in the Persian period*. Winona Lake: Eisenbrauns, 2006.

Liver, Jacob. *Chapters in the History of the Priests and Levites: Studies in the Lists of Chronicles and Ezra and Nehemiah*. Jerusalem: Magnes, 1968.

Loewen, Jacob A. *The Bible in Cross-Cultural Perspective*. Pasadena: William Carey Library, 2000.

Madsen, Deborah L. "'No Place Like Home': The Ambivalent Rhetoric of Hospitality in the Work of Simone Lazaroo, Arlene Chai, and Hsu-Ming Teo." *Journal of Intercultural Studies* 27, no. 1/2 (2006): 117–132.

Mafico, Temba L. J. "The Divine Yahweh 'Elohim from an African Perspective." Pages 21–32 in *Reading from this Place: Social Location and Biblical Interpretation in Global Perspective*.

Edited by Segovia, Fernando F., and Mary Ann Tolbert. Vol. 2. Minneapolis: Fortress, 1995.

Māhina, 'Okusitino. "The Poetics of Tongan Traditional History, *Tala-e-fonua*: An Ecology-Centred Concept of Culture and History." *The Journal of Pacific History* 28, no. 1 (1993): 109–121.

———. "*Tufunga Lalava*: The Tongan Art of Lineal and Spatial Intersection." Pages 5–9, 29–30 in *Genealogy of Lines Hohoko e Tohitohi: Filipe Tohi*. Edited by Rees, Simon. New Plymouth: Govett-Brewster Art Gallery, 2002

Maier, Harry O. "A First-World Reading of *Revelation* among Immigrants." Pages 62–81 in *From Every People and Nation: The Book of Revelation in Intercultural Perspective*. Edited by Rhoads, David. Minneapolis: Fortress, 2005.

Mangan, Céline. *1–2 Chronicles, Ezra, Nehemiah*, Old Testament Message. Wilmington: Michael Glazier, 1982.

Marsden, George M. *Understanding Fundamentalism and Evangelicalism*. Grand Rapids: Eerdmans, 1991.

Martin, Dale B. "Social-Scientific Criticism." Pages 125–141 in *To Each Its Own Meaning: Biblical Criticisms and Their Application*. Edited by McKenzie, Steven L., and Stephen R. Haynes. Louisville: Westminster John Knox, 1999.

Martin, J. *Tonga Islands: William Mariner's Account*. 2 vols. Vol. 1. Edinburgh: Constable, 1827.

McConville, J. G. *Ezra, Nehemiah, and Esther*. Philadelphia: Westminster, 1985.

McKnight, Edgar V. *The Bible and the Reader: An Introduction to Literary Criticism*. Philadephia: Fortress, 1985.

Melanchthon, Monica J. *Dalits, Bible, and Method* 2005 [cited November 2005]. Available from http://www.sbl-site.org/Article.aspx?ArticleId=459.

Meo, Jovili. "Gems of Pacific Communities: Sharing and Service." *Pacific Journal of Theology* II, no. 16 (1996): 84–101.

Meyer, Manulani Aluli. "Our Own Liberation: Reflections on Hawaiian Epistemology." *The Contemporary Pacific* 13, no. 1 (2001): 124–148.

Miguez, Nestor. "Apocalyptic and the Economy: A Reading of Revelation 18 from the Experience of Economic Exclusion." Pages 250–262 in *Reading from this Place: Social Location and Biblical Interpretation in Global Perspective*. Edited by Segovia,

Fernando F., and Mary Ann Tolbert. Vol. 2. Minneapolis: Fortress, 1995.

Moala, Masiu. *'Efinanga: Ko e Ngaahi Tala mo e Anga Fakafonua 'o Tonga*. Nuku'alofa: Lali Publications, 1994.

Moore, Stephen D. *Literary Criticism and the Gospels: The Theoretical Challenge*. New Haven: Yale University Press, 1989.

———, and Fernando F. Segovia. *Postcolonial Biblical Criticism: Interdisciplinary Intersections*. London: T&T Clark, 2005.

Mosala, Itumeleng J. "Race, Class, and Gender as Hermeneutical Factors in the African Independent Churches' Appropriation of the Bible." *Semeia* 73 (1996): 43–57.

Mulrain, George. "Hermeneutics within a Caribbean Context." Pages 116–132 in *Vernacular Hermeneutics*. Edited by Sugirtharajah, R. S. Sheffield: Sheffield Academic Press, 1999.

Nair, Supriya. "Diasporic Roots: Imagining a Nation in Earl Lovelace's *Salt*." *The South Atlantic Quarterly* 100, no. 1 (2001): 259–285.

Najman, Hindy, and Judith H. Newman, eds. *The Idea of Biblical Interpretation: Essays in Honor of James L. Kugel*. Leiden: Brill, 2004.

Nayap-Pot, Dalila. "Life in the Midst of Death: Naomi, Ruth and the Plight of Indigenous Women." Pages 52–65 in *Vernacular Hermeneutics*. Edited by Sugirtharajah, R. S. Sheffield: Sheffield Academic Press, 1999.

Nzimande, Makhosazana Keith. "Postcolonial Biblical Interpretation in Post-Apartheid South Africa: The *gvirah* in the Hebrew Bible in the light of Queen Jezebel and the Queen Mother of Lemuel." Ph.D., Texas Christian University, 2005.

Oeming, Manfred. *Contemporary Biblical Hermeneutics: An Introduction*. Translated by Vette, Joachim F. England: Ashgate, 2006.

Olyan, Saul M. "Purity Ideology in Ezra-Nehemiah as a Tool to Reconstitute the Community." *Journal for the Study of Judaism* XXXV, no. 1 (2004): 1–16.

Packer, J. I. *"Fundamentalism" and the Word of God*. Grand Rapids: Eerdmans, 1958.

Patte, Daniel, ed. *Global Bible Commentary*. Nashville: Abingdon, 2004.

———. "Introduction." Pages xxi–xxxvi in *Global Bible Commentary*. Edited by Patte, Daniel. Nashville: Abingdon, 2004.

———. "One text: Several structures." *Semeia*, no. 18 (1980): 3–22.

Perrin, Norman. *What Is Redaction Criticism?*, Guides to Biblical Scholarship. Philadelphia: Fortress, 1969.
Phillips, Gary A., and Nicole Wilkinson Duran. *Reading Communities, Reading Scripture*. Harrisburg: Trinity, 2002.
Pippin, Tina. "Ideology, Ideological Criticism, and the Bible." *Currents in Research: Biblical Studies* 4 (1996): 51–78.
———. "The Heroine and the Whore: The *Apocalypse of John* in Feminist Perspective." Pages 127–145 in *From Every People and Nation: The Book of Revelation in Intercultural Perspective*. Edited by Rhoads, David. Minneapolis: Fortress, 2005.
Plottel, Jeanine Parisier, and Hanna Kurz Charney. *Intertextuality: New Perspectives in Criticism*. Vol. 2. New York: New York Literary Forum, 1978.
Polzin, Robert. *Biblical Structuralism: Method and Subjectivity in the Study of Ancient Texts*, Semeia Supplements. Philadelphia: Fortress, 1977.
Pope-Levison, Priscilla, and John R. Levison. *Return to Babel: Global Perspectives on the Bible*. Louisville: Westminster John Knox, 1999.
Porter, Stanley E., and Dennis L. Stamps. *Rhetorical criticism and the Bible*. London ; New York: Sheffield Academic Press, 2002.
Powell, Mark Allan. *What is Narrative Criticism?* Edited by Dan O. Via, Jr., Guides to Biblical Scholarship. Minneapolis: Fortress, 1990.
Pushpa, Joseph. "Trailblazers: Elizabeth Schüssler Fiorenza and George M. Soares Prabhu." Pages 53–68 in *On the Cutting Edge: The Study of Women in Biblical Worlds*. Edited by Schaberg, Jane, et al. New York: Continuum, 2004.
Rawlinson, George. *Ezra and Nehemiah: Their Lives and Times*, Men of the Bible. New York: A. D. F. Randolph, 1890.
Reimer, David J., and John Barton, eds. *After the Exile: Essays in Honour of Rex Mason*. Macon: Mercer University Press, 1996.
Rhoads, David, ed. *From Every People and Nation: The Book of Revelation in Intercultural Perspective*. Minneapolis: Fortress, 2005.
———. "Introduction." Pages 1–27 in *From Every People and Nation: The Book of Revelation in Intercultural Perspective*. Edited by Rhoads, David. Minneapolis: Fortress, 2005.
Richard, Pablo. "Reading the *Apocalypse*: Resistance, Hope, and Liberation in Central America." Pages 146–164 in *From Every*

People and Nation. Edited by Rhoads, David. Minneapolis: Fortress, 2005.

Ricoeur, Paul. *The Conflict of Interpretations: Essays in Hermeneutics*. Evanston: Northwestern University Press, 1974.

———. *From Text To Action: Essays in Hermeneutics, II*. Translated by Blamey, Kathleen, and John B. Thompson. Evanston: Northwestern University Press, 1991.

———. *Interpretation Theory: Discourse and the Surplus of Meanings*. Fort Worth, Tex.: Texas Christian University Press, 1976.

———, and Lewis Seymour Mudge. *Essays on Biblical Interpretation*. Philadelphia: Fortress, 1980.

Robbins, Vernon K. *Exploring the Texture of Texts: A Guide to Socio-Rhetorical Interpretation*. Valley Forge: Trinity, 1996.

———. *Jesus the Teacher: A Socio-rhetorical Interpretation of Mark*. Philadelphia: Fortress, 1984.

———. *The Tapestry of Early Christian Discourse: Rhetoric, Society, and Ideology*. London: Routledge, 1996.

Said, Edward. "Opponents, Audiences, Constituencies, and Community." Pages 7–32 in *The Politics of Interpretation*. Edited by Mitchell, W. J. T. Chicago: University of Chicago Press, 1982.

———. *Orientalism*. London: Penguin, 1978.

———. *The World, The Text and The Critic*. London: Vintage, 1983.

Schaberg, Jane, Alice Bach, and Esther Fuchs, eds. *On the Cutting Edge: The Study of Women in Biblical Worlds. Essays in Honor Elisabeth Schussler Fiorenza*. New York: Continuum, 2004.

Schneiders, Sandra M. *The Revelatory Text: Interpreting the New Testament as Sacred Scripture*. Collegeville: Liturgical, 1999.

Segovia, Fernando F. "Cultural Studies and Contemporary Biblical Criticism: Ideological Criticism as Mode of Discourse." Pages 1–15 in *Reading from this Place: Social Location and Biblical Interpretation in Global Perspective*. Edited by Segovia, Fernando F., and Mary Ann Tolbert. Vol. 2. Minneapolis: Fortress, 1995.

———. *Decolonizing Biblical Studies: A View from the Margins*. New York: Maryknoll, 2000.

———, ed. *Interpreting Beyond Borders*. Sheffield: Sheffield Academic Press, 2000.

———. "Postcolonial and Diasporic Criticism in Biblical Studies: Focus, Parameters, and Relevance." *Studies in World Christianity* 5, no. 2 (1999): 177–196.

———. "Reading-Across: Intercultural Criticism and Textual Posture." Pages 59–83 in *Interpreting Beyond Borders*. Edited by Segovia, Fernando F. Sheffield: Sheffield Academic Press, 2000.

———, and Mary Ann Tolbert, eds. *Reading from this Place*. Vol. 1 and 2. Minneapolis: Fortress, 1995.

Sell, Edward. *Chronicles, Ezra, Nehemiah*. Madras: SPCK, 1924.

Smith-Christopher, Daniel. "The Mixed Marriage Crisis in Ezra 9–10 and Nehemiah 13: A Study of the Sociology of Post-Exilic Judaean Community." Pages 243–265 in *Second Temple Studies: 2. Temple and Community in the Persian Period*. Edited by Eskenazi, Tamara Cohn, and Kent H. Richards. Sheffield: JSOT, 1994.

Soares-Prabhu, George M. "Class in the Bible: The Biblical Poor a Social Class?" Pages 147–171 in *Voices from the Margin*. Edited by Sugirtharajah, R. S. London: SPCK, 1991.

———. *The Dharma of Jesus*. Edited by D'Sa, Francis Xavier. Maryknoll: Orbis, 2003.

———. "Laughing at Idols: The Dark Side of Biblical Monotheism." Pages 109–131 in *Reading from this Place: Social Location and Biblical Interpretation in Global Perspective*. Edited by Segovia, Fernando F, and Mary Ann Tolbert. Vol. 2. Minneapolis: Fortress, 1995.

Soulen, Richard N., and R. Kendall Soulen. *Handbook for Biblical Criticism*. 3rd ed. Louisville: Westminster John Knox, 2001.

Spivak, Gayatri C. *Death of a Discipline*. New York: Columbia University Press, 2003.

Stamps, Dennis L., and Stanley E. Porter. *The Rhetorical Interpretation of Scripture: Essays from the 1996 Malibu Conference*. Sheffield: Sheffield Academic Press, 1999.

Stanley, Ron L. "Ezra-Nehemiah." Pages 268–277 in *The Queer Bible Commentary*. Edited by Deryn Guest et al. London: SCM, 2006.

Subramani. "Emerging Epistemologies." Paper presented at the Conference on South Pacific Literatures, Emerging Literatures, Local Interest and Global Significance, Theory Politics, Society. Noumea, New Caledonia, 20–24 October 2003.

———. "The Oceanic Imaginary." *The Contemporary Pacific* 13, no. 1 (2001): 149–162.

Sugirtharajah, R. S. "A Postcolonial Exploration of Collusion and Construction in Biblical Interpretation." Pages 91–116 in *The*

Postcolonial Bible. Edited by Sugirtharajah, R. S. Vol. 1. Sheffield: Sheffield Academic Press, 1998.

———. *Asian Biblical Hermeneutics and Postcolonialism: Contesting the Interpretations*. Sheffield: Sheffield Academic Press, 1999.

———. *The Bible and the Third World: Precolonial, Colonial and Postcolonial Encounters*. Cambridge: Cambridge University Press, 2001.

———. "Inter-faith Hermeneutics: An Example and Some Implications." Pages 352–363 in *Voices from the Margin: Interpreting the Bible from the Third World*. Edited by Sugirtharajah, R. S. London: SPCK, 1991.

———, ed. *The Postcolonial Bible*. Sheffield: Sheffield Academic Press, 1998.

———. *Postcolonial Criticism and Biblical Interpretation*. Oxford: Oxford University Press, 2002.

———. *Postcolonial Reconfigurations: An Alternative Way of Reading the Bible and Doing Theology*. London: SCM, 2003.

———. "Thinking about Vernacular Hermeneutics Sitting in a Metropolitan Study." Pages 92–115 in *Vernacular Hermeneutics*. Edited by Sugirtharajah, R. S. Sheffield: Sheffield Academic Press, 1999.

———, ed. *Vernacular Hermeneutics*. Edited by Sugirtharajah, R. S. Sheffield: Sheffield Academic Press, 1999.

———. "Vernacular Resurrections: An Introduction." Pages 11–17 in *Vernacular Hermeneutics*. Edited by Sugirtharajah, R. S. Sheffield: Sheffield Academic Press, 1999.

———. *Voices from the Margin: Interpreting the Bible from the Third World*. London: SPCK, 1991.

Tamez, Elsa. "1 Timothy." Pages 508–515 in *Global Bible Commentary*. Edited by Patte, Daniel. Nashville: Abingdon, 2004.

———. "Reading the Bible under a Sky without Stars." Pages 3–15 in *The Bible in a World Context*. Edited by Dietrich, Walter, and Ulrich Luz. Grand Rapids: Eerdmans, 2002.

Tate, W. Randolph. *Biblical Interpretation: An Integrated Approach*. Revised ed. Peabody: Hendrickson, 1997.

Thangaraj, M. Thomas. "The Bible as Veda: Biblical Hermeneutics in Tamil Christianity." Pages 133–143 in *Vernacular Hermeneutics*. Edited by Sugirtharajah, R. S. Sheffield: Sheffield Academic Press, 1999.

Theissen, Gerd. *The Bible and Contemporary Culture*. Minneapolis: Fortress, 2007.
Thiselton, Anthony C. *New Horizons in Hermeneutics: The Theory and Practice of Transforming Biblical Reading*. Grand Rapids: Zondervan, 1992.
Throntveit, Mark A. *Ezra-Nehemiah*. Interpretation: A Bible Commentary for Teaching and Preaching. Louisville: John Knox, 1992.
Torre, Miguel A. De La. *Reading the Bible from the Margins*. Maryknoll: Orbis, 2002.
Torrey, Charles C. *Ezra studies*. Chicago: University of Chicago Press, 1910.
Trible, Phyllis. "Exegesis for Storytellers and Other Strangers." *Journal of Biblical Literature* 114, no. 1 (1995): 3–19.
———. *Rhetorical Criticism: Context, Method, and the Book of Jonah*. Guides to Biblical Scholarship. Minneapolis: Fortress, 1994.
Tsagarousianou, Roza. "Rethinking the concept of diaspora: mobility, connectivity and communication in a globalised world." *Westminster Papers in Communication and Culture* 1, no. 1 (2004): 52–66.
Tucker, Gene M. *Form Criticism of the Old Testament*, Guides to Biblical Scholarship. Philadelphia: Fortress, 1971.
Tull, P. K. "Rhetorical Criticism and Intertextuality." Pages 156–180 in *To Each Its Own Meaning. An Introduction to Biblical Criticisms and Their Application*. Edited by McKenzie, Steven L., and Stephen R. Haynes. Louisville: Westminster John Knox, 1999.
Ukpong, Justin. "Inculturation Hermeneutics: An African Approach to Biblical Interpretation." Pages 17–32 in *The Bible in a World Context*. Edited by Dietrich, Walter, and Ulrich Luz. Grand Rapids: Eerdmans, 2002.
———. "The Parable of the Shrewd Manager (Luke 16:1–13): An Essay in Inculturation Biblical Hermeneutic." *Semeia* 73 (1996): 189–210.
———, et al., *Reading the Bible in the Global Village: Cape Town*. Vol. 3, Global Perspectives on Biblical Scholarship. Atlanta: SBL, 2002.
Ulrich, Eugene, et al., eds. *Priests, Prophets and Scribes: Essays on the Formation and Heritage of Second Temple Judaism in Honour of Joseph Blenkinsopp*. Sheffield: JSOT, 1992.

Vaka'uta, Nasili. "Religion and Politics: Issues Surrounding Ecclesiastical Politics and Political Development in Tonga." MA Thesis, University of the South Pacific, 2000.

VanderKam, James C. "Ezra-Nehemiah or Ezra and Nehemiah?" Pages 55–75 in *Priests, Prophets and Scribes*. Edited by Ulrich, Eugene, et al. Sheffield: JSOT, 1992.

Vanhoozer, Kevin J. *Is There a Meaning in This Text?: The Bible, The Reader, and the Morality of Literary Knowledge*. Grand Rapids: Zondervan, 1998.

Wainwright, Elaine M. "A Voice from the Margin: Reading Matthew 15:21–28 in an Australian Feminist Key." Pages 132–153 in *Reading from This Place: Social Location and Biblical Interpretation in Global Perspective*. Edited by Segovia, Fernando F., and Mary Ann Tolbert. Vol. 2. Minneapolis: Fortress, 1995.

———. and Philip Leroy Culbertson, eds. *The Bible in/and Popular Culture: A Creative Encounter*. Atlanta: SBL, 2010.

———. *Women Healing/Healing Women: The Genderization of Healing in Early Christianity*. London: Equinox, 2006.

Washington, Harold C. "Israel's Holy Seed and the Foreign Women of Ezra-Nehemiah: A Kristevan Reading." *Biblical Interpretation* 11 (2003): 427–437.

———. "The Strange Woman (אשה זרה/נכריות) of Proverbs 1–9 and Post-Exilic Judaean Society." Pages 217–242 in *Second Temple Studies 2. Temple and Community in the Persian Period*. Edited by Eskenazi, Tamara Cohn, and Kent H. Richards. Sheffield: JSOT, 1994.

Watson, Francis. *The Open Text: New Directions for Biblical Studies?* London: SCM, 1993.

Weinberg, Joel. *The Citizen-Temple Community*. Translated by Smith-Christopher, Daniel L., JSOTSup 151. Sheffield: JSOT, 1992.

West, Gerald O. *The Academy of the Poor: Towards a Dialogical Reading of the Bible*. Vol. 2, Interventions. Sheffield: Sheffield Academic Press, 1999.

———. "Local is Lekker, but Ubuntu is Best: Indigenous Reading Resources from a South African Perspective." Pages 37–51 in *Vernacular Hermeneutics*. Edited by Sugirtharajah, R. S. Sheffield: Sheffield Academic Press, 1999.

———, ed. *Reading the Bible Other-wise: Socially Engaged Biblical Scholars Reading with Their Local Communities*. Atlanta: SBL, 2007.
———, and Musa W. Dube. *The Bible in Africa: transactions, trajectories, and trends*. Leiden: Brill, 2000.
———. "An Introduction: How Have We Come to 'Read With.'" *Semeia* 73 (1996): 7–17.
West, Mona. "Outsiders, Aliens, and Boundary Crossers: A Queer Reading of the Hebrew Exodus." Pages 71–81 in *Take Back The Word: A Queer Reading of the Bible*. Edited by Goss, Robert E., and Mona West. Cleveland: Pilgrim, 2000.
White, Hugh C. *Speech Act Theory and Biblical Criticism*. Atlanta: Scholars Press, 1988.
Williamson, H. G. M. *Ezra, Nehemiah*. Vol. 16, Word Biblical Commentary. Waco: Word Books, 1985.
Wood-Ellem, Elizabeth. *Queen Salote of Tonga: The Story of an Era 1900–1965*. Auckland: Auckland University Press, 1999.
———, ed. *Songs & Poems of Queen Sālote*. Nuku'alofa: Vava'u, 2004.
Wood, Houston. "Cultural Studies for Oceania." *The Contemporary Pacific* 15, no. 2 (2003): 340–374.
———. "Three Competing Research Perspectives for Oceania." *The Contemporary Pacific* 18, no. 1 (2006): 33–55.
Wortham, Robert A. *Social-scientific Approaches in Biblical Literature*. Lewiston: E. Mellen, 1999.
Wright, John W. "A Tale of Three Cities: Urban Gates, Squares and Power in Iron Age II, Neo-Babylonian and Achaemenid Judah." Pages 19–50 in *Second Temple Studies III: Studies in Politics, Class and Material Culture*. Edited by Davies, Philip R., and John M. Halligan. Sheffield: Sheffield Academic Press, 2002.
Yee, Gale A. *Judges and Method: New Approaches in Biblical Studies*. 2nd ed. Minneapolis: Fortress, 2007.
Yoo, Yani. "*Han*-Laden Women: Korean 'Comfort Women' and Women in Judges 19–21." *Semeia* 78 (1997): 37–46.
Young, Robert C. *Postcolonialism: A Very Short Introduction*, Very Short Introductions 98. Oxford: Oxford University Press, 2003.

GLOSSARY OF TONGAN TERMS

'ā-ki-loto	inner limit
'ā-ki-tu'a	outer limit
'ātakai	limit, boundary
'uhinga	meaning, related, relevance
angafai	method, strategy
fa'ahinga	kind, type, group
fa'unga	structure, component
fatunga	textures, fabrics
faka-'uhinga	to interpret, interpretation
fakamatala	to explain, clarify
faka-motu	way of the island
faka-tu'a	way of the commoners
fala	mat (made from pandanus leaves)
fe'unu	fabric
fonua	land, people, womb, home
fōtunga	form, appearance
founga	method, theory
hikifonua	to depart from one's place
kakai	people
kakai-e-fonua	people of the land
kalasi malanga	lay preachers' fellowship
kulupu tālanga	bible discussion group
kumifonua	land/place seekers
lalava	lashing of coconut fibre
lau faka-motu	island way of reading
lau	to read, count, complain, gossip
lea	rhetoric, utterance, language; to speak, to utter
lōlenga faka-motu	way of the island
lōlenga	way of being
mana	miracle, life–transforming energy
manava	womb
matāpule	orator, chief's attendant
moana	ocean
ngalu	wave
pakipaki folofola	breaking scriptures

ta'ovala	waist mat
tākanga	community (variants: tā-ka'anga; taka-'anga)
tala-e-fonua	way of the land, custom, tradition
tālanga	orality; conversation; verbal engagement; debate (variants: tala-'anga; tā-langa)
talanoa	informal conversation, story, re-telling
tangata	humanity, man
tapu	holy, sacred, prohibited, forbidden
taufonua	to arrive and settle
tō'onga	way of presenting oneself (in speech and in deed)
tohi	to write, book, letter
tu'a	commoner, outsider, exterior, behind, beyond
tu'unga	standing place, position, status, location
tūkunga	situation, occasion
vā	relation, space
vete	to untie, divorce, release; to interpret

www.ingramcontent.com/pod-product-compliance
Lightning Source LLC
Chambersburg PA
CBHW031253230426
43670CB00005B/164